MONTICELLO, THE HOME OF THOMAS JEFFERSON
(Designed by himself)

HEROES OF PROGRESS

IN AMERICA

BY

CHARLES MORRIS

AUTHOR OF "HISTORICAL TALES," "HALF-HOURS WITH AMERICAN AUTHORS," ETC.

SECOND EDITION REVISED AND ENLARGED

PHILADELPHIA AND LONDON
J. B. LIPPINCOTT COMPANY

COPYRIGHT, 1906, BY J. B. LIPPINCOTT COMPANY

COPYRIGHT, 1919, BY J. B. LIPPINCOTT COMPANY

PRINTED IN UNITED STATES OF AMERICA

PREFACE

In the history of every nation there is much more going on than wars and revolutions. These are brief in duration and rapid in effect, but in the long intervals between the years of strife the work of peace goes steadily forward, producing its changes more deliberately but with equal utility. The pioneer and the warrior are not the only figures that stand prominent in national archives, not the only individuals that rise to the surface of things. There are many persons who attain heroic proportions not as results of bold adventure or military skill and daring, but through aid to the progress of mankind in less showy but equally important ways. The careers of these workers for good usually present little of the striking or dramatic. Their histories are not of the coruscating order and their lineaments and proportions not those usually given to the heroic figure. Yet they are often heroes in the noblest sense, and do more for the advancement of mankind than he who draws the sword in his country's defence or plunges into the untrodden wilderness in efforts to extend the borders of his nation's dominion.

Broad are the realms of peace and many paths are open to those who traverse its confines. There are the highroads of statesmanship, of invention, of scientific research, of benevolent activity, of moral earnestness, and many besides, and on all these at times heroic figures appear to dwarf the forms of

PREFACE

ordinary men, the heroes of thought and devotion to a great purpose as opposed to the heroes of the embattled field. Our own history brings up to our mental vision many men and women of this kind, heroic in act and effort though no banners waved over them and no trumpets heralded them on their quiet course. It is deemed appropriate here to put on record the life stories of the more prominent among these, to tell in which field of effort they excelled, what new paths they opened, to what form of supremacy they owed their fame. The tale of these lives is often plain and simple, not marked by the telling events and striking deeds that give spice and variety to the biography of the soldier and the pioneer. It is often what they were rather than what they did that makes their characters great and notable. Their lives were given to the advancement of their country among the nations of the earth or to the benefit of their fellow citizens, and this in every field of quiet and persistent human effort. With a valor and self-sacrifice equal or superior to those of the warrior they led us up to nobler heights and planted the banner of achievement on loftier altitudes than those usually reached by the pathway of the sword.

In the uplifting of the United States to its present high level many men of many parts have borne a share. First came the discoverer and the pioneer, the daring traversers of unknown seas and savage wilds. Then, as occasion arose, came the fighter by land and sea, striking for liberty and union and sowing the land with memories of valiant deeds. But during our whole history heroes of daily life or national development have arisen, cementing the edifice of our government, issuing in thunder tones the call for right and

PREFACE

justice, working in various ways for the happiness and benefit of their fellows. There are many of these. We have been obliged to confine our attention to those of chief prominence and to deal with these but briefly. But we trust that the records of noble life and useful achievement here given may prove interesting and inspiring to readers, and serve to show that the heroes of mankind are of many types, and that the conqueror is not only he who leads victorious armies over prostrate realms, but also he who faces hostile circumstances or braves threatening situations, winning through sheer force of energy and intellect where men of smaller mould would have shrunk back in dismay. Of such stuff are made the heroes of peace and progress, and we here present some of the chief among those who have nobly helped to make the United States great among the nations of the earth.

CONTENTS

	PAGE
Roger Williams, the Pioneer of Religious Liberty....	9
John Eliot, the Apostle to the Indians...............	16
William Penn, the Friend of the Red Men...........	21
James Oglethorpe and the Debtors' Refuge..........	27
Benjamin Franklin, the Father of the American Union	33
Patrick Henry, the Orator of the Revolution........	44
Samuel Adams, the Pioneer of American Liberty.....	51
Thomas Jefferson, the Author of the Declaration of Independence	56
Robert Morris, the Financier of the Revolution.....	66
Alexander Hamilton, the Architect of American Finance	76
John Adams, the Leader of the Boston Patriots......	85
Eli Whitney, America's first great Inventor.........	91
Robert Fulton, the Inventor of the Steamboat.......	96
John Jacob Astor, the Monarch of the Fur Industry	101
Stephen Girard, the Friend of the Orphan..........	107
John Marshall, the Expounder of the Constitution..	115
Henry Clay, the great Advocate of Compromise......	120
Daniel Webster, the Giant of the American Senate	129
John C. Calhoun, the Champion of Southern Institutions	138
Samuel F. B. Morse, the Discoverer of Electric Telegraphy	145
Cyrus W. Field, the Designer of the Atlantic Cable..	153
Elias Howe, the Inventor of the Sewing Machine....	159
Cyrus H. McCormick, the Developer of the Reaping Machine	166
Charles Goodyear, the Prince of the Rubber Industry	171
DeWitt Clinton, the Father of the Erie Canal......	177

CONTENTS—Continued

	PAGE
Horace Wells and the Discoverers of Anæsthesia	184
William Lloyd Garrison, the Great Emancipator	192
Wendell Phillips, the Silver-Tongued Orator of Reform	199
Charles Sumner, the Champion of Political Honor	214
Lucretia Mott, the Quakeress Advocate of Reform	219
Elizabeth Cady Stanton, the Women's Rights Pioneer	226
Susan B. Anthony, the Old Guard of Women Suffrage	232
Dorothea Dix, the Saviour of the Insane	239
George Peabody, the Banker Philanthropist	245
Peter Cooper, the Benefactor of the Uneducated	253
Abraham Lincoln, the Emancipator of the Slave	260
William H. Seward, the War-time Secretary of State	270
James G. Blaine, the Plumed Knight of Republicanism	278
Horace Greeley, the Premier of American Editors	287
John Ericsson, the Inventor of the Monitor	296
Thomas A. Edison, the Wizard of Invention	301
Frances E. Willard, the Woman's Temperance Leader	309
Clara Barton, the Red Cross Evangel of Mercy	317
Andrew Carnegie, the Apostle of the Gospel of Wealth	325
Booker T. Washington, the Pioneer of Negro Progress	335
Theodore Roosevelt as America's All-around Man and Champion	345

LIST OF ILLUSTRATIONS

MONTICELLO ....*Frontispiece.*

	PAGE
TITLE-PAGE TO ELIOT'S ALGONQUIN BIBLE................	16
WEST'S PICTURE OF PENN'S TREATY.....................	22
HOUSE IN WHICH FRANKLIN WAS BORN..................	34
HANOVER COURT HOUSE...............................	48
ASTORIA	102
GIRARD COLLEGE.....................................	108
WEBSTER, CLAY, AND JACKSON.........................	130
COMBINED HARVESTER AND THRASHER...................	168
"ROADSIDE," THE HOME OF LUCRETIA MOTT..............	220
LINCOLN'S BIRTH-PLACE...............................	260
BATTLE OF THE MONITOR AND THE MERRIMAC............	296
EDISON'S MAGNETIC ORE SEPARATOR....................	302
DINING-ROOM AND OFFICE IN CLARA BARTON'S HOME....	318
THEODORE ROOSEVELT IN HIS LIBRARY AT OYSTER BAY...	346
BIRD'S-EYE VIEW OF PANAMA CANAL LOCKS.............	362

HEROES OF PROGRESS

ROGER WILLIAMS, THE PIONEER OF RELIGIOUS LIBERTY

The Pilgrims and Puritans, who made their homes at Plymouth and Boston and were the first settlers of New England, were pious and God-fearing people, but with all that they were hard folks to live with for people who did not think just as they did. Though they had left England in the cause of religious liberty they were not ready to give religious liberty to any one who came among them. The Quakers, who were persecuted in England, were treated worse still in Boston, and when a young Puritan minister named Roger Williams came to Boston and began to preach in favor of liberty of thought he soon found himself in trouble.

The Puritans passed laws to punish every one who did not go to church. Williams said this was not right. He also said that the Indians were very badly treated, and that the king of England had no right to give away their land without paying them for it. These and other things which he was bold enough to say made the rulers very angry, and he was first obliged to leave Boston and afterwards ordered to leave Salem, where he had started a church.

The daring young preacher now declared that he

would start a colony of his own where every one might believe what he thought right. This and other things said by him made the Puritan rulers so furious that they determined to seize him and send him back to England. They would not have any man in their colony who chose to think for himself and would not let them think for him.

Officers were sent to arrest him, but he was told of their coming just in time to make his escape. It was midwinter. The weather was very cold. Snow covered the ground. Wild beasts roamed the woods in search of food. But Roger Williams was determined to keep his freedom even at the risk of his life, and he fled alone into the wilderness, leaving his wife, children, and friends behind in Salem. There was danger from the elements, danger from the wolves and bears, but he cared less for them than he did for the harsh and bitter Puritans of Boston.

He had no fear of the Indians. He had lived among them, learned their speech and ways of living, listened to the story of their wrongs and spoken boldly in their favor. They looked upon him as their best friend, and he set out to find Massasoit, one of their great chiefs, whose love he had won by acts of kindness in former years.

The poor fugitive had a hard journey before him. Massasoit lived about eighty miles to the south, and a wide wilderness lay between, freezingly cold in that winter season, and with few inhabitants. Now and then he came to the hut of an Indian, who gave him food and shelter, but at other times he had to take refuge in hollow trees, or sleep on a bed of leaves beside a woodland fire. It was a cold and miserable journey, one which even the Indians did not care to take at that season, and he was glad enough when,

HEROES OF PROGRESS

after long days of wandering, he reached the cabin of the friend and kind-hearted chief.

Massasoit greeted him joyfully as the friend of the red man, gave him shelter and a royal welcome till spring, and then presented him a tract of land beside the Seekonk River. When the spring opened five of his friends from Salem joined him, and they began to build a cabin on their land and plant a field with corn. But the corn had not begun to sprout before he learned that the ground he was on was within the limits claimed by the Plymouth settlement. Governor Winthrop, who was secretly a friend of the fugitive, sent him a letter advising him to cross to the other side of the water, where he might have the whole country to himself and do as he pleased.

When this word came Williams and his friends abandoned their partly-built cabin and planted field and set off in a canoe in search of a place where they could be safely out of the reach of the Puritans.

As they paddled along the Indians by the riverside greeted the good pastor as their friend, hailed him cheerily, and when he landed and talked with some of them they told him to go a little farther down, saying that he would find a good place to build and a fine spring of water. The spot was soon found. It was on the west side of the Rhode Island peninsula, near the mouth of the Moshassuck River. Williams named it Providence, saying that a good Providence had helped him. On that spot stands to-day the fine city of Providence.

Roger Williams had now an opportunity to carry out the liberal ideas which had given so much offense to the Boston Puritans. In Providence, he said, religion should be free. It should be a place of refuge for all who wished to worship God in their own way.

All he would ask of the people would be to obey the laws made for the good of the settlement. But this was to be "only in civil things." In religion conscience was to be the only law. No one had the right to try and force any man to think in his way, or to punish him for not doing so.

We of to-day, who are accustomed to full liberty in religion, may not understand how great a thing this was at that time. Then no such thing had been thought of. Every country in Europe had its own religion and bitterly persecuted all who set up other creeds. And there was no liberty of thought in America, among either the Spanish, French, or English. Even the Puritans, who had come to America to escape persecution, began, as we have seen, by persecuting the first man who taught new doctrines. Roger Williams was the pioneer in setting up a colony that had no fixed form of religion. Afterwards Lord Baltimore and William Penn wisely did the same.

No one can say that Roger Williams was not a good Christian, a better one than those who drove him from his home, for he soon risked his own life to save them from danger. The fierce and warlike Indians of the Pequot tribe had made an attack on the settlers and were trying to get the large and powerful tribe of the Narragansetts to join them. They wished to kill all the white people of the Plymouth colony and drive the pale-faces from the country.

The people of Plymouth, and of Boston too, were in a great fright when they heard of this. They knew that Roger Williams was the only white man in that region who had any influence with the Indians, and they sent to him, begging him to go to the Narragansett camp and ask them not to join the Pequots.

HEROES OF PROGRESS

Many men would have refused to go into a horde of raging savages for the safety of their enemies, but Roger Williams was too noble to refuse, though he knew that his life would be in the utmost danger, for some of the bloodthirsty Pequots were then with the Narragansetts. He promptly went to the Indian camp and spent three days in the wigwams of the sachems, though he expected every night to have the treacherous Pequots "put their bloody knives to his throat."

But the Narragansetts were strong friends of the honest pastor; they listened to his counsel, and in the end they and another tribe, the Mohicans, joined the English against the Pequots. Thus it was chiefly due to Roger Williams that the colonists were saved from the scalping-knives of the Indians. Yet when Governor Winthrop asked that the fugitive should be called back from banishment and rewarded in some way for his services the rulers at Boston refused to do so. A hard-hearted and stiff-necked people were those old Puritans. They had made laws for heaven and earth and would have no man among them who did not yield to these laws.

When, later on, the other colonies of New England joined in a league for defence, they would have nothing to do with the little colony at Providence. This band of rebels must take care of themselves. Their only friends were the Indians, and they had hard work to keep on good terms with these when the other colonies were treating them with injustice. To many of the savages all white men were alike.

In the end the people of the Providence settlement, to which had come all those who did not like the hard rule of the Puritans, sent Roger Williams to England to get them a charter that would protect them from the despots of Boston, who were not willing to let them alone. Williams set sail in 1643, and was soon back with his charter. He had been kindly greeted in the home country and brought back many good wishes for his little colony of religious rebels.

But the charter did not say enough; trouble with the other colonies did not end. They treated the people of Rhode Island with contempt and injustice. Three men from Newport, who went to visit an old friend at Lynn, were fined and imprisoned. So Williams was begged to go to London again to get a better charter.

But the people were too poor to pay his way. He went on their business, but they could not raise the money for his expenses, and to get the necessary funds he had to sell the trading house he had started. When he got to England he found that country in such disorder from its civil war that nothing could be done. He was a good scholar and he taught languages to a number of young men to pay the cost of his journey, but after three years he had to go back without his charter. But he had met and become the friend of Cromwell, Milton, and other great men.

Trouble had broken out among the towns of Rhode Island. Some wanted one thing and some another, and they quarrelled and wrangled until it seemed as if nothing could settle their dispute. It was this that brought Williams home to his colony, but it took even him a number of years to make peace among them. At length he succeeded. The towns formed a union, he was chosen for their president, and all went well. But it was ten years after he left England before the new charter was received.

After that for twelve years peace and prosperity existed in Rhode Island. The colony grew. No man

HEROES OF PROGRESS

interfered with another man's religion. All those who did not want to be forced to go to church or to accept a special creed came to the colony of Roger Williams. He was their principal pastor, and was so kind, gentle, and good that everybody respected and loved him. They were his children. He had brought them together and spent his time in working for their good, and they looked on him as their best friend.

When Williams grew quite old he was still strong and able, attending to his public duties and his private business, writing religious tracts, and preaching to the people and the Indians. But now a terrible Indian war began. The natives of the country, furious at the bad treatment they had received, rose in arms and tried to kill all the whites or drive them from the country. This was what is known as King Philip's War. There were many terrible scenes while it lasted. In this war the Narragansetts joined the other Indians, and the savage warriors marched towards Providence.

Williams, then over seventy years old, went out once more to meet them, as boldly as he had done years before. The old chiefs of the Narragansetts knew him well and told him that they were still his friends, but that the young warriors were so furious against all the white men that it would not be safe for him to go among them. They were determined and nothing could be done to stop the war.

Roger Williams went sorrowfully home again and told the people they would have to fight for their lives. The war ended after a year, King Philip and most of the Indians being destroyed. The good old pastor lived seven years longer, and died in 1683, loved by all who knew him.

JOHN ELIOT, THE APOSTLE OF THE INDIANS

THE white men who came to America had two ways of dealing with the Indians. One way was with the musket and the sword; the other was with the Bible and the voice of justice and peace. Most men took the first way; a few only took the second. One of these was Roger Williams, whose story we have told. Another was John Eliot, whose story we have now to tell.

While Roger Williams was raising his voice for justice to the Indians and going among them in the interest of peace, John Eliot was carrying to them the Word of God and devoting his life to bringing them into the fold of Christ. He was one of those noble-hearted heroes of good to whom life means only work for the benefit of the poor and ignorant, and he won fame by his earnestness in doing his duty.

John Eliot was born in England of a Puritan family. He was educated at the University of Cambridge, where he showed much quickness in the study of languages. It was this that helped him in later years, when he began his famous work of translating the Bible into the speech of the Indians.

He was one of the early settlers of Boston, where he preached for a time, afterwards going to a church in Roxbury. The people he preached to thought a great deal of him, and he was very successful among them, but all the time, in his home and in the pulpit, there was another matter in his mind. He could not help thinking of the poor pagan savages, the old owners of

MAMUSSE
WUNNEETUPANATAMWE
UP-BIBLUM GOD
NANEESWE
NUKKONE TESTAMENT
KAH WONK
WUSKU TESTAMENT.

Ne quoshkinnumuk nashpe Wuttinneumoh *CHRIST*
noh asoowesit

JOHN ELIOT.

CAMBRIDGE,
Printeuoop nashpe *Samuel Green* kah *Marmaduke Johnson*.
1 6 6 3.

TITLE-PAGE TO ELIOT'S ALGONQUIN BIBLE

the land. From the day he landed and saw for himself the ways of life of the ignorant natives his soul was filled with the desire to teach and uplift them. He longed to convert them from superstition to Christianity and to bring them out of their wild and savage ways.

This matter got into the good man's heart and soul. It was with him day and night. Finally he could bear it no longer, but made up his mind to give up his church and to go out into the wilderness among the Indians, to live with them, preach to them, and teach them the truths of the Christian faith.

But before doing this he felt that he must learn their mode of speech, so that he could talk to them in their own tongue and be sure that they understood him. He wanted to speak like them and live like them, and in this way to gain influence over them. He had, as we have said, a talent for languages, and after a good deal of hard study he got to know that of the neighboring Indians very well. It is doubtful if any other white man ever knew it so well, as will be seen when you have read all that he did with it.

When he was able to talk with the Indians easily he left the settlements and went among them, to spend his life in their wigwams, telling them what the Bible contained and teaching them better ways of living. They gathered around him in their villages and listened eagerly to him, ready and glad to hear all he had to say, for they saw that this white man was their friend. On mossy banks and in quiet dales, on the verdant shores of streams or among the dwellings of the natives, he would talk to them of virtue and honor and good living, and he soon had many ardent followers.

When we read of his work, in the quaint old record

he made of it, we are interested in the curious questions they asked him. One Indian did not think that Jesus Christ could understand a prayer in the Indian language. And when he told them the story of the deluge, he was asked how the world became full of people after they had all been drowned. These and others of the kind were natural questions, but it is likely he found easy answers to them. Of course he had to talk in a very simple way to make his uneducated hearers understand him.

You may be sure that Eliot did not find his new life an easy or comfortable one. All the red men were not his friends. Some of them doubted and suspected him, others were angry with him for asking them to give up their old beliefs. He needed to be a brave and daring man, for his life was often in danger. Some of the chiefs did all they could to stop his work, telling their people that he was seeking to bring them under the rule of the white man, and trying to frighten him by threats. And the medicine men, the priests of the Indians, were bitter against him, for they feared that they would lose their power if he went on with his teachings.

But nothing could stop the ardent missionary in his work. He went from village to village and from tribe to tribe, dwelling in their wigwams, living on their food, and adopting their ways. He made long journeys on foot through the wilderness, enduring the hardships of cold and hunger, passing through many perils, but always cheerful, never repining. He was held up by faith and confidence in his mission, and said, " I am about the work of God; I need not fear."

But we have not told the greatest work done by John Eliot, one of the most difficult tasks ever undertaken

HEROES OF PROGRESS

by any missionary to the Indians. Finding that he needed written as well as spoken words to aid him in his duties, he undertook the enormous labor of translating the whole Bible into the Indian language. This wonderful performance was done not for his own benefit, but to aid all Christian laborers among the Indians. And to make this easy for others, he also wrote an Indian grammar to assist them in learning the speech of the natives.

This would seem enough for any one man, but it was a small part of Eliot's work. What he most wished to do was to collect the men and women he converted to the Christian faith into separate towns, that they might give up their savage life and take up the habits of civilized people. But he did not want these towns to be too near the English settlements. He thought it best to have his converts live by themselves, and away from the influence of the white people.

So he settled his " praying Indians," as they were called, on tracts of land far from the settlements, taught them how to raise other crops than corn, and gave them instruction in many of the industries of the whites.

The first town founded by him was at Natick, Massachusetts. This was in the year 1660. The meeting-house there was the first ever built by Protestants for Indian use, though the Jesuits of Canada had several in their settlements along the Great Lakes and the St. Lawrence River. Before Eliot's work ended he had established thirteen or more little Indian settlements, in which he aimed to make peace and industry the rule and the Bible the law and guide of the people.

But the disturbances and the wars among the Indians interfered greatly with the work of this noble and devoted pioneer of the Christian faith. The injustice of the whites troubled him exceedingly, and the bloody struggle known as King Philip's War went far to destroy all the good he had done. At that time, it is thought, America had about five thousand "praying Indians."

After the war the whites were very bitter against the Indians and treated them cruelly, many of them being sold into slavery. Eliot did all he could for the protection of his peaceful converts, but his life's work was ruined by the war, and it was too late to begin it again. He was now an old man, too feeble to preach, yet he continued to do what he could, and to the end of his life went on writing religious books, not willing to cease while a hope of doing good was left.

The great work of his life, the Indian Bible, was published in 1663. No man had ever accomplished a greater or more unselfish task. Only two editions of it were ever printed, for with the destruction which fell upon the Indians of that region few were left who could speak the Indian dialect in which it was written. But it remains an imperishable honor to the memory of the great John Eliot.

He lived to be eighty-six years of age, dying ripe in years and honors on the twentieth of May, 1690, at Roxbury, Massachusetts. In his death passed away one of the noblest of men.

WILLIAM PENN, THE FRIEND OF THE RED MEN

It made no small stir in English society when young William Penn, whose father was a famous admiral and the friend of the King, joined the poor and despised society known as the Quakers. They called themselves Friends, and tried to be the friends of all the world, but they did not find the world very friendly in return, for they were very badly treated, many of them being sent to jail for daring to have a religion of their own.

It was while William Penn was at college that he took up these new ideas, and he was turned out of college for doing so. When his father heard of this he was furious. He beat the boy and turned him out of doors, and the poor lad would have fared very badly but for his mother, who sent him money. Finding that his severity had no effect on the young rebel, his father let him return home and soon after sent him to France, hoping that in that gay country he would get rid of his foolish notions.

When the young man came back he seemed to be cured of Quakerism, but it was not long before he took it up again, and his father once more turned him into the street. William Penn now had to suffer like the poorer Quakers. He was arrested for attending their meetings, and was kept for eight months in prison for writing in their favor. But all this had no effect on him, and he continued to write and preach.

Admiral Penn died at length, and his son became

the head of the house. He now wished more than ever to help his fellow sufferers. He became one of the owners of New Jersey, in America, and aided some of them to go there. And the idea soon came to him to get a place of his own in the New World that might be a haven of refuge for all men of his faith.

Charles II., the King, had owed Admiral Penn a large sum of money. This was now due to William Penn, but the king had other uses for his money than to pay his debts, and the young man asked him to settle the claim by granting him a tract of land in America.

King Charles was ready enough to do this. It was very easy for him to give away land which did not belong to him, and he made over to Penn a large tract of territory north of Lord Baltimore's colony. All the right the king kept for himself was a payment of two beaver-skins a year and one-fifth of all the gold and silver found. As there was no gold or silver there, the king had to be content with his beaver-skins.

Charles was well satisfied with this easy way of getting out of debt. He named the country Pennsylvania, or " Penn's Woods." Penn was equally well satisfied. He had got a fine home for his fellow Quakers, and he easily persuaded a number of them to cross the ocean to America. The next year, 1682, he sailed himself with a company of emigrants in a ship well-named the "Welcome," and landed with them on the green banks of the noble Delaware River.

He landed at a place called Upland by the Swedes who lived there at that time, but which he named Chester. Before leaving England he had formed a system of laws for the new colony, and these he now made known. Like Roger Williams, he declared that every man was free to worship God in his own way

WEST'S PICTURE OF PENN'S TREATY

and that no one should be made to suffer for his religion. The people were also free to make their own laws, but they must obey them when once made. No one should be put to death except for murder or treason, and every prison was to be made a workshop and place of reformation—a new idea in prison management. Such were some of the principal features of Penn's " Great Law."

Another very just thing William Penn did. Although Charles II. had made him a grant of the land in America, he knew very well that the king had no right to give away what did not belong to him. The Indians, the old owners of the soil, thought the same thing. So he and those with him met a large party of the Indians under a great elm tree on the banks of the Delaware and offered to pay them for the land which he wanted for his colony.

They were quite ready to sell it, and a treaty of peace and friendship was made which was to last as long " as the creeks and rivers run and while the sun, moon, and stars endure." No oaths were taken to bind this treaty; it was simply signed by the Indian chiefs and the Quaker leaders; and some one has said of it that it was " the only treaty in history that was never sworn to and never broken."

From that time forward the Friends and the Indians lived in peace. No Friend ever robbed or hurt an Indian, and no Indian ever hurt a Friend. They dwelt together for many years in harmony, the Indians looking upon Penn and his people as friends and brothers. Long afterwards they bore in memory the great " Mignon," as they called Penn, and told their children of his justice and goodness. They had trouble with other people, but not with the peace-loving Quakers.

When William Penn died, years afterwards, the Indians of Pennsylvania sent some beautiful furs to his widow in memory of their great and good brother. These, they said, were to make her a cloak, " to protect her while she was passing without her guide through the thorny wilderness of life."

The elm tree under which this treaty was made stood on the river bank near where Penn founded his city of Philadelphia, or " Brotherly Love." When the British held Philadelphia during the Revolution a sentinel was stationed by this tree to prevent the soldiers from cutting it down for firewood. It blew down in a storm in 1810, and the spot where it stood is now marked by a monument and a small public park.

The land where Philadelphia stands was held by the Swedes, who bought it from the Indians. Penn bought it from them, and laid out there the site of a handsome city, with broad and straight streets, crossing each other at right angles, and many of them named after the trees of the forest. In the centre and in each of the four quarters spaces for public squares were left. Along the river houses were rapidly built, and soon a small city arose.

When everything was in order and all was moving well, and when new settlers were coming rapidly to the new city in the New World, William Penn bade his people good-by and sailed back to England. He was wanted there. The Quakers were being very badly treated. He went to the king and asked him to have these persecutions stopped, and Charles ordered that this should be done.

But there were many people shut up in the prisons on account of their religious belief, which differed from that taught by the ministers of the Church of England.

HEROES OF PROGRESS 25

Twelve hundred of these were Quakers, and there were many of other sects. When Charles II. died, which he did soon after Penn's return, his brother James took the throne. He and Penn had always been friends, and when the latter asked the king to have these poor sufferers set free, it was done. The prison doors were opened and they were allowed to go out.

William Penn had done a splendid work for the good of humanity, but he was made to suffer in many ways. James II. proved a bad king and was driven from the throne, and William of Orange took his place. As Penn had been the friend of King James, he was accused of treason and was put in prison. He was soon set free, but then new charges were brought against him, and he had to keep out of the way of his enemies. The government of his province in America was also taken from him, but King William gave it back when he found that Penn had been falsely accused.

Penn went back to America in 1699. He found the colony very prosperous. Philadelphia had got to be quite a flourishing city, and people were settling in many other places. But many of these were not Quakers, and there was bad feeling between the different members of the colony. Other things had gone wrong, and many asked for greater privileges than the charter gave them. William Penn was willing to grant them all the liberty he could, and a new and very liberal constitution was made, which gave much of the power in the government to the people. Another treaty was made with the Indians, their condition and that of the negro slaves in the colony was made better, and then, in 1701, Penn returned to England. He was never to see his colony again.

The good friend of the Indians and the oppressed

was growing old now, and his troubles increased. Many of the settlers did not pay their rents, and he got so deeply in debt that he was obliged to mortgage his province. There were new troubles in his colony, there was more persecution of the Quakers at home, his property was badly managed, and when the Pennsylvania Assembly was asked to loan him some money to help him out of his difficulties it refused.

Finally the noble old man was put in prison for debt, and was kept there till some of his friends raised enough money to procure his release. One cannot help thinking that William Penn was a very poor business man, and that, while doing so much for others, he neglected to look out for his own interests. This has been the way with many of the best of men, and it is greatly to their honor.

It was certainly a great sorrow to him that those for whom he had given his work, his time, and his money had proved so ungrateful. Now that he was old and in distress none of those for whom he had done so much came to his aid. Worn out with his troubles, he was about to sell his province to the king when he was stricken with paralysis. He died in 1718, leaving the province to his sons.

We cannot say much in favor of Penn's sons. Their policy was much less just and liberal than his, and their actions caused much irritation and bad feeling in the colony. Disputes continued until after the war of the Revolution, when the State of Pennsylvania bought out the interest of the Penns for the sum of six hundred and fifty thousand dollars. A small price this, but all colonial rights were then at an end and the State might have refused to pay anything.

JAMES OGLETHORPE AND THE DEBTORS' REFUGE

In the days of our forefathers, two or three hundred years ago, England was not a pleasant place to live in. And not only England, but all Europe. It is hard for us to appreciate in these days of merciful laws and kindly customs how cruelly people were treated only that short time ago. In former stories we have told of the severe way they were dealt with if they did not worship God in the manner the government told them to do. And men then were punished very severely for the smallest offences. Great numbers were hung for crimes that would be thought of little importance in our days.

As for the prisons, they were terrible places. The prisons of to-day are palaces compared with them. Close, dark, foul smelling, full of the germs of disease, and crowded with poor wretches of all kinds and classes, they were the most horrible places one could think of. And into these dreadful homes of filth and pestilence were thrust not only the law-breakers and the religious dissenters, but also the debtors—poor men who owed money they could not pay.

There were hundreds of miserable debtors in the prisons, kept where they could not earn the money to pay their debts. Many of them took sick and died, and some were starved to death by cruel jailers, who would not give them food if they had no money to pay for it. The law said that creditors should find food for those they put in jail for debt, but this was often not done, and the poor debtors suffered dreadfully.

In the days when George II. was King of England some of these debtors found a friend. He was a brave English soldier named James Oglethorpe, a general in the British army. He asked about a friend of his who had been put in prison for debt, and was told that he had died there. When he heard this he went to the debtors' prison to see how they were treated, and what he saw there made him sick at heart. Here were numbers of honest men, willing to work if they could, many of them kept in misery and want because their creditors were angry and revengeful.

When General Oglethorpe saw this he determined to do what he could for these poor fellows. If they were set at liberty many of them would find no work to do, but a home might be made for them in America, where they would have the chance to make a fresh start in life.

So the good general went to King George and asked him for a grant of land in America to which he could take some of the most deserving of these debtors, with their families. This was in 1732. Most of the land in the British part of America had already been settled. There only remained the region between South Carolina and Florida, which was still left to the Indians. The British and the Spanish both claimed it, but neither had occupied it, and Oglethorpe proposed to make his colony a military one, that would keep the Spaniards and the Indians in order and protect the English settlements.

George II. willingly granted him the land, and the new province was called Georgia, after his name. Oglethorpe paid the debts of some of the most worthy of the debtors, and in 1733 took out a ship-load of settlers to America. They were not all debtors, for he opened his place of refuge to all the poor and unfortunate and to those who were ill-treated on account of their religion.

In good time the vessel reached the coast of America and sailed into the waters of a fine river to which Oglethorpe gave the name of Savannah. He also gave this name to a town which he laid out on its banks. Thus it was that the colony of Georgia was begun with some of the poorest and most unfortunate people in England, brought there by one of the most noble-hearted of its men.

The debtors soon showed that all they wanted was a chance to work and earn their living. They had been given new life by being taken from prison, and were like new men. They set to at once to cut down trees, build houses, and plant fields, and in a little time the settlement began to look prosperous and flourishing.

For a whole year General Oglethorpe lived in a tent, set up under four pine trees. He was an upright man, and, like William Penn, he knew that it was not the king, but the natives, who owned the land, and that he had no right to it unless he paid them for it.

So, like William Penn, he called the Indian chiefs together and talked with them and made a treaty, agreeing to buy from them at their own price the land he wanted. As the Indians had much more land than they needed, they were quite willing to sell. They seem to have grown to love Oglethorpe as the Indians of Pennsylvania loved William Penn. Some of them gave him a buffalo skin on the inside of which was a painting of the head and feathers of an eagle. They said to him, " The feathers of the eagle are soft, which signifies love; the skin is warm, and is the emblem of protection; therefore love and protect our little families." After that the people of Georgia lived in harmony with the Indians of the colony. All the trouble they had was with the Florida Indians, whom the Spaniards stirred up to molest them.

It was not long before new settlers came to the debtors' colony. Some of these were German Moravians and Lutherans, who had been persecuted at home. Others were Highlanders from Scotland, who had also been ill-treated. Oglethorpe welcomed them all and gave them lands where they could form new settlements. He was proud of his colony of Highlanders, and whenever he visited them he wore the Highland dress, which pleased them highly and won him a warm Scotch welcome.

Georgia soon began to thrive. The climate was warm, so there was no suffering from bitter winter weather, as in the north. Some of them planted corn, others began to raise rice and indigo. Mulberry trees grew wild in the forest, and silkworms were brought from England to feed on their leaves. People also came out who understood silk making. The silk culture was kept up till the Revolution, but not much money was made by it. A silk dress was made for the Queen of England out of the first silk produced. In the end cotton took the place of silk and proved far more profitable.

Among the people who came to the new colony were John and Charles Wesley, who had founded the new sect of the Methodists in England. Their purpose was to try and make Christians of the Indians. After-

HEROES OF PROGRESS 31

wards there came to Georgia another noted Methodist, named George Whitefield, a preacher of wonderful eloquence, who made his way through the colonies, preaching to great multitudes of people. With the money they gave him he supported an orphan asylum which he had established near Savannah.

There were some very curious and very unusual things in the government of the Georgia colony. Slaves were then in common use in all the colonies, but Oglethorpe would not let any be brought into his settlements. He looked on human slavery as a great evil. And he also knew what a bad thing liquor drinking was in England, and would not let any one bring rum into Georgia. All religions were free except the Roman Catholic, but he forbade any Catholics to come into his colony.

Another law that was made was that no man should own a farm beyond a fixed size. He did not want either rich or poor men, but tried to keep all on one level. A curious law was that no woman should have land left her by will. Georgia was to be a military colony, and every one who held land was bound to serve as a soldier when called upon. This was why women, who could not act as soldiers, were forbidden to own land. That was not all. There was no political freedom. All laws were to be made by Oglethorpe and the company he had formed, and the people were deprived of self-government.

Before saying what became of these laws and regulations there is another matter to speak of. Though Spain had not sent a settler into the region of Georgia, she laid claim to it by the right of discovery, for Narvaez and De Soto had journeyed over it two centuries before. The Spaniards of Florida were very angry when they found the English settling there, and when a war broke out between England and Spain there was some hard fighting in that region. Oglethorpe raised an army of white men and Indians in 1740, and tried to take the Spanish city of St. Augustine. He failed in this, and two years afterwards a Spanish army of three thousand men and a fleet of many vessels were sent north to take Georgia from the English. This failed also and the colony was saved.

Some time after this Oglethorpe went back to England. He never returned to America again. In fact, he had plenty of trouble at home. The people complained so bitterly about the severe laws he had made that in time they were all repealed, for they were injuring the progress of the colony. People were then permitted to keep negro slaves, the laws about landholding were changed, and the settlers were allowed to make laws for themselves. It would have been a good thing if the law to keep out rum had been kept, but strong drink gradually made its way in. In fact, Oglethorpe grew so tired of the complaints that in 1752 he gave his province back to the king, and from that time Georgia was a royal colony.

James Oglethorpe was a good and noble-hearted man, but he did not know just how to govern colonists and was wise enough in the end to give up the effort and leave them to govern themselves. He lived to be a very old man, not dying till long after the Revolution, when Georgia was a flourishing State of the American Union, and the little town he had started on the Savannah River was a fine city, its broad streets planted with beautiful shade trees. No doubt he took great pride in the handsome city and the large State which owed their origin to him.

BENJAMIN FRANKLIN, THE FATHER OF THE AMERICAN UNION

FAR back in colonial days there lived in Boston a poor candle-maker named Josiah Franklin, who, like many poor men, was rich in children. There were seventeen of them in all, but only one of these, the youngest son, was ever heard of afterwards. But this one made up for all the rest, for he grew to be one of the greatest men in the whole history of the American colonies.

Little Benjamin showed himself a bright boy, but he had not much chance for schooling. His father had so many children that they had to help him make a living, and Benjamin was put into his father's soap and candle shop when he was ten years old, his school life lasting only two years. He had learned little more than how to read and write, but, like Abraham Lincoln, many years afterwards, he made very good use of this small learning.

He was very fond of books, but had to do all his reading at night by the light of the kitchen fire, or perhaps by a tallow candle of his own making. He was an active and industrious lad, though as fond perhaps of play as of work and, like a true boy, at times given to mischief. He loved the water, and after a while took a fancy to be a sailor, as he was getting very tired of candle and soap making. His father was afraid he might run away to sea, and therefore, as the boy thought so much of books, he took him out of the shop and put him to learn the printing trade with his brother, who had a printing office.

This suited Benjamin very well. He soon learned to set type, but he liked most of all to go to the bookstore, where he got an opportunity to borrow books for his evening reading. The quick-witted little fellow in time fancied that he could write himself, and he began to compose verses, which his brother thought so much of that he printed them and sent the young poet out to sell his own verses. This made him very proud of his talent, until his father laughed at him, saying, "Verse makers are likely to be beggars."

It may be this that caused Benjamin to give up poetry and take to prose. His brother printed a small newspaper, one of the first in America, and the boy began to write small things for it. These he slipped under the office door at night, so that no one should know who wrote them. He grew very proud again when he saw them in print and heard a gentleman in the office talk of them as very good.

Printing a newspaper was not always a pleasant thing in those days. Something James Franklin put in his paper made the governor so angry that he sent him to prison for a month. While he was in jail Benjamin got out the paper and printed some sharp things which seem to have made the governor more angry than ever, for when James Franklin was let out of prison he was forbidden to publish a newspaper any longer.

James got around this by publishing the paper in the name of Benjamin Franklin. This was another thing to make the boy, then only seventeen, proud. It may also have made him a little saucy and rather too independent for an apprentice, for after this there were

HOUSE IN WHICH FRANKLIN WAS BORN

HEROES OF PROGRESS 35

many quarrels between the two brothers, and finally Benjamin left the office, saying he would not work there any longer.

He tried to get work in other printing offices in Boston, but none of them would have him, as they knew that he was apprenticed to his brother. As he could get no employment in Boston, he resolved to leave there. He had to do it secretly, for by law his brother could hold him, so he got some money by selling part of his books, and took passage in a sloop for New York. There was no work to be had in that city, and he next set out for Philadelphia, then the largest city in the colonies.

In his very entertaining autobiography Benjamin Franklin has told us all about this part of his life. We read there the story of how he crossed New Jersey, walking much of the way and going down the Delaware in a boat. When he reached Philadelphia he was in his working clothes, with his very small baggage stuffed into his pockets. He walked up the street, munching at some rolls of bread he had bought at a baker's shop and gazing about curiously at the Quaker city. A girl named Deborah Read, standing at the door of her father's shop, laughed to see this queer-looking boy, with his hands full of bread and his pockets full of clothing. She got to know him better in later years, and in the end became his wife, and a very good one she made.

All this is of interest, as dealing with the early life of a very remarkable man. That he was not a common boy may be seen by what he did in his brother's office before he was seventeen years of age. The remainder of Franklin's autobiography is full of interesting matter and shows us that from the start he was a leader of men and a starter of new things. But we cannot go into the details of these, as his life is full of more important matter, about which something must be said.

The runaway printer's apprentice was not long in finding work to do in Philadelphia. He was an excellent type-setter, and had read so much and had such a fund of information that he was very useful in a printing office.

He was only a year in Philadelphia when the governor of Pennsylvania, seeing how bright and able he was, promised to help him set up a shop of his own, and he took ship for England to buy type and other materials for this purpose. But the money promised him did not come, and he had to go to work as a printer in London, where he stayed for more than a year. The governor had treated him very badly, but in 1729, when he was twenty-three years old, some friends helped him to start in business in Philadelphia and to buy out a newspaper. The next year he married Deborah Read.

Franklin's paper, *The Pennsylvania Gazette,* was soon popular and profitable, and his own writings in it were much appreciated. In a few years he began to publish an almanac, put out under the name of Richard Saunders. It became known as " Poor Richard's Almanac," and was full of useful facts and clever hints and bright sayings, telling people how to live frugally. It was a sort of book of proverbs, and of shrewd common sense, and had a multitude of readers for many years.

Young as he was, Franklin was wide awake to all that was going on, and was well up in literature. He was a friend of the brightest people in the city, and formed a number of them into a social and literary club called the Junto. Simplicity and common sense marked all the doings of the club, for Franklin was its leader and there was never a man of better judgment. It kept together for forty years, and out of it grew the American Philosophical Society, which still stands high among scientific bodies. And the small collection of books made by the members was the beginning of the noble Philadelphia Library, the first subscription library in America.

These were two of the things which Franklin started, but they were not all. He had his eyes on everything, and there was no public movement in which he did not take part. He laid the foundation of the University of Pennsylvania, he formed the first fire company in the city, he was the first to propose street paving, and in fact he was the busiest and most alert citizen of America's greatest city. Any one who wanted anything done went to Franklin first of all.

All this time he was pushing his business and making money. He never put on airs or was too proud to do honest labor, and might be seen in the street wearing a leathern apron, and wheeling goods to his shop in a wheelbarrow, not caring who saw him or what they might think.

Benjamin Franklin soon got to be known as something more than a mere business man. He became an able writer, what he wrote being so full of shrewd sense and discretion that it was read all through the colonies. In addition there was a quaint simplicity about it and a vein of homely and pleasant humor that made it very good reading. People read his writings with satisfaction to-day, and that is more than can be said of the other writers of colonial times.

He was much more than a business man and a writer; he was a keen observer of the ways of nature, and if he had not been so busy in other ways might have made a great figure in science. As it was, he made many discoveries of importance. Thus he pointed out the course of storms over the American continent, he studied the course and character of the Gulf Stream, and he investigated the powers of the different colors in absorbing the heat of the sun.

But his greatest service to science was in the field of electricity. This was then a very young science, and people knew hardly anything about it. No one, for instance, knew that lightning had anything to do with electricity, though some suspected it. Franklin, in his practical way, set himself to find out, and he did it in a very simple manner. He raised a kite into the clouds during a thunder-storm, and when a current of electricity came down the string and a spark flew from a key at the end to his knuckles he was a very happy man, for he knew that he had made a great discovery.

His experiment was talked of and repeated all over Europe and made him a famous man. One man tried it in Russia and brought down so much of the lightning that he was killed by the stroke. But Franklin was quite satisfied with his first trial, and set himself at work to make his discovery of use to mankind. He proposed that buildings should be protected by lightning rods, to carry the electric charge to the earth, and this is one of his practical ideas that are still in use.

One might think that Benjamin Franklin, with his business, and his newspaper, and his looking after the affairs of the city, and his studies in science, and his literary labors and social duties, had quite enough to occupy his time, but he found leisure to do many other things. He was interested in all the affairs of the colonies, and became so active in them that he made himself one of the greatest public men of the time. The shrewd common sense and broad ideas which he applied in his business were also applied in public affairs and proved as useful in one as in the other.

In 1736 he was appointed clerk of the Pennsylvania Assembly, in 1737 was made postmaster of Pennsylvania, and some years later was appointed postmaster general of all the colonies. Soon after he was made clerk he was elected a member of the Assembly, which then met in Philadelphia, and later was one of the commissioners sent to treat with the Pennsylvania Indians.

A very important event in his life took place in 1754, when there was great danger of war with France. A congress of deputies from the colonies was held at Albany to treat with the chiefs of the Iroquois Indians of New York. Pennsylvania sent Franklin as its most important man. What he did was to propose a plan for the union of all the colonies for mutual defence. If they were united, he said, they could take care of themselves and would not need troops from Europe. It was the first step taken towards an American Union.

Franklin, in his quaint way, illustrated the position of the colonies by the figure of a snake broken up into thirteen sections. He wished to make them see that a whole snake was much stronger than one cut up into thirteen bits, each acting for itself, and that a whole union would be the same. His plan was rejected by the congress, whose members were jealous for their several colonies. It was also rejected by the British government, which did not want the colonies to become united and powerful. Franklin was much disappointed, for he felt they were all making a mistake. Thus this first step towards a union in America fell through.

Franklin was now recognized as the ablest statesman in the colonies, and during the remainder of his life he was kept busy in the public service. When General Braddock wanted wagons for his army and could not get them in Virginia, Franklin obtained them for him from the Pennsylvania farmers, promising to pay for them himself if they were lost. The farmers were more ready to trust him than the English general. In 1757 he was sent to England by Pennsylvania to try to make the sons of William Penn pay their share of the tax for the war with the French and Indians, then going on. This was a very different visit from that of some thirty years before, when he went to London as a boy to buy type. He was now in a position to deal with the great men of England, and succeeded in making the Penns do their duty. Seven years later he was sent back to England, this time by all the colonies, to protest against the taxes that were being laid upon Americans. He stayed there over ten years, doing all he could to have the unjust taxes repealed, and before he came back the battle of Lexington had been fought and the whole country was in a wild fever of excitement.

A man of Franklin's ability was wanted now. While brave men were needed in the army, wise men were needed in the councils, and the day after he landed, on May 6, 1775, he was chosen as a member of the Continental Congress. Pennsylvania fully recognized the excellent work he had done in Europe, and in this way rewarded him for it.

HEROES OF PROGRESS

The next year he was one of the famous committee of five to prepare the Declaration of Independence, and soon after was one of the noble fifty-four who risked their lives and all they owned by signing this great paper. When one of the members said after the Declaration had been signed, " Now we must all hang together," Franklin replied, with his ready wit, " Yes, or we will surely all hang separately."

Franklin made himself active and prominent in the Congress, as he did in everything in which he was concerned. His plan to unite the colonies in 1754 had been defeated, but he helped to unite them now by drafting the form of union that was called the Articles of Confederation. He was made the first Postmaster General of the Confederation; he visited Washington's camp and consulted with him upon ways and means; he went to Canada to see if the people there would join the colonies; he worked on important committees, and his influence was felt in everything that was done.

But the great ability of Dr. Franklin, as he was now called, was best recognized when, near the close of 1776, he was sent to France with the hope of gaining its support in the war with England. He was now seventy years old, and was looked upon as one of the foremost people in the world. He had won great fame both as a scientist and as a statesman, and when he appeared in Paris he was greeted with a delight and enthusiasm enough to turn the head of many men.

His simple ways and quaint American manners charmed the French. Though the great University of Oxford had made him a Doctor of Laws, though he was renowned for his learning, his inventions, his discoveries in science, his homely proverbial wisdom, his ability as a statesman, he was only a plain colonist in his dress and manners and won esteem wherever he went. He completely won over the people to favor the American cause, but the government held back from openly aiding the colonists, though it secretly helped them with money. It was not till 1778, after the capture of Burgoyne's whole army, that a treaty was signed and France sent soldiers and ships to the aid of the Americans.

Franklin stayed in Paris, working in a dozen ways for the good of his countrymen. Among other things, he helped to fit out the fleet of vessels with which Paul Jones won his great naval victory. In 1783 he was one of the commissioners to make peace with England, and signed the treaty which gave liberty to the United States.

It was 1785 when Franklin returned from France. He was then in the eightieth year of his age, and the infirmities of old age were telling upon him. His reception in America was enthusiastic. Even Washington was not regarded with more honor and esteem. These two men, the one in war, the other in the council chamber, had been the leaders in gaining liberty for the colonies, and both were looked up to as America's greatest men.

Franklin had barely landed when he was elected President of Pennsylvania, and he filled this office for three years. While he was president it became very evident that the Articles of Confederation were too weak to hold the States together, and a convention was called to form a stronger union. Franklin, as may well be imagined, was elected a member of this convention, and he took a leading part in forming the Constitution of the United States. Thus he aided in completing the work which he had begun in Albany in 1754. The broken sections of the snake were at length firmly united, and a sound union was formed.

This work done, Franklin retired from public life. He had now passed the age for active service, and two years later, on the 17th of April, 1790, the wise old sage passed away, in the eighty-fifth year of his life.

It would be hard to find in history another man who became as eminent in various ways. He was equally great as a statesman, a scientist, and a practical man of affairs, while as a philosopher of homely common sense he has rarely had his equal. His writings continue to this day to be republished in almost every written tongue. They were nearly all produced during his years of editorial work, and they constitute the best and most original literature coming to us from colonial times. Finally, he deserves very great credit for his services in the cause of American liberty, and his persistent efforts in bringing about a union of the colonies and the states.

PATRICK HENRY, THE ORATOR OF THE REVOLUTION

IN 1765 there was an important meeting of the House of Burgesses of Virginia, as the law-making body of that colony was called. They had come together to debate upon a great question, that of the Stamp Act passed by the British Parliament for the taxation of the colonies. Most of the members were opposed to it, but they were timid and doubtful, and dreadfully afraid of saying or doing something that might offend the king. They talked all round the subject, but were as afraid to come close to it as if it had been a chained wolf.

They were almost ready to adjourn, with nothing done, when a tall and slender young man, a new and insignificant member whom few knew, rose in his seat and began to speak upon the subject. Some of the rich and aristocratic members looked upon him with indignation. What did this nobody mean in meddling with so weighty a subject as that before them, and which they had already fully debated? But their indignation did not trouble the young man.

He began by offering a series of resolutions, in which he maintained that only the Burgesses and the Governor had the right to tax the people, and that the Stamp Act was contrary to the constitution of the colony and therefore was void. This was a bold resolution. No one else had dared to go so far. It scared many of the members, and a great storm of opposition arose, but the young man would not yield.

He began to speak and soon there was flowing from his lips a stream of eloquence that took every one by surprise. Never had such glowing words been heard in that old hall. His force and enthusiasm shook the whole Assembly. Finally, wrought up to the highest pitch of indignant patriotism, he thundered out the memorable words: "Cæsar had his Brutus, Charles the First his Cromwell, and George the Third ——" "Treason! Treason!" cried some of the excited members, but the orator went on—" may profit by their example. If this be treason make the most of it." His boldness carried the day; his words were irresistible; the resolutions were adopted; Virginia took a decided stand; and Patrick Henry, the orator, from that time took first rank among American speakers. A zealous and daring patriot, he had made himself a power among the people.

Who was this man that had dared hurl defiance at the king? A few years before he had been looked upon as one of the most insignificant of men, a failure in everything he undertook, an awkward, ill-dressed, slovenly, lazy fellow, who could not even speak the king's English correctly. He was little better than a tavern lounger, most of his time being spent in hunting and fishing, in playing the flute and violin, and in telling amusing stories. He was an adept in the latter and made himself popular among the common people.

He had tried farming and failed. He had made a pretense of studying law, and gained admittance to the bar, though his legal knowledge was very slight. Having almost nothing to do in the law, he spent most of his time helping about the tavern at Hanover Court-House, kept by his father-in-law, who supported him and his family, for he had married early, with little means of keeping his wife.

One day there came up a case in court which all of the leading lawyers had refused. It was called the " Parsons' Cause," and had to do with the claim of the ministers of the Established Church to collect dues from all the people, whatever their religious faith. A refusal to pay these had brought on the suit. The parsons had engaged one of the ablest lawyers of the county town on their side, and none of the lawyers seemed willing to take the opposite side.

What was the surprise of the people when the story went around that Patrick Henry had offered himself on the defendants' side! His taking up the case was a joke to most of them, and a general burst of laughter followed the news. What did this fellow know about the law? He was a good talker, no doubt, in his low Virginia dialect, but what kind of a show would he make in pleading a case before a learned judge! The case of the people seemed desperate indeed when intrusted to such hands as these.

When the young lawyer appeared in court smiles went round among the lawyers and the audience. The idea of this awkward, backward, slovenly, untrained man attempting to handle such an important case! It seemed utterly absurd, and the opposing lawyers felt that they would make short work of him. They had the law on their side, their plaintiffs' case was a good one, their opponent was a mountebank, the defendants would be made to pay.

It is likely enough that Patrick Henry felt much the same way. His powers had never been tried except before a bar-room audience, and he could not have had much confidence in them. Doubtless he would have been glad enough, now it was too late, to get out of the court and back in the friendly tavern of his father-in-law.

When he rose to speak he faltered and hesitated. It looked as if he would break down utterly. But he had spoken before his friends; he was not quite a tyro in oratory; as he went on his timidity vanished and his confidence returned. He warmed up to his subject and a change seemed to come over him. His form straightened, his face filled out, his eyes blazed, the words poured from his mouth, clear, forcible sentences, that carried everybody away with admiration and astonishment, came from his lips. There was not much statute law in what Patrick Henry said, but there was much of the eternal principles of right and justice. What right in equity had these plaintiffs to make the people pay for what they did not want and what they refused to accept? The argument was masterly and irresistible. It was poured forth in a flood of burning eloquence. The plaintiffs could not bear the storm of his accusations. They left the court in confusion. The specious plea of the opposing lawyers was quite overslaughed. The jury, carried away by his argument, returned the plaintiffs a verdict of one penny damages; and the people, filled with enthusiasm, lifted the young advocate on their shoulders and carried him out of the court-house in triumph.

Patrick Henry was a made man. He no longer had to lounge in his office waiting for business. Plenty of it came to him. He set himself for the first time to an earnest study of the law, he improved his dialect and his command of language, the dormant powers of his mind rapidly unfolded, and two years after pleading his first case he was elected a member of the House of Burgesses. We have seen how, in this body, he " set the ball of the Revolution rolling."

The idle tavern orator suddenly found himself launched into greatness. With all his careless habits and rural manners, he was a man of honor and integrity. Those who knew him respected him. For the first time he had learned what was in him, and he worked hard to make the best of his powers. Not many years passed after that great scene in the country court before Patrick Henry was transformed into a new man, one of culture and learning and of extraordinary powers of oratory.

It was the time for such a man to make his force felt. The country was in a critical state. The people were on all sides demanding their rights, and would soon be demanding their liberty. Excitement spread everywhere. Fearless leaders were needed, men full of the spirit of patriotism. Patrick Henry had shown that he was both. In his spirit-stirring oration before the House of Burgesses he had put himself on record for all time. His defiance of the king stamped him as a warrior who had thrown his shield away and thenceforward would fight only with the sword.

The patriot leaders welcomed him. He worked with Thomas Jefferson and others upon the Committee of Correspondence, which sought to spread the story of political events through the colonies. The Virginia Assemblies which were broken up by the governor and called together again by the people welcomed him as a member. He was sent to Philadelphia as a member of the First Continental Congress, and his voice was eloquently heard in that body. In fact, he became one of the most active and ardent of the American patriots.

HANOVER COURT-HOUSE
(Built of brick in 1735. Scene of Henry's maiden leap for fame.)

HEROES OF PROGRESS

Of Patrick Henry's early speeches we know nothing beyond that intense blaze of eloquence with which he electrified the House of Burgesses. The first speech of his on record was that noble one given before the convention held at Richmond in March, 1775. But this was an effort almost without a parallel in the annals of oratory. He had presented resolutions before the convention in favor of an open appeal to arms. To this the more timid spirits made strong opposition. The fight at Lexington had not yet taken place, but Henry's prophetic gaze saw it coming. In a burst of flaming eloquence he laid bare the tyranny of Parliament and king, declared that there was nothing left but to fight, and ended with an outburst thrilling in its force and intensity:

"There is no retreat but in submission and slavery! Our chains are forged! Their clanking may be heard on the plains of Boston! The war is inevitable—and let it come! I repeat, sir, let it come! It is in vain to extenuate the matter! Gentlemen may cry, Peace, peace,—but there is no peace! The war is actually begun! The next gale that sweeps from the north will bring to our ears the clash of resounding arms! Our brethren are already in the field! Why stand we here idle? What is it that gentlemen wish? What would they have? Is life so dear, or peace so sweet, as to be purchased at the price of chains and slavery? Forbid it, Almighty God! I know not what course others may take; but as for me, give me liberty or give me death!"

Where was the idle fisher and fiddler, who had amused himself in telling stories to tavern loungers? Was this the man, this burning orator, whose voice was capable of moving great audiences like a cyclone, and the echo of whose words still thrills our hearts? Certainly in the career of Patrick Henry we have a remarkable example of mental evolution. He was asleep in the early days, an idling dreamer. When he awoke he made the world rock with his voice.

As for Virginia, it listened to his fervid appeal, and when the news of Lexington reached its soil its sons were ready to spring to arms. Henry helped to gather a force of ardent patriots and led them to prevent the royal governor from carrying away the military stores of the state. He was elected Governor of Virginia in 1776, and held the office till 1779, actively aiding the popular cause. He was Governor again in 1784 and 1785.

In 1788, when the Federal Constitution had been formed and the States were called upon to adopt it, Henry, as a member of the Virginia Convention, appeared in a new rôle. He was bitterly opposed to the Constitution, which he said had "an awful squinting towards monarchy," and he opposed its adoption in a number of speeches of extraordinary eloquence. Fortunately he did not succeed, the demand for a stronger Union being too great for even his powers of oratory.

He died June 6, 1799, with the reputation of being the greatest of American orators. John Randolph of Roanoke, himself one of Virginia's famous orators, has said that Patrick Henry was Shakespeare and Garrick in one, with their genius applied to the actual business of life.

SAMUEL ADAMS, THE FATHER OF AMERICAN LIBERTY

FROM 1760 to 1775 Boston was the hotbed of resistance to British oppression. George III., furious at the rebellious spirit of his unruly subjects beyond the seas, laid his hand on that unquiet city with crushing weight, while a stalwart group of patriots resisted and defied the efforts of their oppressors. At the head of these was a daring son of the soil named Samuel Adams, the man who had more to do in inspiring the minds of the people with the spirit of independence than any other man in the colonies. It has been truly said that if the title of Father of America belongs to any one man Samuel Adams was the man.

It was he that led in all the movements against "taxation," and he was ever earnest in efforts to keep the spirit of resistance alive. Poor though he was, he could not be bought. Efforts to bribe him to desert the cause of liberty were made, but they only served to make him more determined still.

Mather Byles, a Tory clergyman of Boston, one day said to him with insidious pleasantry: "Come, friend Samuel, let us relinquish republican phantoms and attend to our fields."

"Very well," said stalwart Sam, to give him his familiar title, "you attend to the planting of liberty and I will grub up the taxes. Thus we shall both have pleasant places."

Adams was an educated man. Born in 1722, he graduated from Harvard College in 1740. Afterwards, when he took the degree of master of arts, his thesis showed the prevailing trend of his thoughts. He chose the question, " Whether it be lawful to resist the supreme magistrate if the commonwealth cannot otherwise be preserved?" We need not say which side of the question he argued for.

Adams engaged in business, but did not succeed. He was afterwards collector of taxes in Boston. He was elected to the Assembly of Massachusetts in 1765 and remained there nine years, winning great influence by his courage, talents, and energy. Before this he had gained a reputation as a political writer. He was not a great orator, but he was a bold and daring one, and early became a leader of the people. At the very first whisper of opposition to the designs of the king Adams was in the field, ready and eager to act whenever occasion served, a fervid, active, independent spirit, knowing what to do and how to do it, and ready to give his services and his life in the cause of his country.

Such a man was Sam Adams, Boston's popular leader. John Adams, his cousin, referring to the patriots, wrote of him as early as 1765: "Adams, I believe, has the most thorough understanding of liberty and her resources in the temper and character of the people, though not in the law and constitution, as well as the most habitual radical love of it, of any of them."

It was this radical love of liberty that made him a thorn in the side of George III. and his myrmidons. No sooner was a party formed opposed to the British yoke than Adams came to the front as its leader. In 1764, ten years before the Revolution, we hear his voice protesting in the name of Boston and all America against the plan for taxing the colonies. In the words of John Adams, he was " always for softness, prudence, and delicacy where they will do, but stanch and stiff and strict and rigid and inflexible in the cause."

It was Adams who in 1765 suggested the idea of a Colonial Congress, and who afterwards became a strong advocate of the Continental Congress. As events became more critical, he became more resolute and outspoken. At the time of the " Boston Massacre " he was spokesman of the committee that demanded that the troops should be removed from Boston, and it was his boldness that forced them out.

The most dramatic event in his life occurred on that memorable night of December 16, 1773, when the ships lay in Boston harbor laden with the tea which the king and his advisers were seeking to force on the Americans. That night a great town-meeting was held at Faneuil Hall, with Adams as one of its principal speakers. The hour advanced, the efforts to induce the authorities to remove the tea-ships peacefully had failed, it was known that the tea would be forcibly landed in the morning. Compromise, persuasion, had failed. Action was demanded. Adams rose to his feet and said, " This meeting can do nothing more to save the country."

Were these words a prearranged signal? It seemed so. Scarcely were they spoken when a shrill war-whoop was heard in the street, and a party of men disguised as Indians and armed with hatchets rushed impetuously past, seeking the wharves. Here they boarded the ships, carried the tea-chests from the hold, broke them open with their hatchets, and poured the tea into the harbor. It was the famous " Boston tea-party," which did more than any one thing besides to speedily bring on the Revolution.

This was only one of his acts. " Step by step, inch by inch, he fought the enemies of liberty during the dark hours before the Revolution." On that dark night in April, 1775, when the British in Boston were plotting to send out a force of soldiers to seize the stores at Concord, they had another purpose in view. Samuel Adams and John Hancock were then in the village of Lexington, whither they had fled from arrest, and General Gage was as eager to lay hands on these patriot leaders as upon the Concord stores. But before the soldiers reached Lexington the birds had flown. Paul Revere had ridden through that fateful night, roused them from sleep, and warned them of the coming troops.

To this day the house in which they slept that night is preserved as a memorial of American liberty, and on the village green near by stands a statue which marks the spot where the first British shots were fired and the first patriots fell. The beginning of the struggle for liberty dates from that night and the day that followed.

Adams was elected to the First Continental Congress in 1774, and was one of the two popular leaders excepted from the general pardon offered by the British government in June, 1775. He was one of the two who had sinned beyond forgiveness. Yet at first, in the Continental Congress, he spoke in favor of a peaceful settlement of the difficulty with England. This mood of softness did not last. Later, when some members of the Congress grew hopeless of success, Adams ardently exclaimed: " I should advise persisting in our struggle for liberty though it were revealed from Heaven that ninety-nine would perish and only one of a hundred were to survive and retain his liberty.

One such freeman must possess more virtue and enjoy more happiness than a hundred slaves, and his children may have what he has so nobly preserved."

When the Declaration was prepared he was one of the most ready to sign it, and his signing was the occasion for the delivery of the only example of his eloquence which we possess. He closed with the words: " For my own part, I ask no greater blessing than to share the common danger and the common glory. If I have a wish dearer to my soul than that my ashes may be mingled with those of a Warren and a Montgomery, it is that these American States may never cease to be free and independent."

Adams continued in Congress until after the surrender of Yorktown, working so diligently and with such judgment and order that some have called him " the helmsman of the Revolution." He withdrew after liberty had been gained, and afterwards helped to form the constitution of Massachusetts, was a senator of that State, its Lieutenant-Governor from 1789 to 1794, and Governor from 1795 to 1797. Always poor, he died so in 1803. John Adams has said of him as a speaker and writer, that in his works may be found " specimens of a nervous simplicity of reasoning and eloquence that have never been rivalled in America."

THOMAS JEFFERSON, AUTHOR OF THE DECLARATION OF INDEPENDENCE

The name of Thomas Jefferson always calls up to us a vision of the Declaration of Independence, that famous state paper which has never been surpassed in this or any country. Jefferson was its author, and his name will ever remain associated with it. Elected to the Continental Congress, he took his seat in that body on the day when news reached Philadelphia of the battle of Bunker Hill and of the splendid fighting of the "rebel" troops. Washington was then on his way to Boston to take command of the army, and the hope of liberty burned high in the people's hearts.

Eight months later, when the British army sailed away from Boston and left it to the Continentals, this hope burned still stronger, and men began to feel that it was time to cut loose for good and all from British rule and sail onward in a ship of independence of their own. So a resolution in favor of such a course was offered in Congress, and five men, Thomas Jefferson, John Adams, Benjamin Franklin, Roger Sherman, and Robert R. Livingston, were chosen to draft a declaration to be given to the world.

This declaration was to show why and on what grounds the American colonies claimed freedom, and Thomas Jefferson was chosen by his four fellow members to write it. He was known by them to be an able writer on such subjects, and two years before he had published "A Summary View of the Rights of

British America," which had attracted great attention and was full of the sentiments they wished.

So Jefferson was selected to write the paper, and did so. He did it so well that his fellow members felt more like clapping him on the back than making changes in it. Hardly a word was rewritten, either by the committee or by Congress, and it was quickly passed and signed, as America's declaration to the world. It is to-day regarded as one of the ablest documents ever written, and as the most important state paper in modern political history, and it will make the name of Thomas Jefferson famous for many centuries to come.

On a Virginia plantation near the present city of Charlottesville, Thomas Jefferson was born in the year 1743. Not far away rose the Blue Ridge Mountains, and broad forests spread for miles around, for the country was then very thinly settled. Here the young Virginian grew up, learning to ride, swim, and shoot, and reading every book he could get. He was fond of music, too, and spent many hours learning to play on the violin. He was a tall, straight, slender boy, with reddish hair; no beauty, but a pleasant-looking lad.

At seventeen he entered William and Mary College, studied like a young Trojan, graduated in two years, and then began to study law as diligently. When admitted to the bar he quickly won a place among the foremost lawyers of the time.

The young lawyer soon became active in politics. These were the days of the Stamp Act and the Tea Tax, and America held no more ardent patriot than our bright youthful Virginian. A fine-looking fellow he had then grown to be, over six feet tall, with square, well-cut features, ruddy skin, and a face full of intelligence. He had a quick, positive way of speaking and paid little heed to the over-formal politeness of the day, characteristics that made him prominent. A rigid republican, he did not even like the formality of " Mr." Anything like a title displeased him.

He believed in the equality of all men, and was bitterly opposed to slavery. He said, " I tremble for my country when I remember that God is just, for this is politically and morally wrong."

Jefferson was no orator. He never made a formal speech in his life. But he was a deep and able thinker, an adept with the pen, and he soon ranked with the ablest political leaders of the age. He took an active part in all the movements of that period of excitement, was seen in all the conventions and congresses called, was always active, zealous, and capable, and crowned his work at length with the noble Declaration of Independence, the writing of which formed the high-water mark of his life.

Jefferson soon left Congress to enter the legislature of his native State. Descended from the best stock of Virginia, and as well born as its greatest aristocrat, he was still a democrat to the core. He did not believe in the privileges claimed by the proud old families. Liberty and equality were his watchwords. He had put them in the Declaration, and he worked for them in his State. He fought for religious freedom till he got it, and he stopped the importation of slaves. He also drew up an excellent plan for the education of all the children of Virginia. If he could, he would have put everybody on the same plane and have them all start equal in life.

When Patrick Henry gave up the office of Governor Jefferson succeeded him. But he was not a military

HEROES OF PROGRESS 59

man and was not suited to this office in time of war, and at the end of his term he declined to serve again and was succeeded by a soldier, General Nelson, of Yorktown. But in 1783, when the treaty of peace with Great Britain was made, he had the honor of reporting it to Congress, and thus completed the work he had begun with the Declaration of Independence seven years before. It must have been a great joy to him to proclaim that the world now acknowledged this independence.

Let us here give some anecdotes which are told of Jefferson. In 1770, when he was practicing law, his old home at Shadwell took fire and burned down. When word was brought him of it his first thought was for his favorite books, and he eagerly asked if they had been saved.

"No, massa," said the ebony servitor. "Dey is burned up; but de fire didn't git yo' fiddle. We sabed dat."

To the simple-minded negro a fiddle was of more account than a whole library of books.

The burning of the old Jefferson mansion was a serious loss. A new one had to be built, and for it he chose the top of a forest-covered hill near by, five hundred and eighty feet high, on the side of which was a favorite spot where he had loved to sit and read and converse with his special college friend. Here, under a great oak, this friend, Dabney Carr, was afterwards buried, for the two had made a compact that he who died first should have his grave under their favorite oak. Many years later Jefferson was buried on the same spot beside his old friend.

The hill was named Monticello, or "Little Mountain." Jefferson had its broad, round top leveled off, and he built there a handsome manor-house, of his own designing, which has since been known as Monticello. It is to-day a place of pilgrimage for patriotic Americans. A few miles away stands the University of Virginia, of which he was the founder. Not far away is the old Virginian town of Charlottesville.

An interesting story is told of how, in 1772, Jefferson brought his young wife home to this newly finished mansion. They had more than a hundred miles to travel in midwinter, with no easier way of doing it than in a two-horse carriage. At least, the only easier way of traveling in those days would have been to put more horses to their carriage.

Much of the way ran through the forest, the trees often meeting over the road. As they went on it began to snow, and long before their home was reached a thick white carpet covered the ground. Night had fallen and the hour was late when the high hill was reached and they began to climb the steep roadway up its side to the house on the summit. As they drew near the darkness was deep and not a light to be seen. The servants, not expecting their master and mistress at that hour, were all asleep in their cabins, and there was not a fire in the house.

A gloomy and chilly welcome was that which Monticello gave to its young mistress. Fortunately, they were at that age when ill hap does not weigh heavy and discomfort can be easily borne. The shivering pair had to go straight to bed to keep from freezing. The next morning the fires were all blazing, the house was bright and cheerful, they were able to laugh at their predicament of the night before, and they began what was to be a long and happy life in their mountain home.

There is another story told of Monticello that might

HEROES OF PROGRESS 61

have led to a more tragic ending. Years later, when the Revolutionary war was nearing its end and the British troops had invaded Virginia, there came with them Colonel Tarleton, the daring cavalry leader who had been fighting with Morgan and Marion and other patriot leaders in the South. Jefferson was then at Monticello, and the Legislature of Virginia was in session at Charlottesville, a few miles away. It seemed to Tarleton a good chance to catch all the Virginia leaders in one nest.

While the family at Monticello were at breakfast, up the hillside came a frightened horseman at full speed. When he reached the door he shouted: "The British are coming! Fly for your lives! Tarleton will soon be here with his dragoons!"

When the man was questioned he told Jefferson that Tarleton, with two hundred and fifty men, had galloped into Louisa, twenty miles away, at midnight. The family was in a panic, but Jefferson coolly told them to finish their breakfast, as there was time enough. He then sent the family away to a place of safety, but stayed behind to gather certain precious papers.

Soon came another messenger, shouting that the British were coming up the mountain. Jefferson listened. No sounds of hoofs could be heard. He rode to a place where he could look down on Charlottesville. All was quite and peaceful there. Deeming it another false alarm, he turned back, intending to get more of his papers.

As he did so he saw that his sword was missing, having fallen from the scabbard. He turned to search for it, and, looking down on Charlottesville again, saw that a great change had taken place in that little borough. Armed horsemen filled its streets. He could see some of them already on the road to Monticello, galloping at full speed. Jefferson put spurs to his horse and rode swiftly away. His fallen sword had saved him from capture. A brief delay longer and the author of the Declaration would have been a prisoner in British hands.

Another story is told of this raid which, if true, goes to show how faithful to their masters were the old Virginian slaves. Two of them, Martin and Cæsar, were trying to save the silver plate of the house by hiding it in a secret place closed by a trap-door. Cæsar entered the hole, and Martin handed him down the plate. They had not finished when they heard the British bursting into the house. Martin quickly closed the trap, and the faithful Cæsar lay without a sound in the dark hole until the British were gone. He was a sorry figure when he was drawn out.

To go back now to history, we may say that Jefferson went to Congress in 1783, and in 1784 was sent abroad as Minister to France from the young republic. He remained five years in France, so that he was not home at the time of the making of the Constitution. But those were exciting days in France. The great French Revolution was at hand, and everybody was talking of liberty and the rights of man. What he saw and heard there made him a greater lover of human rights than ever. He was active in other ways. A practical farmer, he sent home seeds, plants, and everything which he thought would be of use to grow in American fields and gardens.

He came home in 1789 to find that Washington had been made President and had chosen him for Secretary of State. It was an honor he did not want, but the President would not let him off, for he was anxious

HEROES OF PROGRESS 63

to have the ablest men in the country in his Cabinet. Jefferson was Secretary of State for five years, and then he resigned. There had been quarrels between him and Alexander Hamilton, Secretary of the Treasury. Hamilton was a strong aristocrat, Jefferson a strong democrat, and the two men could not agree. At last, in 1794, Jefferson, tired of the constant disputes, gave it up and went home to Monticello.

Like Washington, he was fond of home life and farming. He enjoyed landscape gardening and architecture, and was never more happy than when he was adding new beauty to his place. He did not lack company. Many visitors came to see the great statesman, despite the fact that Monticello could be reached only by a long and wearisome carriage journey.

He would have liked to spend his life at Monticello, but when Washington gave up the presidency and John Adams was elected in his place, Jefferson was chosen for Vice-President. So he had to go back again to Philadelphia, then the capital of the country, and devote himself to public duties. He did not enjoy it any more than before, for Adams was hard to get along with, and the old bad feeling between him and Hamilton was kept up.

Four years later, in 1800, Jefferson was chosen for the highest honor the country had to bestow. He was elected President. A new Democratic party had been formed, of which he was the leader, and the old aristocratic Federal party, of which Hamilton was the head, was losing its power.

Now was the time for the great believer in democracy and the simple life to show his feeling. He hated all pomp and display. Washington, when inaugurated, had gone to the Capitol in a carriage drawn by six cream-colored horses. Adams had also gone there with pomp and ceremony. Men now looked for another grand parade, and great was their surprise when they saw a plainly-dressed man, without servant or guard, ride up to the Capitol grounds, spring from his horse, fasten its bridle to the fence, and walk up to the Capitol. This was Thomas Jefferson, the great democrat, coming to be inaugurated as President of the United States. He wanted the people to see that he was a man like themselves, free from all pride and ostentation.

Jefferson was President for eight years. They were exciting years, for the great wars of Napoleon were going on in Europe, and England and France gave so much trouble to America, by interfering with its commerce, that it was hard to keep this country from going to war with one or the other of them. The people were very angry with England for taking sailors out of American vessels to serve in their warships, and Jefferson, who was a man of peace, found this very hard to bear.

The troubles in Europe did one great good for this country. France held the great region between the Mississippi River and the Rocky Mountains, then known as Louisiana. Napoleon had taken this region from Spain, but he was now much afraid that England, with her strong fleet, would take it from him, so he offered to sell it at a small price to the United States. Jefferson was glad to purchase it, for he was wise enough to see how valuable it would become.

To-day this great domain is divided into a number of states, with millions of people and many thriving cities, and what is known as the Louisiana Purchase has been celebrated by a splendid World's Fair, held at

HEROES OF PROGRESS

St. Louis, its principal city. Jefferson's name is as fully associated with this great addition to our territory as it is with the Declaration of Independence.

A happy man was Thomas Jefferson in 1809, when, his public life ended, he was free from the cares of office, and could go home to his family, his books, and his farm. The wife he had brought home that stormy night had died many years before, but there were children in the house, both his own and those of his friend Dabney Carr, who had married his sister Martha. She was left poor, and Jefferson took her home with her six children, bringing them up as tenderly as though they were his own.

He had abundance of company, too. He was so hospitable that his house was always full of guests, some of whom stayed for months at a time. He was so free-handed in this and other ways that in his old days he became poor and was forced to sell his precious library to save his home. Fortunately, his friends came to his aid and money was sent him to pay his debts.

The end came on the Fourth of July, 1826, exactly fifty years from the day the Declaration of Independence was adopted. At noon on that day the great patriot breathed his last. It is singular that John Adams, who was on the committee with him to prepare the Declaration, died on the same day.

ROBERT MORRIS, THE FINANCIER OF THE REVOLUTION

War is to us a picture, a brilliant show of material splendor, a glorious display of daring deeds. We see the flash of weapons and the waving of banners. We hear the stirring sounds of music and the measured beat of marching feet. We read of valiant deeds on the fields of battle and of men giving their lives for their country's cause, and hearing and seeing all this we are too apt to forget what lies behind.

The bright picture of war has an opposite side, on which are painted the dark forms of misery and suffering and death in all its terrors. But aside from this there is something else that lies behind the show. War is costly. We are told that " money is the sinews of war." All the " show and circumstance of glorious war " has to be paid for, and the country in which we live might not have won its freedom had there not been a noble man ready to pay the cost, a man whose story every patriot should read. There were three men to whom American liberty was chiefly due: Washington, the general; Franklin, the statesman; and Morris, the financier, and without the work of the latter, freedom might not have been won.

Like many others who took part in the Revolution, Robert Morris came from England, his native place being the city of Liverpool, where he was born in 1734. But he was still a young boy when his father brought him across the sea, and he grew up to be as true-hearted a patriot as any son of the soil. No man did more than he to save the country from ruin and to aid the patriot soldiers on the field of battle.

The city of Philadelphia was his home, and there, as he grew up, he showed a marvellous talent for business. He began at the age of fifteen in the counting-house of a firm of Philadelphia merchants, and worked with such diligence and ability that at the age of twenty he was made a member of the firm. This was an excellent beginning for an ambitious boy, and we may be sure that he made the most of his opportunity. At any rate, the firm thrived after he became a member, and he soon began to grow rich.

Time went on, and troubles came to the country. War broke out with the French; then came the disputes with England, the stamp tax, the tea tariff, the insolent soldiers in Boston, the war spirit in the people. All this time Robert Morris was attending to his business with diligence and enterprise and making money fast, while everybody praised him as a man of integrity and uprightness. Willing & Morris was the name of the firm. No other firm in Philadelphia, then the largest city in the country, did a larger business, so that by the time the war with England began Morris was a very wealthy man. But it must be remembered that it did not take as much money to make wealth in those days as it does now. A million dollars counted for as much then as a hundred millions do now.

In the midst of his business Robert Morris never forgot the country that had given him a home. He was an earnest patriot through all the troubles of the time. His firm did a large business with England, buying there to sell in America, but in 1765, when the Stamp Act was passed, and the colonists vowed they would buy no article made in England, Morris supported them in this, though he knew it would be a great loss to him.

When the Revolution began he was looked upon as a stanch friend of the country. In 1775 he was elected a member of the Continental Congress, and in 1776 he was one of those bold patriots who signed the Declaration of Independence. In his own mind he felt that it was too soon for this, and that the members were too hasty and had better feel their way. But there it was, the work was done, and as a true American he put his name to it. In doing this he cut loose from all allegiance to England and threw in his lot with the land he had made his home.

Morris was one of the kind of men the young country sadly needed. He had great business ability and judgment, and as a member of the Committee of Ways and Means his knowledge of money matters and skill in affairs of finance made him of the greatest service to the cause of liberty.

But this was only through good advice and careful handling of the funds. The time came when more were wanted. The country was poor; Congress had no means of raising money; yet the soldiers in the field had to be fed and clothed, even if they were not paid; arms and ammunition had to be supplied, for they could not fight without them, and the Treasury at times was empty. Paper money was issued, printed promises to pay, but there got to be so much of this afloat that few were willing to take it. Its value in time went down almost to nothing.

It was then that Robert Morris showed the kind of patriot he was. He helped the Government with his own money. He borrowed large sums from his friends. When people of means were not willing to lend their

HEROES OF PROGRESS 69

money to Congress, Morris came to its support, and he used the credit of his firm to borrow for its needs. The word of Robert Morris was as good as gold, and people who would not trust Congress were ready to trust him.

On that brilliant Christmas Day of 1777, when Washington turned the tide of the war by the splendid victory of his ragged Continentals at Trenton, the army chest was empty, there was not a penny to pay the troops. The victor could not follow up his success without some cash in hand, and he wrote a letter of earnest appeal to Robert Morris, who responded nobly. " Whatever I can do for the good of the service shall be done," he replied, and on New Year's morning he went from house to house among his friends in Philadelphia, raising people from their beds to borrow money for the troops in the field.

In this way $50,000 in hard money was obtained and sent to Washington. It saved the army from falling to pieces and was a wonderful aid to Washington in following up his victory. Morris had a warm admiration for the grand soldier whom he thus helped, and said of him, " He is the greatest man on earth."

A strong, large, fine-looking man was Robert Morris, active in business, but speculative in disposition. There are few anecdotes of his private life, but here is one. In his earlier business days he went out on several voyages as supercargo on ships of the firm, and once, during the war with France, the ship he was on was captured and he was taken prisoner. He had no money with which to pay ransom. But he knew how to do things and secured his release by repairing a watch of one of the French officers.

He was made a member of the Council of Safety in

1775, and during the Revolution did valuable service on various committees of Congress. In 1778, when Lord North offered terms of settlement with the colonies if they would yield to the king, he wrote these strong words: " No offer ought to have a hearing for one moment unless preceded by acknowledgment of our independence. We can never be a happy people under their domination."

During all this time he continued to supply the Government with money, either his own or that borrowed on his credit. When the paper money issued by Congress grew to be worth little more than rags, Morris kept things going by the hard cash of himself and his friends. He is said to have raised much more than one million dollars in all, with no assurance that he would ever get a penny of it back. But he was too sincere a patriot to let any such thought as this trouble him.

This was not all. He did his utmost to arrange some system under which the necessary funds might be raised and the nation gain credit instead of sinking into bankruptcy. He wanted a strong central government, with the right to collect the revenues, instead of leaving this right to the States, and he got the brilliant author Thomas Paine to write in support of this. He wished to establish a solid continental system of finance which would make Congress more than a mere figurehead to the thirteen independent States.

In 1781 Congress saw that the war could not go on unless some very able man should be put over the money matters of the country, and Robert Morris was the only man anybody thought of for this work, so he was appointed Superintendent of Finances. Congress could not have pleased the people better. Every-

HEROES OF PROGRESS

body was satisfied with their choice. Many looked upon Morris as a sort of magician, who knew how to get something from nothing. As for him, he did not see his way clear to do anything of the kind, and the prospect ahead was not very pleasant.

It was his duty to look after the funds in the Treasury and to do his best to add to them. It was a hard task. There was very little to look after, and it was almost impossible to add anything to it. He appealed to the States for money, but grew sick of the delay in getting it. Cash came in pennies instead of dollars, and his demands and appeals were alike in vain.

One of the first things he did was to establish the Bank of North America, the first bank in the country. This was chartered by Congress on the last day of the year 1781. Morris lost no time in getting it under way, and spared no pains in inducing people of wealth to buy its stock and put gold and silver money into its vaults. Thomas Paine put $500 of his own money in it and used his brilliant pen and his persuasive powers to get others to do the same.

The credit of the bank was soon established, and before long Morris was able to help the suffering army. During the first six months of the bank's existence he loaned the Government $400,000 from it, and $80,000 more to the State of Pennsylvania. His brilliant plan had proved a complete success.

For three of the most trying years the country ever went through in money matters Morris was at the head of its finances, working like a giant to help it through. He had not only the needs of the army to look after, but those of the navy as well, for money was needed to fit out vessels and pay the sailors. Even after peace came his duties went on. The country was very poor. Congress had no power to collect money from the States or to lay taxes of any kind. He resigned at length in 1783, worn out with his work and disgusted with the doings of Congress and the States. He said: "To increase our debts while the prospect of paying them diminishes does not consist with my idea of integrity."

Morris did not come out of the war a poor man. He was still wealthy, as wealth was regarded in those days. He lived in a handsome house, with doors and furniture of finely-wrought mahogany, but he was not the man to make a grand display. On the banks of the Schuylkill he built a pleasantly situated country residence which was not finished until after 1787. It stood upon the bluff above Fairmount, and was called by him "The Hills." It still stands and is now known as the Lemon Hill mansion. Here thousands collect in the summer season, for near by is a large music pavilion where bands play several times weekly.

Robert Morris did not give up his interest in the country in his later years. Twice he served as a member of the Pennsylvania legislature, and he was one of those who helped to make the Constitution of the United States. When the new government was organized, with Washington for President, Morris was asked to take the responsible position of Secretary of the Treasury. He declined and named Alexander Hamilton for the difficult post, saying that he was a better man in finance than himself. He was elected, however, to the United States Senate and served one term in the first Senate of the country.

Morris had given much of his fortune to the country and had neglected his business to devote himself to poorly paid public duties. But his business capacity remained and after the war he went to work again, now engaging in the East India trade. In the year he resigned the office of financier he sent the "Empress of China" from New York to Canton, this being the first American vessel that ever entered that port. He marked out a route to China by which the dangerous winds that at certain seasons blow over the Pacific might be avoided, and to prove that he was right he sent a vessel over this route. The voyage proved successful and profitable.

We have said that Morris was speculative in disposition. He proved this after 1790 by going very largely into land speculations, buying a great deal of wild land in the western part of New York. He bought lands also in Pennsylvania and elsewhere, but his investments proved failures, his lands could not be sold, and the once wealthy merchant lost all his money and fell deeply into debt.

Before telling the story of his later life there is an interesting episode that must be narrated. In 1795 he bought the square of land in Philadelphia between Chestnut and Walnut and Seventh and Eighth Streets, paying for it $50,000. To-day it might take fifty millions to purchase it. Here he began to build a large house, on such a scale that it came to be known as "Morris's Folly." One envious man says of it: "A person is just now building at an enormous expense a palace in Philadelphia."

Was it a palace or a folly? It was probably neither. It was built of brick, with light stone trimmings to doors and windows, its depth being between 80 and 100 feet and its width between 40 and 60. According to Morris's account, the amount spent on it was only $16,370. Begun in 1795, work went on in a slow way until 1800, when it was abandoned unfinished, its doors and windows being boarded up. It was never finished, and in time was torn down to make way for other buildings.

The only folly in it was that Morris was hopelessly in debt when he began to build it. He held many square miles of wilderness, but could not pay his debts with this. In those days people could be imprisoned for debt, and this was poor Morris's fate. In 1798 he was put in prison and remained there for three years and a half. The debts proved against him are said to have amounted to $3,000,000. Great as they were and poor as was the country, it has ever since been looked upon as a shameful disgrace to the United States that its great benefactor should be allowed to suffer from poverty and imprisonment in his old age. It is one of the dark spots on our banner that can never be wiped off.

Debtors had to pay their own way in prison if their creditors did not, and Morris was destitute. He wrote at one time, "Starvation stares me in the face." Rooms in the prison were high in price, and he could not afford a room to himself. He could not even buy paper to write on and had to borrow it from his fellow prisoners. Washington visited him in prison during a visit to Philadelphia in 1798, but no one took any steps for his release. A pathetic story is told about his prison life. He was allowed to walk in the prison yard and walked around it fifty times a day. To count the number, he carried pebbles in his pocket and dropped one at each round. It seems, however, that the poor prisoner did not become careless and despairing, for one who visited him said that he was always neat and careful in dress.

Morris was adjudged a bankrupt in 1801 and was released on August 26 of that year. He was now old and poor, his life approaching its end. He died in Philadelphia, May 8, 1806, a striking example of the ingratitude of nations. The country for which he had done so much suffered him to languish for years in a prison cell, and only one monument of his work remains, the Bank of North America, in its early days the salvation of the Government, to-day a flourishing banking institution of Philadelphia.

ALEXANDER HAMILTON, THE ARCHITECT OF AMERICAN FINANCE

In those dark days before the American Revolution, when the colonies were choosing delegates to a congress to offer their protest to the king, an open-air meeting—" the great meeting in the fields," it was afterwards called—was held in New York to select delegates for that colony. Speech after speech was made, but none of the speakers got to the pith of the matter. At length a new speaker appeared on the platform, who seemed to be pushed forward by his friends. The audience looked at him in surprise. A small, slight, boyish fellow, with dark skin and deep-set eyes; what could this boy have to say?

He had much to say. Faltering and hesitating at first, he was soon speaking freely and to the point. He laid down clearly the principles involved, strongly depicted the oppressions of England, and in a burst of fervid eloquence went on to point out the duty of the people, to resist to the last drop of their blood.

" The sacred rights of mankind are not to be rummaged for among old parchments and musty records," declared this wonderful boy; " they are written as with a sunbeam in the whole volume of human nature, by the hand of Divinity itself, and no mortal power can erase or obscure them."

As he went on, ardent and glowing with youthful fire, describing " the waves of rebellion, sparkling with fire, and washing back on the shores of England the wrecks of her power, her wealth, and her glory," the

HEROES OF PROGRESS 77

whole audience took fire, and cheer after cheer responded to the orator's words. "It is a collegian!" they said, as they looked with wonder on the boyish speaker.

A collegian he was, a student at King's College (now Columbia University), Alexander Hamilton by name. In the College halls he had soared over all his fellows in acuteness of reasoning and fervor of eloquence, and it was to their admiration that he owed this first public appearance. With it Hamilton began his career in the world of affairs, in which he was to occupy a marked position during the remaining thirty years of his life.

Alexander Hamilton was a West Indian by birth, born in the little island of Nevis, of a Scotch father and a French Huguenot mother. This was in 1757. A frightful hurricane desolated the Leeward Islands in 1772, and an account of it was published that attracted wide attention by its force and vivid description. The surprise was greater when it was found to be the work of a boy of fifteen—the same one who at seventeen electrified the great audience in New York.

He was then a counting-house clerk in the island of St. Croix, but his relatives thought that so bright a boy ought to have a chance for the best education, and they raised money and sent him to Boston. From there he made his way to New York, entered an excellent school at Elizabethtown, N. J., and in 1773 was admitted to King's College. Here he progressed with remarkable rapidity in his classes. He had read and written much while in the West Indies, and now devoured every scrap of learning that came to his hands, wrote hymns and burlesques, defeated all his fellows in the debating hall, was a pious youth who prayed as passionately as he spoke, but among his companions was lively and gay, ready to take part in all that went on.

The clear-minded young West Indian, though a British subject by birth, quickly became infected with the spirit of the colonists, cast his lot with them for good or bad, and became as ardent a "rebel" as the best of them. That speech in the fields was his "coming out" event. He now took to the pen and answered the arguments of the Tory supporters of Great Britain so ably that many thought his writings came from some of the eminent thinkers of the country. When they found who was their author he became famous at once.

From that time forward Hamilton was active and prominent in all the exciting doings of the times. Even in college his patriotic fervor led him to organize a military corps among his fellow students, who called themselves "Hearts of Oak," and wore a green uniform and a leather cap, on which was the motto "Freedom or Death!" With all this he was a busy student, an active writer, a frequent speaker, bold, zealous, yet cool and self-repressed, often seeking to check the patriotic party when it inclined to violence.

Young, ardent, and patriotic, Hamilton had a strong taste for a military life, joined a company of volunteers, and in March, 1776, was made the captain of an artillery company. We are not here interested in his career as a soldier, and will only say that he showed such courage and skill that Washington appointed him his aide-de-camp, and took so strong a fancy to him that he made him his private secretary. During most of the remainder of those terrible years of war Hamilton was Washington's most intimate friend, adviser, and confidant, the great general often conferring with and seeking the advice of his youthful secretary, whose opinion on military matters he highly valued. In after years he came to value Hamilton for like abilities in matters of peace, and remained his warm friend till his death. The voluminous correspondence of Washington during the war mainly fell upon Hamilton, and Troup says of it: " The pen of our country was held by Hamilton; and for dignity of manner, pith of matter, and elegance of style, General Washington's letters are unrivalled in military annals."

Of Hamilton's military career we shall only say that he took part ably in Washington's principal battles, carried one of the British forts at Yorktown, and as a reward for his bravery was selected to receive the surrender of one division of Cornwallis's army. The war done, he spent some time in Congress, where, as one of the members said, " his winning eloquence was the wonder and delight of friend and foe." Resigning within a year, he engaged in the practice of law in New York. He had given little time to legal study, but his quickness and ability were such that he rose at once to the first rank in his profession, his forceful oratory, his fine powers as a reasoner, his close attention to his cases, winning him success from the first.

Such were the chief features of Hamilton's early life. Now we must pay attention to those qualities and powers which were displayed in his later life and on which his great fame rests. He was born with fine political genius and developed an extraordinary ability in finance. In college much of his time was given to a deep study of political economy, financial systems, and such like practical topics. He was diligently preparing himself for a career of which he could not then have dreamed.

All readers of history are aware of the great difficulty the young government had to raise money to support its army, of the vast sums of paper money that were set afloat, and of the little value this came to have. The money troubles set Hamilton to the study of finance. He wrote on the subject to Robert Morris and proposed a financial scheme for the country that would combine public with private credit and bring all the resources of the people to the aid of the nation. His letters had much to do with the founding of the Bank of North America, afterwards started by Morris. As for the state of the country, he felt bitterly the weakness of the Confederation then existing, and wrote to James Duane a celebrated letter on the needs of the nation, urging the necessity of a new constitution, his opinion being that "Congress should have complete sovereignty in all that relates to war, peace, trade, finance, and to the management of foreign affairs." This letter, written in 1780, was the first step towards the great Constitutional Convention, held in Philadelphia in 1787.

Nothing went on in public affairs in which Hamilton did not take a hand. He opposed the persecution of the Tories, and when a mob in New York sought to capture a Tory, Hamilton kept them back by his eloquence until their intended victim escaped. He did not believe in slavery and was a member of the Abolition Society, of which Benjamin Franklin was president. He felt that they ought to live up to their principles, and moved that every member of the society should prove his sentiments by setting his own slaves free.

When the Constitutional Convention, which he had years before suggested, was called, New York sent

Hamilton as one of its delegates. He was one of the ablest men there; no speaker was listened to with more attention; and yet with all he had gone through, with all his service in war and peace, this remarkable man was still only thirty years old. At that age most men are just beginning to make their force felt, but Hamilton had won his spurs as a thinker years before, and he stood among that famous body of well seasoned statesmen the peer of them all. His chief speech before the Convention was said by Gouverneur Morris to be " the most able and impressive I ever heard."

He had his plan for a Constitution. It was one that would have given the central government great power. It was opposed by those who were jealous for the dignity and power of the States. The plan finally adopted was a compromise between the various views offered. It differed from Hamilton's plan, but he signed the new Constitution and went back to New York to support it with all the power at his command. It needed to be adopted by the States, and a party in New York bitterly opposed it, being in favor of State independence. Many opposed it in other States, Patrick Henry among those in Virginia, and it was far from sure that this great State paper would be accepted.

In this dilemma Hamilton came nobly to the front. He and two other able men, James Madison and John Jay, wrote and published the most brilliant series of political essays ever written in the United States. These were in support of the Constitution. There were eighty-five in all, of which Hamilton wrote more than fifty. They were afterwards published under the title of the " Federalist," and of the three pens that wrote this famous work, that of Hamilton was the ablest and most convincing.

He supported the Constitution with his voice as well as with his pen. When the Convention for the adoption of the Constitution met at Poughkeepsie, New York, Hamilton was the chief speaker in its favor. The opposition was bitter and obstinate. At first it seemed to carry with it the whole body. But Hamilton's luminous and brilliant speeches gradually broke down its force, and when the vote was finally taken nearly the whole body cast their ballots in its favor. Alexander Hamilton had won in one of the greatest contests of his life. Now came to him another opportunity. The new government was formed. George Washington was unanimously elected the President. He looked around him for a body of skilled advisers to help him in his arduous work. One of the most difficult subjects to be handled was that of finances. The country was practically bankrupt. Only a man of exceptional ability could lift it above its difficulties.

Washington consulted Robert Morris, who had been superintendent of finance and had done much to save the country from ruin. " What is to be done with this heavy debt?" he asked.

" There is but one man in the United States who can tell you," said Morris, " and that man is Alexander Hamilton."

Washington, who probably thought the same thing, at once appointed Hamilton Secretary of the Treasury.

The new Secretary had a tremendous task before him. The young nation had no money and no credit. It was deeply in debt and was practically bankrupt. How was it to be got out of this difficulty? It is doubtful if there was another man then in the country that could have solved this problem with half the quickness and completeness of Alexander Hamilton.

He began by a radical measure that startled Congress. He proposed that the general government should assume all the debts of the States. This seemed like adding immensely to a burden that was already too heavy, but Hamilton gave such convincing reasons for it that Congress adopted it.

To pay this debt some plan of taxation had to be devised. A direct tax is always unpopular, and Hamilton proposed an indirect tax, by laying a moderate tariff on imported goods. He also proposed a national bank, like those of England and France. This, too, was adopted, the capital of the bank being made ten million dollars. A mint for the coinage of American money was also established. The next step was the funding of the public debt and the issuing of bonds, a device providing for its gradual payment.

These wise plans had their intended effect. The pressure upon the Government was quickly relieved. Money came in, enabling the government to meet its foreign debts as they became due and to pay its running expenses. As for the internal debt, people were content to take the Government bonds. The credit of the United States was completely restored. When Hamilton withdrew from the Cabinet, five years later, no country had a better fiscal system, and it was all due to him. In the words of Daniel Webster: " He smote the rock of the national resources and abundant streams of revenue burst forth. He touched the dead corpse of public credit and it sprang upon its feet."

When Hamilton left the Cabinet it was to resume his law business, his salary as Secretary barely sufficing to maintain his family. He soon again became the leader of the New York bar. He bought himself a small estate near New York City, which he named

"The Grange." It was shaded with fine old trees, the balcony commanded a beautiful prospect, and he spent many of his leisure hours happily in his garden or with his family and friends.

But he could not escape from politics. Washington frequently consulted him. Party interests occupied his attention. Two parties had grown up in the country, the Federal, of which he was the head, and the Democratic, of which Jefferson was the leader. He believed in a strong central government, and would have liked Washington to have the standing and state of a king. Jefferson was a strong advocate of State-rights. This difference of opinion led to much bad feeling between the two when they were together in the Cabinet and after they had left it.

In New York the leader of the Democrats was Aaron Burr, a brilliant and able man, but not a safe and honest one. After serving as Vice-President under Jefferson, Burr became a candidate for governor of New York in 1804, but was defeated, partly through Hamilton's opposition. A newspaper report said that Hamilton had "expressed a despicable opinion" of Burr and "looked upon him as a dangerous man."

Burr, disappointed and angry, demanded that Hamilton should deny this. Hamilton declined. Then Burr challenged him to fight a duel. In those days, when duels were common, Hamilton would have been looked upon with contempt if he had refused. The duel took place in New Jersey, opposite the city of New York, on July 11, 1804. Hamilton fell before Burr's bullet and died the following day.

Thus died, in sustaining what was falsely called the "code of honor," the greatest statesman and financier of his age.

JOHN ADAMS, THE LEADER OF THE BOSTON PATRIOTS

WHILE Samuel Adams was the leading spirit among the New England patriots in the times before the Revolution, there were others little less prominent. Chief among these was his cousin, John Adams; his co-worker, John Hancock; and the orator of patriotism, James Otis, who, in the words of John Adams, was " a flame of fire." John Hancock shared with Samuel Adams the honor of being left out of the pardon offered the rebels and of being one of the men whom the British troops marched to Lexington to arrest. He was afterwards President of the Continental Congress, and his name stands at the head of the signers of the Declaration of Independence in large, bold letters. When he wrote it he said: " The British ministry can read that name without their spectacles."

Most important among these men in his after career was John Adams, the story of whose life we shall here give. Born in Braintree, Massachusetts, in 1735, John Adams came to bear a great part in American public life. He succeeded Washington as President of the United States. Before he died his son, John Quincy Adams, was elected President. His grandson, Charles Francis Adams, was afterwards nominated for Vice-President. This is certainly a fine record for the Adams family.

The father of John Adams was a poor farmer, but he wanted his son to be educated, and toiled the harder that he might send him to Harvard College. After leaving college Adams studied the law, married a bright and clever young woman, and settled down to practice in his native town. In principles he was a sturdy patriot, and when the British Parliament passed the Stamp Act, and an uproar broke out in America, Adams was one of its leaders. He was an able speaker, with a fine-sounding voice and a clear way of thinking, and he told the people in plain language what he thought about Parliament and the tax. He wrote as well as spoke, and made such a stir that the British leaders tried to buy him over by offering him a good paying position. They made a mistake. Adams was poor, but he was not to be bought.

John Adams believed in justice, no matter on which side it was. When the " Boston Massacre " took place, the soldiers who fired on the people were arrested and tried for murder. Adams did not think this just. They had been attacked by a mob and fired in self-defence. So he became their lawyer, saying that it was the people and not the soldiers who were in fault. He won his case. All the soldiers were set free, though two whose shots had killed men were branded in the hand. The people, when they quieted down, thought all the better of John Adams for what he did.

In 1774 Adams became a member of the First Continental Congress, and in 1776 was one of the committee to prepare the Declaration of Independence. He supported this by a great speech. Jefferson said of him:

" John Adams was the ablest advocate and champion of independence on the floor of the House. He was the colossus of that Congress. Not graceful, not eloquent, not always fluent in his public addresses, he yet came out with a power of thought and expression which moved his hearers from their seats."

In 1774 his friend Sewell had urged him not to engage in the dangerous business of revolution. Adams replied with the memorable words: "The die is now cast. I have passed the Rubicon. Sink or swim, live or die, survive or perish with my country, is my unalterable determination."

On the 3d of July, 1776, he wrote a letter to his wife which had in it this celebrated passage:

"Yesterday the greatest question was discussed which was ever debated in America; and a greater, perhaps, never was nor will be decided among men. The second day of July, 1776, will be the most memorable epoch in the history of America. I am apt to believe that it will be celebrated by succeeding generations as the great anniversary festival. It ought to be commemorated as the day of deliverance by solemn acts of devotion to Almighty God. It ought to be solemnized with pomp and parade, with shows, games, sports, bells, bonfires, and illuminations, from one end of the continent to another from this time forward, forevermore."

His prediction has come true, but not for the 2d of July, the day when the resolution before Congress was adopted, but for the 4th, the day when the Declaration which sprang from this resolution was adopted and John Adams and most of the members signed it. For more than a century and a quarter that day has been celebrated in the way he suggested, and it will probably be for many centuries to come.

There was no busier man in Congress than Adams. He was chairman of twenty-five committees and was at the head of the War Department. In 1777 he was sent to France to help make a treaty with that country. On the way across, the "Boston," in which he sailed, was chased by a British man-of-war, but was fast enough to escape. It had also a fight with a British privateer, and when the two vessels came close together Adams seized a musket and began fighting like a common sailor. When the captain saw him he was angry and roared out:

"Why are you here, sir? I am commanded to carry you safely to Europe and I will do it." Adams was a little man and the captain was a big one, and the big man picked up the little man in his arms as if he were a child and carried him below deck. Soon after the privateer was captured, and the "Boston" sailed onward for France.

It was March, 1778, when Adams got there. He was too late, for Franklin had already made the treaty with France. He went to Europe again in 1780, was Minister to Holland in 1782 and got that country to recognize the United States, and in 1783 was one of the five men who negotiated the treaty of peace with Great Britain. As he had been in at the beginning of the struggle for independence, he was in at its close.

In 1784 Adams had the honor of being made the first United States Minister to Great Britain. It was a dramatic moment when he stood before King George III., as the representative of that nation which had just won its liberty from the king. George received him politely and graciously, but he said something which drew from Adams the proud remark: "I must tell your Majesty that I love no country but my own."

"An honest man will never love any other," was the polite reply of the king.

But there were men at the British court who were

not as gentlemanly as their king and treated Adams coldly. And the British queen was as cold in her demeanor towards Mrs. Adams. So, when he got back home again in 1788, he was glad enough to set foot on American soil. He had seen all he cared to of Europe.

In 1789 a new and greater honor came to Adams. When Washington was chosen for President, Adams was made Vice-President of the new nation, and for eight years he held this office, serving as the first president of the United States Senate. When Washington declined to be President for a third term, Adams was looked upon as the next most prominent man in the country, and was elected to the highest office in the gift of the American people, that of President. Thomas Jefferson, his old associate in Congress, was made Vice-President.

As President, Adams had many difficulties to contend with. One of the worst of these was a trouble which broke out with France. The leaders in that country wanted to see Jefferson, the democrat, made President, and were so angry at the election of Adams that they would not receive the Minister he sent them. They passed an insulting decree against American commerce, and hinted that the American envoys might get what they wished if they paid well for it. But Charles Pinckney, one of the envoys, indignantly exclaimed, " Millions for defence, but not one cent for tribute! "

There arose a cry in the States for War. Adams was in favor of it. He called out an army, and Washington consented to lead it. The navy was ordered to fight, and it captured two French frigates and many smaller vessels. This was more than the French had bargained for, and they were glad enough to withdraw their demands and make a treaty of peace.

The short naval war made Adams very popular, but he did other things that made him unpopular, and in 1800, when the time for the next election came, he was defeated and Jefferson was made President. Adams was bitterly disappointed. He felt so badly that he would not wait at Washington to welcome the new President. That was a very discourteous thing to do, and it made him many enemies.

After that Adams lived quietly at home, where he spent a great deal of time in writing. Despite his patriotism and ability, he was a vain man, one of the kind that always thinks his side is the right one. And he had no soft, smooth ways, but was always blunt and plain-spoken. This helped to make him enemies. In this he was very different from Franklin, who once wrote about him from Europe: " Mr. Adams is always an honest man, often a wise one; but he is sometimes completely out of his senses."

As he grew older he grew softer. The bad feeling between him and Jefferson died out and they once more became friends. He had the satisfaction in 1824 of seeing his son elected President of the United States, and died on July 4, 1826, his last words being, " Thomas Jefferson still lives." He was mistaken. His old associate in the Declaration had died earlier that same day in his home at Monticello. It was certainly a remarkable coincidence that the two members of the committee on the Declaration who afterwards became President should have died on the fiftieth anniversary of its signing.

ELI WHITNEY, AMERICA'S FIRST GREAT INVENTOR

AMERICANS are famous the world over for inventions, for the marvellous products of their genius are to be seen in all lands. The Revolution was barely at an end before their inventive skill began to show itself, and as early as 1787 the first steamboat, that of John Fitch, was seen on American waters, and the pioneer of the locomotive was seen on American soil. But the first successful and famous inventor of this country was Eli Whitney, to whose hand the South owes its agricultural prosperity.

In 1792 a young Yankee of this name was living in Savannah, Georgia, in the home of Mrs. Greene, the widow of the celebrated General Greene of the Revolutionary War. He was teaching her children and studying law. He had come south from New England, after graduating at Yale College, to teach in a Georgia family, but before he got there some one else had filled the place, and the poor fellow was in some trouble until Mrs. Greene took a fancy to him and invited him to make her house his home.

Young Whitney was a born mechanic. While working on his father's farm he had mended all the broken violins in the neighborhood, made canes, hatpins, and nails, and learned all he could about machinery. In Mrs. Greene's house he was as handy. He rigged up an embroidery frame for her, made other things, and mended everything that got out of order. She grew to look upon him as a genius in mechanics.

Such a genius was then badly wanted in the South. The farmers and planters of Georgia had tried several plants in their fields and had settled on cotton as the most profitable one for them to grow. But the cotton plant was giving them serious trouble.. When ripe, as most people know, it has a white, fluffy head, made up of the cotton fibres, which are fast to the seeds of the plant. To use the cotton, these seeds had to be got rid of, and this was slow work. They had to be taken out by hand, and it was a day's work for a negro to pull the seeds out of a pound of cotton. This made the fibre very dear, and it was hard to sell it. In 1784 eight bags of cotton were sent to Liverpool, and the custom-house people there seized it for duties. They said it must have been smuggled from some other country, for the United States could never have produced such a " prodigious quantity."

Mrs. Greene had often heard her planter friends talking about this difficulty and wishing that some way could be found to take out the cotton seeds by machinery. She told them that there was a young Yankee in her house who " could make anything," and showed them some of the things he had done for her. They were much interested and asked him if he could help them. Whitney was quite as much interested, for he loved machinery far more than he did his law books, and he told them he would try.

He knew nothing about cotton. It is doubtful if he had ever seen it growing. He got some of the ripe cotton pods from the planters, and pulled them to pieces to see how the seeds were fixed in them. Then he went to a cotton house and watched the dusky pickers at work taking out the seeds. It was not long before the bright fellow saw just how the work could be done, and he set eagerly to work to make a machine. He had to do everything himself, to make his own tools, and even to draw his own wires, for there was no one in that region who could help him. But he did it all, and did it well.

The plan of the machine he made was very simple. It consisted of a network of wires, at such a distance apart that the cotton could go through them but the seeds could not. A set of circular saws, with sharp teeth, was arranged so that the teeth projected between the wires. When in operation the cotton was fed in so that it ran down the wire grid or network, and the circular saws were made to revolve. Their teeth caught the cotton and pulled it between the wires, tearing it loose from the seeds, which could not go through but slid down out of the way. There was also a revolving brush which swept the cotton from the saw-teeth and kept them clean, so that they could catch more.

Such is the principle of the famous cotton gin, which has been worth so many millions of dollars to the South. Since the days of Eli Whitney many improvements have been made in it, so that it does its work far better than at first, but otherwise it is the same as it was when it was made by Eli Whitney in 1793.

When it became known that the young Yankee inventor was at work on this machine and felt sure that he could make one that would do the work, there was much excitement among the Southern planters. It would be worth so much to them. The news of it rapidly spread, and many wanted to see it, but he would not let them. He was only working on a model, he said, and did not want to show it before it was perfected. Besides, he wished to have his invention patented before it was made public.

Whitney was too honest himself to suspect others of dishonesty. He trusted his precious model in a simple frame workshop, with no guard but a locked door. One night some thieves broke open this door and carried away the model. When he arose the next morning and went to his shop, what was his dismay to find the door wide open and the precious model gone!

It was a bad business for poor Whitney. The principle of the machine was made known and anybody could make one like it. Copies of it appeared on all sides. As Horace Greeley says, " The South fairly swarmed with pirates of the invention, of all kinds and degrees." Before he could make a new model and procure a patent the cotton-gin was widely in use. He prosecuted those who were making his machine, but the juries of Georgia decided that they had the right to do so. The only justice he could ever obtain was from South Carolina, which in later years voted him fifty thousand dollars as a reward.

Whitney's patent was got out in 1794, and a Mr. Miller, who afterwards married Mrs. Greene, went into partnership with him in its manufacture. But the demand for the machines was so great that he could not begin to supply them, so there was a good market for the pirated machines, though they were much inferior to his. Then his shop burned down with all its contents, and he was a bankrupt. In 1812 the patent ran out, and Congress refused to renew it, so that the poor inventor made nothing from his machine but the fifty thousand dollars which South Carolina gave him.

If of little value to the inventor, the cotton-gin proved of the greatest value to the South. In the year when it was made this country produced only 500,000 pounds of cotton. In 1801 it produced 20,000,000 pounds. To-day it produces much more than 10,000,000 bales, of nearly 500 pounds each.

Eli Whitney was too ingenious a mechanic to be content with one invention. After trying for five years to obtain justice, he went north to New Haven, Connecticut, and began to make fire-arms for the government. He so greatly improved the machinery and methods used in this business that he fairly revolutionized it. He was the first to divide factory labor so that each part of a machine is made separately and will fit in any machine. If one of his fire-arms was broken, a new part, which would be sure to fit, could be had from the factory, and this is the case with many other things now.

If Whitney was unfortunate in his first invention, his fire-arms proved very successful, and he made a fortune out of them. Thus he did not die in poverty, as many other inventors have done.

Whitney was born at Westborough, Massachusetts, December 8, 1765, and lived till his sixtieth year of age, dying in New Haven in January, 1825.

ROBERT FULTON, THE INVENTOR OF THE STEAMBOAT

On Friday, the 11th of August, 1807, there was an exciting scene on the shores of the Hudson River, at New York City. A crowd of people thronged the water's edge, and in the stream outside lay a strange-looking vessel, on which all eyes were fixed. Above the deck rose a smoke-stack from which volumes of black smoke poured, while queer-shaped paddle-wheels stood out from its side. It was the famous "Clermont," Fulton's side-wheel steamboat, the first of its kind ever seen on American waters.

Years before paddle-wheel steamboats had been tried in Europe, but without success. In America other kinds of steamboats had been used. James Rumsey in 1786 drove a boat in Virginia waters at the speed of four miles an hour by pumping with steam power a jet of water through the stern. John Fitch in 1787 was more successful. His boats were moved by paddles like those used in Indian canoes, and made seven miles an hour. They ran on the Delaware for a number of years, but did not prove a permanent success. Many other inventors were working on the same subject, but the true era of steamboating began with Fulton's "Clermont" on that morning in 1807.

As the crowd looked on, some in interest, some ready to laugh at the queer craft, the wheels of the vessel began slowly to turn. They were uncovered and they sent the spray flying on all sides. Moving slowly at first, in a little while the "Clermont" was fairly under way, gliding up the Hudson at the rate of five miles an hour. This was no great speed, but to the lookers on, who had never seen a vessel move without sails, it seemed magical, and cheers went up from the great crowd. Nobody felt inclined to laugh now. There were many who had thought it ridiculous to try to move a boat with a steam engine; but—it moved, and there was no more to be said.

Only twelve people took passage for that trip. Men did not like to trust their lives to a new-fangled craft with a steam-puffing demon in its inside. Along the stream, above the city, everybody was out. At every town the banks were crowded, hats and handkerchiefs were waved, and cheers greeted the enterprise. They were proud to see that an American had invented a workable steamboat, and that the Hudson was the scene of its triumph. Albany, nearly one hundred and fifty miles distant, was reached in thirty-two hours, and the return voyage to New York was made in thirty hours, an average of about five miles an hour for the trip.

There were other scenes on the Hudson during that eventful journey. There were many sailing vessels on the river, the crews of which did not know of the great experiment, and as the strange water-monster, pouring smoke and sparks into the air, churning the water into foam, and moving against the tide without sails, met their eyes, they were filled with surprise and apprehension. Some flung themselves in a spasm of terror on the decks of their vessels while the fire-dragon passed, while others took to their boats and rowed lustily for the shore. It was worse still at night, when flames seemed to redden the smoke, and that pioneer voyage of the "Clermont" was a sensation not soon to be forgotten.

Who was Robert Fulton, do you ask? He was an American, born in Pennsylvania in 1765, the same year that Eli Whitney was born in Massachusetts. He made up his mind to be an artist, became a friend of Franklin in Philadelphia as a boy, and at the age of twenty-one went to London to study art under the great Benjamin West. While there he met James Watt, the greatest genius among the inventors of the steam-engine, and new ideas came into his young head. He felt that he had a genius for invention, too, and abandoned art to become a civil engineer. He made experiments and inventions, wrote a work on "Canal Navigation," showed in Paris the first panorama ever seen there, and did some drawing and painting besides. Much of the first money he made in his younger days he used to buy a little farm for his mother, then a widow and poor.

At that time many experiments were being made in the effort to move boats by aid of the steam-engine. Rumsey and Fitch had made some progress in America, and several others were trying in Europe. With what Fulton knew of the steam-engine, this seemed to him a fair field for his inventive powers. He began experimenting, Robert R. Livingston, our Minister to France, who believed in Fulton, furnishing the money. Fulton was sure he knew why other inventors had failed, and that he saw the way to success. He built a trial boat on the Seine, furnished it with a steam-engine and paddle-wheels, and early in 1803 was ready for its first trial.

He made one sad mistake: the engine was too heavy for the boat. One morning he was roused from sleep by the distracting news that the boat had broken to pieces and the engine gone to the bottom. He sprang up and hurried to the river, to find that the news was true. The boat had broken in half and was resting with its engine on the bottom of the Seine.

Fulton succeeded in raising the engine, and found it was not damaged. The boat was ruined, and he had to build a new and stronger one. When it was finished, in August, 1803, the new boat was tried with much success, the members of the National Institute of France and a great crowd of citizens looking on as it made its way down the stream, with a great deal of bluster, but not with any great speed.

Much yet was needed, and the next experiments were made in New York, where they excited as much ridicule as they did interest. The idea of moving a vessel by steam power seemed to many of the good citizens only fit to be laughed at, and their surprise was not small on that day in 1807 when they saw the "Clermont" start away against wind and tide and move up stream.

The problem of steam navigation, which had occupied the time and talent of so many inventors, was solved. The sail and oar, for the first time in history, were thrown out of duty. Regular trips between New York and Albany were made too or three times a week, a larger boat, named the "Car of Neptune," being built and put on the route, and in a few years the steamboat was puffing its way along the waters of many American rivers. It had this time come to stay, and with successive improvements soon became a swifter and more serviceable craft. Fulton took out his first patent in 1809 and his second in 1811. All they called for was the way he employed the crank of the engine in the moving of paddle-wheels. For years he had a monopoly of steam navigation on all the waters of New York State.

During the remainder of Fulton's life he was kept busy inventing and improving. He was employed by the United States Government upon engineering work connected with the navigation of rivers and canals. While in Europe he had made torpedoes for blowing up vessels under water, and these he now improved and they were accepted for naval use by the United States.

In 1814 Fulton was delighted with an order from the government to build a steam frigate or ship of war. This he had long worked to obtain, and Congress now voted three hundred and twenty thousand dollars for the work. The work was finished the next year, and his steam-frigate, the "Fulton," the pride of his life, was successfully launched.

Poor Fulton was not there to see it. He had been exposed to severe weather some months before and taken a violent cold. Before he recovered he went out in inclement weather to give some orders about the frigate, and his sickness came back more severely than before. It grew rapidly worse, and on the 24th of February, 1815, the great inventor died.

His life had been a marked success. Though his steam frigate was never made use of in war, his commercial steamers were to be seen on all the rivers of the United States, and in time began to drive sailing vessels from the seas. Other noted engineers arose to perfect the invention, and to-day steam navigation is one of the most important industries of the world.

JOHN JACOB ASTOR, THE MONARCH OF THE FUR INDUSTRY

In the year 1779 a sturdy German lad of sixteen might have been seen trudging along a country road near his native village of Waldorf, a small bundle of clothes over his shoulder, and German coins worth about two dollars in his pocket. With this slender equipment he was going out to seek his fortune in the great world. His father was a butcher, poor, shiftless, and good for nothing, and the boy had set out to do something for himself.

Though he had very little money, he had something of more value. He was strong and hearty, had a good, plain education, was not afraid of work, had a head full of common sense, and was free from bad habits. He tells us this: "Soon after I left the village I sat down under a tree to rest, and there I made three resolutions—to be honest, to be industrious, and not to gamble." Three very good ones, most people will say. Such was the equipment with which John Jacob Astor left home to win his way in the world. To-day his name and that of his native village are commemorated in the Waldorf-Astoria, the greatest hotel in New York.

With no thought of great hotels in his young brain, the boy made his way along. He went down the Rhine on a raft, and got ten dollars at the river's mouth for his help. One of his brothers was in London, a maker of musical instruments, and with him the young adventurer stopped for some years, learning a good deal about instrument making, and how to speak English. At length, in 1783, with a good suit of clothes and seventy-five dollars in money, he set out for America, spending one-third of his money for a steerage passage and another third for seven German flutes from his brother. With these flutes for a stock in trade and twenty-five dollars in money, he landed at Baltimore in March, 1784.

On the ship he met a German fur-trader, a man who had made much money in the business and who advised young Astor to go into the same line. The boy went to New York, where he had another brother engaged in butchering, and with his aid and that of his German friend he got a position in a fur-store, where he set himself to work to learn all about furs. He studied their qualities and value and the methods of curing and preserving them. The trappers who came to the store were ready to tell him all about fur-bearing animals, their modes of life and the best way of taking them. He was constantly looking around and asking questions.

A diligent and intelligent worker, his employer got to trust him, rapidly advancing him in position, and finally sending him to Montreal to buy furs. This was an important errand. The German fur-trader had told him what to do. He was to buy trinkets, go among the Indians, bargain with them, and get his furs at first hand. When he got back to New York he surprised and pleased his employer by the great number of fur-skins he had bought with the money given him.

Two years after coming to New York Astor felt that he knew the business well enough to start for himself. He took a small store on Water Street, borrowed some money from his brother to stock it with such

ASTORIA

things as the Indians liked, and began to buy. When the peltries did not come in fast enough he set out himself with a pack of trinkets and visited the Indians and trappers of Central New York, with whom he usually made a good trade. Several such journeys were made each year, and on his return he would cure the skins and prepare them for market himself.

After some years of dealing with New York traders, he took ship to London, where furs sold for much more than could be got for them in America. He made arrangements with good houses there to ship furs to them, thus greatly increasing his profits. He also engaged to sell his brother's musical instruments in America, and in time built up a profitable trade in these goods. At home he lived over his store. He had married a New York girl who was as wide awake as himself, and who grew to know as much about furs as he did and to be his match in a business deal.

This was the way that John Jacob Astor's great fortune began. He was now making money rapidly. Instead of going out himself, he employed agents to buy furs and ship them to New York, and as soon as possible he bought a ship, in which he sent his furs to London. The little trudger on the German highway was fast growing rich. The beaver skins that he bought for a dollar apiece from the New York trappers brought more than six dollars apiece in London, and the money got for them was invested in British goods on which he made another profit in New York. From Europe his ships made their way as far as China, where large prices were to be had for furs, and from which they brought back teas and silks. A voyage to China would net him a profit of thirty thousand dollars; sometimes much more.

When he had been in business fifteen years he moved his store to 233 Broadway—where the Astor House now stands. He was now worth a quarter of a million of dollars, but was the same cautious and enterprising business man as when he began. When the treaty of 1795 was made, which fixed the northern frontier of the United States, Astor took quick advantage of it. It limited the field of the Hudson Bay and other Canadian fur companies, and Astor soon had his agents out buying furs all along the Great Lakes, and far to the west of the lakes.

He planned a great scheme of setting up a line of trading posts across the country, by way of the Missouri and Columbia Rivers, as far as the Pacific, and in 1811 he founded the town of Astoria at the mouth of the Columbia. It was his design to make this a starting point for his vessels, supplying China with furs directly from the Pacific coast, instead of following the long, roundabout course from New York. He proposed to make one of the Hawaiian Islands an intermediate station.

This ambitious scheme fell through from the dishonesty of his agents, who played him false and betrayed his plans to a British fur company, which got possession of Astoria and the Oregon business for a trifle. Astor's loss was more than a million dollars, but he bore it calmly.

A shrewd, far-seeing, adventurous man was John Jacob Astor. His business judgment amounted to genius, and he rarely if ever made a mistake. He gave incessant attention to his business, and not until he was quite wealthy would he leave his store or warehouse before the close of the day. Then he got to leaving at two o'clock in the afternoon, and, after an early dinner, taking a horseback ride, of which he was very fond. His other favorite recreation was the theatre. He was plain and simple in all his habits, and the strict economy with which he began clung to him long after it had ceased to be necessary.

He grew to be very rich, not wholly in the fur trade, though he made about two million dollars in this. But a greater source of wealth was his shrewd purchases of real estate in the upper part of New York. If he bought a piece of land he built upon it and made it pay by rents. These rents he used to buy new property. He had an instinctive judgment of the best localities for an increase in value by the growth of population, and by holding on to his properties he added many millions to his estate. The Astor estate came in time to have as many as seven thousand houses in New York City.

During the last twenty years of Astor's life he lived in quiet retirement, employing business agents to look after his property, which grew to be worth at least twenty million dollars. Some of this money he gave away. All his relatives were placed in comfort. For the poor of Waldorf, his native place, he gave fifty thousand dollars. The Astor Library, founded by him, was endowed with four hundred thousand dollars in land and funds. He made other public gifts, but the great bulk of his immense estate was left to his eldest son, William B. Astor. Since then it has been sedulously kept together and increased, until its value has become immense.

Mr. Astor's great success was largely due to his remarkable business powers, his temperate habits, punctuality, perseverance, care that no money should be wasted and no enterprise undertaken until thoroughly understood. This done, he was daring and enterprising in his operations. He was prompt in all engagements, and cool and cheerful even under severe losses. Always an early riser, not until he was fifty-five years of age did he ever fail to appear at his store before seven o'clock in the morning.

Such is the record of the boy who made wise resolutions as he sat resting by the wayside when he set out to make his fortune. He kept those resolutions strictly, and was always prudent, sagacious, tactful, quick in grasping and courageous in carrying out an enterprise. He was never liberal, being very careful and close in money dealings, the gifts which he finally made being given after his wealth was so great as to render them matters of small moment to him. Death came to this remarkable man on the 29th of March, 1848.

STEPHEN GIRARD, THE FRIEND OF THE ORPHAN

A QUEER old fellow, one-eyed, and one-sided in his nature, was Stephen Girard, the famous Philadelphia merchant of a century ago. Rich, eccentric, miserly in his habits, yet ready to spend his money and even risk his life for the good of mankind, such was the odd make-up of the old merchant. In our days a fortune of more than a hundred millions of dollars is not thought remarkable, but in his days Girard, with a few millions, was looked upon as a world's wonder, stupendously rich, and he became famous as the Crœsus of his day. This much more we may say, that no man, except Benjamin Franklin, ever did so much to benefit the great city in which he made his home. Miser as he lived, he left his great wealth with wise discrimination for the benefit of his fellow citizens after his death.

The life of Stephen Girard was in one way like that of John Jacob Astor. Both poor boys, born a few years apart in Europe, they both made their way to America and there, by aid of a genius for business, built up great fortunes. Girard was born in Bordeaux, France, in 1750, and set out to win his fortune at the age of thirteen, as a cabin boy on a ship bound for the West Indies and New York. For thirteen years he followed the sea, becoming a thorough sailor, and making his way upward step by step, until he became captain and owner of a vessel in the American coasting trade.

In 1776 he left New Orleans on a voyage to Canada. The colonies of America were then fighting for liberty, and ships like his were in danger of being captured as prizes by British ships of war, many of which were prowling about. On reaching the waters off the mouth of Delaware Bay the ship was becalmed, and Girard feared some British cruiser might swoop down on him like a sea-hawk. So with the first breath of air he sailed into the bay and on up the Delaware River until Philadelphia was reached.

Thus it was more accident than anything else that made Girard a citizen of William Penn's city, then the metropolis of America. Sea traffic was just then too dangerous for a cautious man, so he sold his vessel and cargo and went into business in a grocery and liquor store.

From the very start his cautious, saving habits and business judgment were shown. He saved his money carefully, and as soon as the war was over and the seas were safe, he invested his savings in the New Orleans and San Domingo trade, which he knew to be profitable. At the same time he looked carefully around him for chances. The war had ruined business in Philadelphia, but he was shrewd enough to know that it would soon revive, and he was ready to take advantage of the change.

One sharp thing he did was to rent a block of buildings on Water Street at a very low rate, which, as soon as business grew better, he leased to others for a much larger rent. But his chief inclination was towards the ocean trade, which he thoroughly understood, and he joined his brother in trading ventures to West Indian ports. Cautious, shrewd, far-seeing in business operations, he went on until he had accumulated thirty

HEROES OF PROGRESS

thousand dollars, a small fortune in those days. He then left his brother and began dealing for himself.

A remarkable accident about this time more than doubled Girard's fortune at a single stroke, one of those strange chances which come in the lives of some men. In 1791 the negroes of the island of Hayti broke out in insurrection against the French, and a war for liberty began which lasted for years. Many of the planters were killed, and all that could fled for their lives to the vessels in the harbor.

It happened that two vessels belonging to Girard lay there, and to these came several planters carrying what they could bring of their wealth. Leaving this, they returned for more, but never came back again. They were probably met by armed negroes and killed. When the vessels reached Philadelphia Girard's captains told him of what had happened and handed over the treasure. He put it safely away, advertised it long and widely, but no one ever came to claim it, and the treasure became his. This strange stroke of fortune added some fifty thousand dollars to his growing wealth. He had become heir of the unknown dead.

Girard by this time was looked upon as one of the merchant princes of the Quaker City and as one of its most enterprising citizens. His wealth was steadily growing, his enterprises were so carefully managed that they all proved successful, and he was fast growing rich. But he did not make friends. He was of a sour, unhappy disposition, was looked upon as a miser, avoided society, and lived in a sparse way over his Water Street store, giving every hour of his time to his business, harsh and penurious to those under him, and exacting the best service at the smallest cost. He was not a lovable man.

And yet below all this coldness and harshness, this grasping for dollars and driving of hard bargains, there was much that was good and noble in the man, and the time was at hand when he was to show a courage in danger and a love for his fellows which put to shame many others of more specious show of philanthropy.

In 1793 a terrible epidemic of yellow fever broke out in Philadelphia. Thousands were down with the dread disease, the hospitals were overcrowded with sufferers, multitudes were fleeing in terror from the city, great distress prevailed among the sick, and few could be found willing to take care of them. An appeal was made for nurses and money, and, to the surprise of everybody, Stephen Girard was one of the first to respond. He paid freely for help and supplies of all kinds, and, more than this, he offered his own services as a nurse.

Entering a hospital filled with victims of the terrible pestilence, he took tender care of the sick, giving his earnest and unwavering attention to his duty during the whole continuance of the scourge. Daily his own life was in danger, but he never swerved from his work, fortunately escaping infection. When the epidemic ended one-sixth of the people of the city had fallen victims to it, and many helpless orphans were left. To these Girard became like a second father, two hundred of them being provided for by him in an orphans' home.

Four years later the disease returned. This time it was not so bad, and the authorities knew better how to manage it. But Girard came forward in the same brave and devoted manner as before, aiding the sick with money and personal service. After the disease was finally overcome, it left behind it a new and better opinion of Stephen Girard. Men no longer looked upon him as a heartless and penurious money-maker, and though still not liked, he had won admiration and respect.

This yellow fever episode was the one illuminating event in Stephen Girard's life. The crust was removed and men saw the true nobility of his nature. The remainder of his life was devoted to what he deemed the one important business, that of money-making, in which he grew more and more successful as time went on.

He became a great sea merchant. Vessel after vessel was added to his fleet, until he had ships in all seas. There was hardly a port in the world where things were to be bought and sold that his ships did not reach. He was an adept in ocean trading, and knew just how to make the most of his ventures. With China and the East Indies he had a large trade, for there goods of great value in the West were to be had. Careful directions were given to his captains, which they were to obey on pain of dismissal. Thus they were told to buy fruits in the fertile islands of the south and sell them in northern ports. Here other goods were to be bought and carried again where they would bring the best price. Thus in each voyage two or three separate profits were made, and almost every venture added a notable share to his wealth.

His captains must obey orders. He would take no excuses, even if much money was made by their taking a chance on their own account. This was one of Girard's fads. Any captain who broke his orders lost his place. He thought he knew best, and left no discretion to his captains. " Once it might succeed," he said, "but if followed up it would likely lead to losses, and at last ruin me." He was an old merchant and deemed his own judgment better than that of men who, however well they understood the sea, had had no training in trade.

Girard went into a new business in 1812. He bought the building and most of the stock of the old United States Bank and became a banker, the new institution becoming known as the Girard Bank. He made money in it, as he did in everything, in time increasing the capital to four millions and doing a large and profitable business.

This was the time of the second war with Great Britain, and in the third year of this war Stephen Girard came to the aid of the Government, as Robert Morris had done in the Revolutionary War. Money was badly needed and a loan of five millions was offered the people. Liberal inducements were presented, but only the paltry amount of twenty thousand dollars was bid for.

In this dilemma Girard came forward and agreed to take the whole loan, lending the Government the total sum. This act made the loan popular, and the far-seeing banker soon found a profitable market for the bonds. As his biography says: "He was the sheet anchor of the government credit during that disastrous war." Whether he had the aid of the Government in view, or his shrewd business judgment saw in this a way to add to his own wealth, this much is certain, that the Government found him a helper in its extremity.

As his wealth rose into the millions it was used in new enterprises. He was active in obtaining a charter for the second Bank of the United States, and served on its board of directors. Several handsome blocks of buildings were built by him in the city, he subscribed liberally to the fund for the improvement of the Schuylkill, and invested largely in other directions. His wealth, which in the end reached the then enormous sum of about nine million dollars, needed a profitable output in various directions, and he was on the alert for good investments.

Many anecdotes might be told of Girard's eccentricities if we had space for them. He was a queer fellow throughout, testy and often ill-natured, caring nothing for society and paying no attention to religious services. Money was his god, and to that he gave his life, except in the one noble case of self-sacrifice cited.

He married, it is true, but his wife found him far from being a cheerful companion, and his penuriousness and testy ill nature made his household anything but a scene of domestic comfort. The poor woman in the end lost her mind and spent the last years of her life in an insane asylum, while Girard shut himself up more closely in his shell than ever.

When old age came upon him the question of what he should do with his wealth occupied his mind. He had no children, his wife was dead, and when his will came to be read, after his death on the 26th of December, 1831, the people of Philadelphia were astonished and delighted with its provisions. After leaving legacies to his relatives, to such of his captains as should bring their vessels safely home, to his apprentices and old servants, the great bulk of his estate was left to found a college for orphans, to improve the streets of Philadelphia and develop canal navigation, to a fund for the distressed masters of ships, and to various city and state schools and asylums. His public bequests amounted to nearly seven million dollars, his private ones to several millions more.

The city of Philadelphia was his chief heir, and Girard College his great bequest. Forty-five acres of land and two millions of dollars were left for this benevolent purpose, to be devoted to the care and education of fatherless white boys, who were to be carefully reared and apprenticed to some suitable occupation.

Girard College, as the first of importance, is the most famous institution due to benevolence in the United States, and its great main building is the finest example of Corinthian architecture now standing in the world.

It has started some thousands of boys upon the upward track in life, and its mission for good grows with the years, while the Girard Trust Fund, carefully managed and fostered, has proved of great value to the city of Philadelphia. Girard showed excellent business judgment in the disposition of his money, and the results have all been for good. No man in America has won greater fame as a benefactor of mankind than the eccentric and money-grabbing merchant of Water Street, Philadelphia, and Girard College stands as a noble monument to his memory.

JOHN MARSHALL, THE EXPOUNDER OF THE CONSTITUTION

JOHN MARSHALL, one of the greatest among the great Virginians of the early days of this country, won his fame in a field in which there is not much of incident to relate, that of the Supreme Court of the United States, of which he was Chief Justice for the last thirty-four years of his life. The greatest of all our Chief Justices, he is known as the ablest expounder of the Constitution, and this noble State paper owes its acceptation very largely to the wise and luminous decisions of John Marshall.

Born in Germantown (now Midland), Virginia, on the 24th of September, 1755, Marshall spent a life of considerable activity before he reached the bench of the Supreme Court, and there are many things of interest to be told of him during the first half of his life.

In figure John Marshall was not striking or commanding. Tall and thin and usually erect, he often took very awkward attitudes. His face, swarthy in hue, with low forehead, black hair, and twinkling eyes, was not handsome, though kindly in expression. His voice was dry and hard in tone, and his manner of speech plain and forcible, but devoid of the graces of oratory. Often, indeed, he was embarrassed in speech. Yet the sound sense, lucid reasoning, and fine powers of argument of his speeches gave him command over his audiences, and were especially telling in his court decisions, in which wisdom rather than oratory is demanded.

This will serve to introduce the great figure of John Marshall to our readers. In his younger days he was one of the most spirited of patriots, and served as a soldier throughout the Revolutionary War, winning distinction by his courage and ability. In seeking for the early life of the great Chief Justice, we should scarcely look for him as a dashing lieutenant of volunteers, yet that is the way Marshall began at the age of twenty-one.

He became Captain Marshall in 1777, and fought boldly and gallantly in many campaigns. He was present at the battles of Brandywine, Germantown, and Monmouth, was at Valley Forge during the terrible winter spent there, and by his patience and liveliness helped to give spirit to his fellow officers amid its hardships and sufferings. He took part with General Wayne in the daring assault on Stony Point, and served gallantly in various other actions.

Near the end of the war, while he was out of the army for a time, Marshall attended a course of lectures on law and philosophy at William and Mary College. He had never been to college, having been taught at home by his father, and this was his first introduction to the law. But his keen mind and quick judgment enabled him readily to take it in. During the war he had often aided as an arbitrator to settle disputes among the men; and he now took up seriously the study of law. Before the war ended he was admitted to the bar.

Marshall quickly showed that he had now fallen into his true vocation. In a brief time he gained the reputation of being a promising young barrister, and a year of legal practice raised him to the position of one of the leaders of the Virginia bar. His elevation had been phenomenally rapid, but was a natural consequence of the great ability he displayed.

He became a member of the Legislature of Virginia in 1782, and there, too, quickly made his mark. It was apparent to the members that they had a man of no common powers among them. There was work enough then for men of ability to do. The State needed reorganizing, and Marshall took an active part in the work. In doing so he came into close relations with Patrick Henry and other leaders of the day, and impressed them strongly with the commanding qualities of his mind.

But his first great opportunity to make his force felt came in 1788, when the Constitution was before the Virginia Convention for adoption. In its support, next to James Madison, he was the leading advocate. Patrick Henry opposed it with all his wonderful eloquence, making pyrotechnic orations that his audiences listened to with wonder and delight. Marshall, on the contrary, had no eloquence to offer. He simply talked, but reason and argument formed the basis of his talk, and his words had a convincing influence upon his hearers. The Constitution was adopted, and he shared with Madison the chief honor in the result.

A still greater display of his power was made in 1794, when Jay's treaty with Great Britain was under discussion, and was bitterly opposed in all parts of the country. Marshall made so able a speech in its support that the influence of it was felt as far away as Europe, and when, the next year, he was sent on a special mission to France, he was received there as a statesman of great distinction.

In 1799 he was elected to Congress, and there strongly defended President Adams for giving up Thomas Nash, whom Great Britain claimed as a fugitive from justice. Marshall's speech on this subject was marvellously able in its exposition of international law, and settled decisively the status of such questions.

In 1800 he became Secretary of State in President Adams's Cabinet, and on the 31st of January, 1801, was appointed by the President to the office in which he was to gain a fame unsurpassed in this country, that of Chief Justice of the Supreme Court of the United States. This was a life position, in which he remained for the remaining thirty-four years of his stay upon earth. The profound knowledge, wisdom, and judgment which Marshall displayed in this high office gave him rank as the ablest of all who have filled it. He interpreted the Constitution upon just and liberal principles, his writings and arguments being of the greatest value to the courts of the nation. Its legal machinery was not yet running very smoothly, and the true significance of the Constitution, as applied to actual questions, was little understood.

Marshall interpreted it in many famous cases, one of the most important being the trial of Aaron Burr, late Vice-President of the United States, for high treason. Here the Chief Justice presided, and in many points stood against the opinions of the leading lawyers of the day. Time has proved that he was right, and that his decisions were "a sound, even-handed administration of the law."

Judge Story, referring to some of his famous decisions, praises him in the highest terms as a just and luminous expounder of the Constitution, and says:

HEROES OF PROGRESS

" If all others of the Chief Justice's judicial arguments had perished, his luminous judgments on these occasions would have given an enviable immortality to his name."

Aside from his legal standing, he was distinguished for his benevolence, modesty, urbanity, and simplicity. His one contribution to literature is a " Life of George Washington," in five volumes, which is highly esteemed. His home was in Richmond, Virginia, but he died in Philadelphia, having gone there for medical advice, on the 6th of July, 1835.

HENRY CLAY, THE GREAT ADVOCATE OF COMPROMISE

In those historic days when Washington was settling himself in his seat as first President of the United States, and this great country was slowly getting used to its new government harness, there entered the office of the Court of Chancery at Richmond, Virginia, a boy clerk whose ungainly appearance created a smile among the older lads in the office. He was fifteen years old, very tall for his age, very slender, very awkward, yet with a prepossessing face. And he was dressed in country fasion, wearing a pepper-and-salt suit, with stiffly starched shirt and collar and an equally stiff coat-tail. No wonder looks and winks of amusement went round among the clerks.

Such was Henry Clay at fifteen. Before he was twenty all his awkwardness had vanished and he had learned to dress and carry himself as well as the most fashionable of his fellows. He was never a handsome man, but he had an expanded forehead and a countenance beaming with intelligence, while his every movement had gained a winning grace. The ungainly boy had developed into the well-poised man. And his voice, always musical, now seemed to hold the rich tones of an organ. It had a depth, a volume, a harmony, a compass, rarely heard, and was destined to fill large audiences with delight in future years.

Henry Clay's early life had been one of penury and privation. He was born in 1777, during the war of

HEROES OF PROGRESS 121

the Revolution, in a low, swampy district of Virginia called the "Slashes," not far away from Richmond, the capital city. The boy had a hard life of it. He was one of seven children, his father, a poor Baptist preacher, dying when he was four years old, leaving his wife to a desperate struggle for life with her young family.

Henry had plenty of time for work, but very little time for study. We see him first sitting, one of a score of barefooted urchins, in a little log school-house, with a teacher who was good-natured enough when he was sober, but cross and irritable when he was drunk. Here the boy learned to read, write, and cipher, going into the arithmetic only as far as the rules of "Practice."

That was the whole of his schooling. His mother had to take him from school at an early age and put him to work on her little farm. At thirteen we see him again, still barefoot, clad in a homespun butternut suit of his mother's making, riding to mill on the family pony, and carrying before him a bag of the corn he had helped to raise in the fields. From this he afterwards got the title of the "Mill-Boy of the Slashes."

He was put into a Richmond drug-store as errand boy at fourteen, and a position was obtained for him in the Court of Chancery at fifteen. Here, despite the ridicule of the clerks, he made his way so well by study and industry that he was chosen by the Chancellor for his private secretary. The Chancellor liked the boy, taught him many things, and gave him a chance to study law. This he did so earnestly that he was practicing as a lawyer before he was twenty-one.

Long before this the boys in the office had ceased to smile at Henry Clay. He had made friends among some of the best families of Richmond, was grave and studious in disposition, and had already shown himself a ready and able debator. Tradition tells us that he was the peerless star of the Richmond Debating Society in 1795, when eighteen years of age.

Kentucky was then a rapidly growing state. Settled by Daniel Boone and his followers in Revolutionary days, it was now fast filling up. Clay's mother, who had married again, had moved to that fertile land in 1792; and Clay himself, finding business anything but brisk in Richmond, followed her in 1798, when twenty-one years of age. Like many others, he thought it would pay to "grow up with the country."

The young lawyer hung out his sign over an office in Lexington, Kentucky, and waited for business. He had plenty of ambition, but his pocket was empty. He had not money enough to pay his board, and his first fifteen-shilling fee filled him with delight. But he was versed in the law, was a good pleader, and so successful in his cases that business came to him fast. In less than two years he married a woman of excellent standing and character, and soon after had money enough to buy an estate of six hundred acres near Lexington, named Ashland. It afterwards became famous as the home of Henry Clay.

Thus was the future great orator launched in life. He soon became active in politics, advocating the policy of President Jefferson, whom he esteemed as one of the best and ablest of men. His native powers as a speaker had now greatly developed, his rich, resonant voice was heard widely on stump and rostrum, and his powers of rhetoric and oratory unfolded so rapidly that he soon became highly popular as a public speaker. The people of Lexington thought that a man of his powers

HEROES OF PROGRESS

ought to represent them in the legislature, and he was elected by a large majority in 1803.

As a law-maker Clay's ability was so marked that three years later, when one of the Kentucky Senators resigned, he was chosen to fill the balance of his term in the Senate of the United States. He was re-elected to this body again in 1809, another Senator having resigned.

Up to this time Henry Clay had not especially made his mark, though he was becoming widely known as an orator of unusual powers and a statesman of fine ability. His great career began in 1811, when he was elected to Congress as a member of the House.

It was a time of great political activity. Troubles were growing between England and the United States. War was in the air, and Clay became such an ardent and powerful advocate of appeal to the sword that the war-party in the House immediately elected him Speaker. He attained to his important office at thirty-four years of age.

From that time on Clay's voice fiercely denounced Great Britain for its injuries and insults to this country, and he had more to do with bringing on the war of 1812 than any other individual. He often left his seat as Speaker to arouse the House by his clarion voice. He put new spirit into President Madison. When the war began and the soldiers set out for the field, Clay warmed their hearts with inspiring words, and they read his speeches with delight by their camp-fires. At a later date, when all seemed going wrong in the army, the President wished to appoint him commander-in-chief, but Gallatin objected, saying, "What shall we do without him in the House of Representatives?"

In 1814 Russia, as a friend of both countries, tried to bring about a peace, much as the United States did for Russia and Japan in the war of 1905. Both parties were tired of the war, and "Harry of the West," as Clay was then called, was chosen as one of the commissioners to the peace conference at Ghent. The treaty was agreed to on the day before Christmas, 1814. In settling its terms Clay gained many advantages for the United States.

On his return, in 1815, he was at once sent back to Congress, where he was re-elected Speaker, and for the years that followed he was the leader of the House, leaving it in 1825 to become Secretary of State. Never has the House known his superior as a presiding officer. There was a charm of manner, a dignity, and a reserved power in the way in which he held together the excitable members, and during his whole career not one of his decisions was reversed. Party feeling was intense during his early years as Speaker, and all his strength and resolution were often needed to keep order, but he never failed.

The great event of this period in Henry Clay's career was the famous Missouri Compromise of 1821. It was a result of the first great struggle over the subject of Slavery. New territories were opening in the West, and the planters of the South claimed the right to take their slaves into this region. Missouri applied for admission as a State in 1820, and at once there arose a bitter contest as to whether it should be admitted as a slave or a free State. The dispute grew so hot and violent that there was almost a war on the floor of Congress.

Finally a compromise was suggested under which Missouri was to be a slave State, but no other slave

HEROES OF PROGRESS   125

States were to be made in the Western country north of the parallel of 36° 30′, the southern boundary of Missouri. Clay, a peace-maker in spirit, despite his advocacy of war ten years before, became the great advocate of this compromise. He did not confine himself to speeches, but went in person from member to member, talking with them, reasoning, beseeching, and persuading, in his most winning way. He succeeded, the Compromise Bill was passed, and the difficulty was settled for the next thirty years. Clay was praised as the " great pacificator."

In the year 1824 Jackson, Adams, Crawford, and Clay were candidates for the Presidency. Jackson got the largest number of votes, but none of the candidates had a majority, and the choice of a President was left to the House of Representatives. The choice was to be made from the three highest candidates, of which Clay was not one. He was still Speaker, his influence in the House was very great, and as Jackson had long been his bitter enemy he naturally used his influence in favor of Adams, who was declared elected.

Adams, on forming his Cabinet, selected Clay for the highest place in it, appointing him Secretary of State. In consequence of this the charge was made that Clay had sold his influence to get this high post, and that there had been a bargain between him and Adams before the election. The charge was false and malicious, as has since been shown, but it was widely believed at the time, and it hurt Clay for all the rest of his career. For years the cry of "bargain and sale" was not allowed to drop.

The next great question that came before the country was that of a protective tariff. Henry Clay was one of its ablest supporters. In a few years a new tariff party was formed, called the Whig party, which looked upon Clay as its leader. The tariff question became urgent after 1829, when Jackson was made President, and so much hostile feeling was stirred up that South Carolina attempted to secede from the Union. This was checked by the vigorous action of "Old Hickory," who took hold of the affair with a warlike grip.

But the tariff contest remained before the country, and something needed to be done with it. Clay ceased to be Secretary of State when Jackson became President, but two years afterwards he was elected to the Senate. The agitation was great, and Clay did his best to allay it, offering his second great compromise measure. This was the compromise tariff of 1833, under which the duties were gradually reduced till they reached the level of twenty per cent.

Clay ran for President against Jackson in 1832, though he had no chance of election against a soldier of such popularity. He ran again in 1844, and this time seemed sure of an election, for his popularity was immense. But the question of the annexation of Texas came up, and by trying to satisfy both parties Clay lost votes in both, and, to the utter surprise of the whole country, was defeated.

Never was there another Presidential defeat that excited such intense feeling. The Whigs were utterly overwhelmed. " It was," says Nathan Sargent, " as if the first-born of every family had been stricken down." Henry Clay was not only admired, he was loved, worshipped almost, and his defeat gave rise to an extraordinary grief. Men and women alike wept bitterly when they heard the news. The busiest places in the cities were almost deserted for a day or two, people gathering to discuss in low tones the result. The victorious party made no show of triumph, the feeling being that a great wrong had been done.

Clay was bitterly disappointed, and just then other cares arose to add to his depression of feeling. He had fallen deeply into debt, and it seemed as if he might have to sell his beloved home at Ashland to satisfy his creditors. The old man of sixty-seven, whose life had been given to the service of his country, was in no condition to start life afresh.

But if his friends could not make him President, they could save him from poverty. To his utter surprise, he suddenly found that money had come to the bank at Lexington to pay all his debts. Where it came from the banker did not know, and Clay therefore could not return the gift, as it was his first impulse to do. He was forced to accept it, and Ashland was saved.

Then followed the last great event in Henry Clay's life. From 1842 to 1849 he was out of Congress, but in the latter year he was again elected to the Senate. He came there in time to face a momentous question. The dangerous slavery contest was thrown open again. Texas had been annexed, and new territory gained from Mexico. There arose a hot dispute as to whether or not slavery should be admitted into this territory. There was talk of disunion. No one knew but there might be war. The old warrior had to fling himself into the breach again. Once more he offered a compromise measure with the hope of again removing the slavery question from politics.

A sick and feeble old man, often needing a friend's arm to help him up the steps of the Capitol, he was never absent from the Senate on the days when the compromise question was up for debate. During that session of 1849-50 he spoke seventy times. On the morning of his greatest speech on the question he was so weak that he could hardly climb the steps. When he arose to speak his feebleness was evident. But as he went on his cough left him, his frame became erect, and his voice rolled through the Senate chamber with its old musical resonance. Never had he spoken with such pathos and grandeur. That great speech lasted two days. It won the contest and put off the Civil War for ten years, but it wrecked the "great compromiser." He never recovered from the effects of the effort, though he lived two years more, dying June 29, 1852.

As an orator Henry Clay's great power lay in his remarkable voice and his eloquent delivery. His speeches do not read well, but as spoken their force was irresistible. The following estimate is from Parton, the biographer:

"Take him for all in all, we must regard him as the first of American orators; but posterity will not assign him that rank, because posterity will not hear that matchless voice, will not see those large gestures, those striking attitudes, that grand manner, which gave to second-rate composition first-rate effect. His speeches will long be interesting as the relics of a magnificent and dazzling personality, and for the light they cast upon the history of parties; but they add scarcely anything to the intellectual property of the nation."

DANIEL WEBSTER, THE GIANT OF THE AMERICAN SENATE

On the 26th of January, 1830, was heard in the hall of the United States Senate the greatest oration ever delivered on the American rostrum. It was Daniel Webster's famous "Reply to Hayne," the noblest effort in the career of our noblest orator, and as great in its way as the world-famed oration of Demosthenes, "On the Crown."

Forty years before this Webster was a poor boy, the son of a New Hampshire farmer, who seems to have had plenty to do, but was so fond of books that he snatched every spare minute of time to read. His father had a saw mill, and Daniel had to set the logs, but while the saw was cutting through them he kept his eyes on the pages of a book. It was the same with his odd minutes on the farm or when on an errand, and at night he read diligently by the light of a log fire. In this way the boy ran through the circulating library of the village. He read the Bible so ardently that he had much of it by heart.

It is said that the first twenty-five cents he ever earned he gave to a peddler for a handkerchief on which was printed the Constitution of the United States. This he read again and again, till every word of it was impressed on his memory. He little dreamed in those days how useful this intimate knowledge of the Constitution was to become to him in his later days. As for his memory, it was extraordinary. By the time he grew up his mind was like a great store-house of useful information.

Daniel Webster was born at Salisbury, New Hampshire, January 18, 1782. The Revolution was just ending, and five years more were to elapse before the making of the Constitution, that great state paper which he was so nobly to defend in the years to come.

There were ten children in the family, he being the youngest. He was a feeble little fellow, so weak that the people around said he could not live. In his young days he was not fit to work, so he grew fond of wandering through the fields and woods, his chief comrade being an old British sailor who was as fond of the woods as he. The two would lie on the river banks for hours at a time while the old man told the child long yarns of his life on the sea.

His outdoor life made him strong and fit for work, and he grew up a large, finely formed man. But all his life he kept his fondness for the woods and for the hunting and fishing which he had shared with his childhood friend.

One day while Daniel was in the hayfield with his father a man who was riding by stopped to speak for a few minutes with Squire Webster, as the father was called. When the man had gone his father said:

"Dan, that man beat me by a few votes when I ran against him for Congress, and all because he had a better education. For that reason I intend you shall have a good education, and hope to see you work your way up to Congress."

The squire had a high opinion of his son's ability, from his studious habits, and felt that a boy like him should have every chance. Daniel was delighted with the prospect, but he felt that his elder brother, Ezekiel,

WEBSTER, CLAY, AND JACKSON
(Copy of a steel engraving by John Sartain, from a print in possession of Hon. Hampton L. Carson, of Philadelphia)

a bright boy, ought to have the first chance. In the end Squire Webster mortgaged his farm and sent both boys to the Phillips Exeter Academy.

There they studied heartily, Daniel teaching school for a time and copying law papers to help pay his way and that of his brother. In this way he fitted himself for college, entered Dartmouth College in 1797, and after graduation engaged in the study of law.

The story is told that Squire Webster, who had now advanced to the dignity of judge, got for Daniel, at the end of his college course, the position of clerk of the courts, with a fifteen hundred dollar salary. This was a great temptation for the boy, whose life had been one of poverty, but he refused it, saying, " I intend to be a lawyer myself and not to spend my life jotting down other men's doings."

The judge argued against this, deeming that a bird in the hand was worth two in the bush. There were already more lawyers than there was any need of, and not half work enough for them, he said. Daniel sturdily replied, " There is always room at the top."

This resolution he kept, against the advice of his father and friends, beginning his law studies at Salisbury and ending them at Boston, when he was admitted to the bar in 1805. Ezekiel, with whom Daniel had taught school to help in his college studies, was already gaining a reputation as a brilliant lawyer. He was a fine-looking fellow, and some say that he was the handsomest man in the United States.

Daniel himself grew to be a man of impressive appearance. As many readers may wish to know what this great man looked like, we quote Senator Lodge's description of him in later years:

" In face, form, and voice, nature did her utmost

for Daniel Webster. He seemed to every one to be a giant; that, at least, is the word we most commonly find applied to him; and there is no better proof of his wonderful impressiveness than this fact, for he was not a man of extraordinary stature. He was five feet ten inches in height, and in health weighed a little less than two hundred pounds. These are the proportions of a large man, but there is nothing remarkable about them. We must look elsewhere than to mere size to discover why men spoke of Webster as a giant. He had a swarthy complexion and straight black hair. His head was very large; at the same time it was of noble shape, with a broad and lofty brow, and his features were finely cut and full of massive strength. His eyes were extraordinary. They were large and deep-set and, when he began to rouse himself to action, shone with the deep light of a forge-fire, getting ever more glowing as excitement rose. His voice was in harmony with his appearance. It was low and musical in conversation; in debate it was high but full, ringing out in moments of excitement like a clarion, and then sinking to deep notes with the solemn richness of organ-tones, while the words were accompanied by a manner in which grace and dignity mingled in complete accord."

Such was Daniel Webster in the years of his fame. He began to win a reputation as an orator even in college, where he was looked upon as the best writer and speaker of his class. While at the bar he added to his reputation by several Fourth-of-July orations. In the law he soon became highly regarded, and in a few years was looked upon as a fit antagonist of Jeremiah Mason, a man many years older and the greatest lawyer in the State.

In 1812 the ambition of Squire Webster was realized, his son Daniel being elected to Congress. He had run as a member of the Federalist party, then in strong opposition to the Democratic war party, led by John C. Calhoun, and supported by Henry Clay, the Speaker of the House. Webster strongly opposed the war. At the same time he advocated an increase in the navy. The force and intellectual power of his speeches on this subject placed him in the first rank as a debater, and he quickly became looked upon as the Federal leader of New England.

After serving through two terms of Congress he withdrew from politics and settled at law practice in Boston, where his former reputation increased so rapidly that he came to be looked upon as the leading lawyer of New England. His first great case was in defence of the charter rights of his old college, Dartmouth. This he argued before the Supreme Court of the United States with a skill, strength of argument, and knowledge of the law which spread his fame over the whole country. He became regarded as a leader among constitutional lawyers, and his services were called for in nearly all important cases before the Supreme Court.

The effect of his arguments was enhanced by the magnificent manner with which they were delivered, his deep-toned and powerful voice, and his great personal magnetism. "His influence over juries was due chiefly to the combination of a power of lucid statement with his extraordinary oratorical force." In criminal law his success was great, alike in pleading, in examining witnesses, and in his skill in baffling deep-laid schemes of perjury and fraud.

During this period of his life Mr. Webster greatly

increased his reputation by a series of splendid orations upon great national events. One of the chief of these was delivered at Plymouth in 1820, on the two hundredth anniversary of the landing of the Pilgrims. Another great one was in 1825, when the corner-stone of the Bunker-Hill Monument was laid. Most brilliant of all was that given in Faneuil Hall in 1826, when he eulogized the two great patriots, Thomas Jefferson and John Adams, who died on the Fourth of July of that year.

Webster returned to the hall of Congress in 1823, quickly resuming there his former standing, and became active in the very important work of revising the United States Criminal Law. He was transferred to the Senate in 1828, then first entering that arena in which his greatest triumphs were to be gained.

The old Federal party had long since vanished, and new parties were arising, with new aims. Webster took his stand by voting for Clay's tariff bill of 1828, and when the Whig party was organized he and Clay became its foremost men.

He reached the acme of his career as an orator in 1830, when the doctrine of the right of a State to "nullify" the acts of Congress was being maintained by Robert Y. Hayne, an able Senator from South Carolina. The excitement in Washington was great. Party spirit ran high. If the doctrine of nullification was sustained the permanence of the American Union would be in serious danger. Hayne, as the champion of the Southern side, made a speech of marked force and eloquence, in which he bitterly assailed New England and made a sharp personal attack on Webster.

Edward Everett tells us of what followed. After the adjournment he hastened to Webster's house, expecting to find him in a state of great excitement, and was surprised at his entire calmness. He spoke of the Hayne speech, asked Webster if he proposed to reply, and finished by asking him if he had taken notes of his speech.

"Mr. Webster took from his vest pocket a piece of paper about as big as the palm of his hand, and replied, 'I have it all; that is his speech.'"

That was enough for Everett. He immediately left, confident that Webster would fully hold his own.

On the morning of the following day the Senate chamber and galleries were packed by an eager crowd. It was felt that a great day in the annals of the Senate had dawned. When Webster rose, calm and grand, there was a dead hush of expectation. He began in a low, even tone:

"Mr. President: when the mariner has been tossed for many days in thick weather and on an unknown sea, he naturally avails himself of the first pause in the storm, the earliest glance of the sun, to take his latitude and ascertain how far the elements have driven him from his true course. Let us imitate this prudence, and before we float farther on the waves of this debate, refer to the point from which we departed, that we may, at least, be able to conjecture where we are now. I ask for the reading of the resolution before the Senate."

Such was the skilful and artistic beginning of the greatest speech the Senate ever heard. When the reading of the resolution was finished Webster resumed. Never had such a flood of masterly eloquence and argument been poured forth. The audience listened with breathless attention, lest a word should be lost. The strong, resonant sentences, the pathos, the sarcasm, the reasoning, the fervent appeals to love of country, flowed in an unbroken stream. On, on, it went, in crushing and overwhelming weight, closing with the most magnificent burst of eloquence that ever fell from human lips:

"When my eyes shall be turned to behold for the last time the sun in heaven, may I not see him shining on the broken and dishonored fragments of a once glorious Union; on States dissevered, discordant, belligerent; on a land rent with civil feuds, or drenched, it may be, in fraternal blood! Let this last feeble and lingering glance behold rather the glorious ensign of the republic, now known and honored throughout the earth, still full high advanced, its arms and trophies streaming in their original lustre, not a stripe erased or polluted, not a single star obscured; bearing for its motto no such miserable interrogatory as, 'What is all this worth?' or those other words of delusion and folly, 'Liberty first and Union afterwards;' but everywhere, spread all over in characters of living light, blazing in all its ample folds, as they float over the sea and over the land, that other sentiment, dear to every true American heart,— LIBERTY AND UNION, NOW AND FOREVER, ONE AND INSEPARABLE!"

The audience left the hall silent and awe-stricken, feeling that it had been given to them to listen to one of the greatest efforts of the human intellect.

During the years that followed Webster's voice was often heard on momentous subjects before the Senate, and always with power and effect. He was one of the most popular leaders of the Whigs, and the great opponent of Calhoun in all tariff debates. In 1833 he vigorously opposed Clay's compromise tariff bill and supported the "Force Bill" of the Jackson administration.

He promoted the election of President Harrison in 1840 by a series of speeches, and in 1841 was appointed Secretary of State, resigning in 1843. He returned to the Senate in 1845, and in 1850 supported Clay's compromise measure in one of his ablest speeches.

The great orator was fast nearing the end of his career. In 1852 his name was presented in the National Whig Convention for the Presidential nomination, but he received only thirty-two votes. His support of Clay's compromise had lost him many friends. In May of that year he was thrown from his carriage and seriously injured, and on the 24th of October, 1852, he died.

Thus passed away our greatest orator. "He was," said *Fraser's Magazine* in 1890, "the greatest orator that ever lived in the Western hemisphere. Less vehement than Calhoun, less persuasive than Clay, he was yet more grand and powerful than either." Another able English writer says: "Our impression is that, excepting for Mirabeau, Chatham, Fox, and Brougham, no speaker entirely the match of Daniel Webster has trod the world-stage for full two centuries."

There are Americans who would not admit these exceptions, Webster surpassing all the orators named in depth and profundity of knowledge and solidity of argument, his speeches being storehouses of thought and learning, lofty sentiment, solid judgment, brilliant rhetoric, and broad and generous views of the history and destiny of his native land.

JOHN C. CALHOUN, THE CHAMPION OF SOUTHERN INSTITUTIONS

In 1832 the great American Union was in danger. The State of South Carolina had declared that it would not obey the tariff laws, would not permit any one to collect revenue in its ports, and would secede from the Union if an attempt was made to force it to obey the law.

Four years before John C. Calhoun, a powerful orator from that State, had declared of the tariff, " We look upon it as a dead law, null and void, and will not obey it." From this expression his party were called " nullifiers " and his doctrine " nullification." Two years before Webster had made his remarkable speech on this subject, powerfully defending the Constitution and the Union. Now there were open threats of war, and in parts of the State troops were drilling and putting their muskets in order. The fire had been kindled; no one knew how far it might spread.

Fortunately President Jackson, " Old Hickory," the hero of New Orleans, was then at the head of the government. More of a soldier than a statesman, he was a man of the kind that strikes first and talks afterwards. When the Carolinians began to threaten war he began to send troops to their State. A Southerner himself, he was an American first of all, and thundered out: " The Union must and shall be preserved." He threatened to arrest Calhoun, the great advocate of nullification, for treason the moment he

HEROES OF PROGRESS 139

heard of resistance to the Government in South Carolina.

This settled the matter. Nullification sank out of sight. But the Free Traders in Congress were strong, and Henry Clay's Compromise Tariff Bill, for a gradual reduction of the tariff, was passed. Thus ended a critical situation which Calhoun was the main agent in bringing about. He was active in bringing on the Civil War, for he was one of the chief champions of slavery.

John C. Calhoun was born in Abbeyville, South Carolina, in 1782, the same year that Daniel Webster was born in New Hampshire. These two men were to become powerful orators and bitter opponents on the floor of Congress; Calhoun as a statesman of the South, Webster of the North.

Calhoun went north to college, working his way through Yale, where he showed such fine mental powers that Dr. Dwight, the president of the college, said he had talent enough to be a President of the United States. Certainly he had much more talent than some who became President, but like the other great orators of Congress he failed to attain this honor, though he was twice Vice-President.

He began his public career in the legislature of South Carolina in 1807, and was elected to Congress in 1810, remaining there till 1817. When he entered the House the great subject of debate was the insults and injuries of England to this country. There was a strong war party and Calhoun soon put himself at its head. His first speech in the House was on this subject and was so powerful that he sprang at once into fame and was quickly ranked among the leading statesmen of his day. With him in the fight for war was Henry Clay, and these two strong speakers swayed the House till war was declared, and did not desist till it was over and peace declared.

Calhoun began with war, and he was always at war. He kept himself at the head in party wars, now fighting for free trade, now for slavery, always in contest, always a leader in some hostile debate.

Eloquent and vigorous as a speaker, he did not, like many others, make his points by personal attacks on his opponents. He was a gentleman in the warmest of his contests, and though he cut his way sharply and fiercely through the arguments of his opponents, dealing them stunning blows, he did not attack the men themselves. A trenchant reasoner, it was always what his opponent said that he assailed, not what he was. He could see no merit or force in angry and rude personal abuse.

It is singular that, in this early period, Calhoun made a long and strong speech in favor of a protective tariff, the policy which he afterwards so bitterly assailed. But at that time the South was not opposed to a tariff. It strongly favored it. The opposition came later.

In 1817 Calhoun was made Secretary of War in the Cabinet of President Monroe. When he took charge of the War Department all was in disorder and confusion, but it did not take him long to set it right. He established a new system, a very simple and very suitable one, and one that has been followed ever since. One thing he did not believe in was the saving of money by paying the men poorly and feeding them on mean food. He held that good pay and good food would bring better service, and this is still held in the army. No soldier in the world is taken better care

HEROES OF PROGRESS 141

of and treated more like a man than the American soldier, and he owes this largely to Calhoun, who first recognised the rights of the soldier.

By 1824 Calhoun had become so prominent that he was elected Vice-President, with John Quincy Adams as President. He was elected again with General Jackson in 1828. During this time his opinions on the tariff changed, and he came to believe that free trade was better than protection for the interests of the South. Very many in the South were of the same opinion, and the agitation began which led to the "nullification" excitement.

Calhoun was now the great leader of the South. He brought out the doctrine of the Sovereignty of the States, holding that they had the right to leave the Union if they had just cause. He was so bitterly opposed to the course of the administration that he resigned from the Vice-Presidency in 1832, was elected to the Senate, and kept up a vigorous agitation which only ended when President Jackson threatened him with arrest for treason.

When the tariff question was set aside, that of slavery loomed up, and Calhoun became its most powerful supporter. He believed in it firmly. He thought that the slave system was morally and politically right. He thought it good for white and black alike, and that the best good of the country depended upon it. In this he was honest and sincere. No man was more upright; he fought for what he believed in, and his influence became immense. For a quarter of a century he advocated the doctrine of the rightfulness and the extension of slavery, and there is no doubt that his arguments had much to do with bringing on the crisis that ended in the Civil War.

"I mean to force the issue on the North," he said, and he did force it. Garrison and Phillips and the other anti-slavery leaders might have found their labors in vain but for Calhoun, who gave them much to talk upon. The denial of the right of petition in the House, the annexation of Texas as a new slave territory, the forcing of slavery into the Territories, these were the things he worked for and aided in gaining. To the end of his life he protested that slavery is a divine institution, and that it must rule this country or ruin it.

A few words will suffice to tell the remainder of his personal history. He was not satisfied with being Vice-President, he was eager to be President, but, like his fellow orators, Clay and Webster, he failed in this. In 1836 he was a popular favorite in his party, but President Jackson was his enemy and defeated his efforts, to his bitter disappointment. The remainder of his life was spent in the Senate, except for a short time when he served as Secretary of State in President Tyler's Cabinet. During this time he was active in securing the annexation of Texas, a movement then very popular in the south.

From 1835 to 1850 the agitation on the slavery question was chiefly kept up by Calhoun, Webster and Clay were earnest in trying to put off the day of strife, but he was as earnest in trying to bring it on. In his view slavery was a righteous and beneficial institution, and any aid given to runaway slaves or legal efforts to restrict the slave system was an interference with the rights of the slave States which would justify their secession from the Union. Ten years after his death, which took place March 31, 1850, the doctrine he so long sustained began to bear fruit, and the

HEROES OF PROGRESS 143

country was on the verge of the great war which put a final end to the system of which he had been the strongest advocate.

We know little about the private life of Mr. Calhoun, though it is said that he was just and kind to his slaves, and an honorable and pure-minded man. As a statesman he had keen judgment, great foresight, and much discretion, and his bitterest enemies gave him credit for splendid talent and ability. Harriet Martineau, in her "Retrospect of Western Travel," has given a fine picture of him and his great opponents which is well worth quoting. She thus photographs the three great statesmen:

"Mr. Clay, sitting upright on the sofa, with his snuff-box ever in his hand, would discourse for many an hour in his even, soft, deliberate tone on any one of the great subjects of American policy which we might happen to start, always amazing us with the moderation of estimate and speech which so impetuous a nature had been able to attain. Mr. Webster, leaning back at his ease, telling stories, cracking jokes, shaking the sofa with burst after burst of laughter, or smoothly discoursing to the perfect felicity of the logical part of one's constitution, would illuminate an evening now and then.

"Mr. Calhoun, the cast-iron man, who looks as if he had never been born and could never be extinguished, would come in sometimes to keep our understanding on a painful stretch for a short while, and leave us to take to pieces his close, rapid, theoretical, illustrated talk, and see what we could make of it. We found it usually more worth retaining as a curiosity than as either very just or useful. I know of no man who lives in such utter intellectual solitude. He meets men and harangues by the fireside as in the Senate; he is wrought like a piece of machinery, set going vehemently by a weight, and stops while you answer; he either passes by what you say, or twists it into a suitability with what is in his head, and begins to lecture again."

She paints his portrait in a few telling words: " Mr. Calhoun's countenance first fixed my attention; the splendid eye, the straight forehead, surmounted by a wad of stiff, upright, dark hair, the stern brow, the inflexible mouth—it is one of the most remarkable heads in the country."

SAMUEL F. B. MORSE, THE DISCOVERER OF ELECTRIC TELEGRAPHY

In 1844 a Whig National Convention for the nomination of a President was in session at Baltimore. Henry Clay, the people's favorite, was the most prominent candidate, and a good deal of interest was felt by those waiting for the news. In Washington, forty miles away, the interest was great, and many waited eagerly for the coming of the first railroad train with tidings of the result.

Suddenly the word went from mouth to mouth that Clay had been nominated. People heard the news with surprise and incredulity. How could any one know? No train had arrived, no mail or messenger reached the capital. When it was told that the news had come by lightning message, flashed over a wire which led from Baltimore to a room in the Capitol building, many laughed in scorn. They would wait for the train, they said. It was impossible for news to come in a minute from Baltimore to Washington.

But when the train came in, confirming the report, there was a sudden change of feeling. An awe spread over the people. What did this mean? Were space and time to be annihilated? Had man made a discovery which would carry thought in a moment from end to end of the land? Men walked home sobered and wondering. All interest in the nomination was lost before the interest in this new and magical discovery. The name of Professor Morse, the discoverer, suddenly rose from obscurity to fame.

Twelve years before this Samuel Finley Breese Morse, an American painter of much talent, was on his way home from Europe in the ship "Sully" to accept the professorship of Literature of the Fine Arts at the University of the City of New York. He was then forty-one years old, having been born in Charlestown, Massachusetts, on the 27th of April, 1791. Until now all his time and attention had been given to the art of painting, and no dream had come to him of the strange history of his later life.

Inspiration came to him in a talk of some passengers on the "Sully," one of whom had seen in Paris some experiments with the electro-magnet. These proved that the electric spark could be obtained by means of the magnet, and that the current of electricity which gave this spark could be carried very rapidly to a distance along an iron wire.

The story immediately interested Mr. Morse. If sparks could thus be obtained at the end of a long wire, could not some system of signals be devised? Morse talked it over with the gentleman, considering how this could be done, and trying to devise a working plan. He thought deeply on the subject himself, walking the deck alone under the stars and debating inwardly on the possibilities of the current and the magnet.

Mr. Morse was not a tyro on the subject of electricity. He knew what had been done in it, and what had been discovered of its ways of action, and his thought bore remarkable fruit. Before the "Sully" reached New York he had worked out in his mind a complete plan, devising "not only the idea of an electric telegraph, but of an electro-magnetic and recording telegraph substantially and essentially as it now exists." He is said to have even invented an alphabet of signs, closely the same as that which is now in use, but it is probable that this was a later device.

Mr. Morse had no time to give to a Fine Arts professorship when he landed in New York. A new idea had taken possession of his mind, and during the rest of his life most of his time and thought was given to telegraphy. He had a desperate struggle before him. It is one thing to lay out a plan in one's mind and another thing to make it work in matter. Many difficulties are sure to arise to trouble the inventor and sadden his soul.

Morse had been something of an inventor already, and had made experiments in electricity and galvanism. This had been for mere pastime; now it was to be serious work. He went into his new labor with vim and energy, but the path before him was long and hard. Wires were stretched, experiments made, but again and again they failed to work. His money went, he had three children to support, starvation threatened him, but he kept on, doing enough painting to bring him some slight support. He had faith in himself, he had sympathy and aid from his brother and friends, but there were days when he had to go hungry for want of food. When his instruments refused to do what he expected, he studied them till he found out what was wrong, and made it right.

At length he had ready a working model, but this was not until 1835, after three years of continued experiment and endless discouragement. He had a wire circling round his room half a mile in length and was able to send signals to its end, but he could not yet bring them back again. A duplicate instrument was needed at the other end of the wire, and he was so poor that two years more passed before he was able to have one made.

Now all was right. His telegraph worked splendidly. He could send signals both ways over his wire and read them easily. In September, 1837, he set it up in the University of New York and exhibited it to large audiences, who saw it with wonder and delight.

But this was only a lecture room experiment. To make it a practical working affair was another matter. Money, far more money than he could hope to command, was needed to bring it into general use. He applied to Congress, but in vain. Some interest was awakened, but no grant of money was made. Most men were disposed to ridicule the whole affair. Then he went to England, but with the same result. "Even if it does work," said one wise man, "what good will it be? Men get news now as fast as any one is likely to want them. Your idea is good, Mr. Morse, but it won't pay."

Back to Washington again, and a new bill in Congress. It was the early spring of 1843. At midnight of March 3 the Congress then in session would end. Morse's bill had passed the House on February 23, but it hung in the Senate, quite crowded out of sight by the rush of bills deemed of more importance. Morse waited about the Senate chamber until nearly midnight, and then, seeing the confusion growing every minute greater, and his case apparently hopeless, he gave it up in despair and walked sadly home.

When he came down to breakfast the next morning his face was a picture of gloom. He was fairly ready to give up the fight and go back to the painter's brush. A young lady met him at the door with a smiling face.

"I have come to congratulate you, Mr. Morse."

"For what, my dear friend?"

"For the passage of your bill."

"What!" He stood aghast. "The passage of my bill!" he faltered.

"Yes. Do you not know of it?"

"Nothing at all."

"Then you came home too soon last night. Congress has granted your claim. I am happy in being the first to bring you the good news."

"You have given me new life, Miss Ellsworth," he exclaimed. "As a reward for your good tidings, I promise you that when my telegraph line is completed you shall have the honor of selecting the first message to be sent over it."

Eleven and a half years had passed since the conversation on the ship "Sully," years of incessant work and bitter discouragement. Now success seemed to shine on the horizon. The grant was for thirty thousand dollars only, but he hoped that would be enough. The plan he had worked out on the "Sully" was the following: There was to be an alphabet of some kind of marks, a revolving ribbon of paper to receive these, and a method of carrying the wires underground in tubes. He had thought also of supporting them in the air, but the other plan seemed to him the best.

What he now wanted was a contrivance to make a ditch to lay the wires in. A man named Ezra Cornell was applied to. No one knew of him then, but he is now known as the founder of Cornell University, for he afterwards became famous and rich. He had an inventive mind, knew much about ploughs, and in a short time devised a machine that would cut a trench in the ground, lay the pipe at its bottom, and cover in the earth behind it.

In ten days the machine was ready. A yoke of oxen was attached to it, one man managed it, and in five minutes it had laid one hundred feet of pipe and covered it with earth. It was a decided success. The pipe, with the wire within it, was laid so rapidly that in a few days ten miles were down.

Here it stopped. Something had gone wrong. No trace of a current could be got through. The insulation of the wire was imperfect. Another kind of pipe was tried. Still the current would not go through. Many experiments were made, a year passed by, only seven thousand dollars of the money remained, the inventor was in despair.

"I fear it will never work." said Cornell. "The pipe plan is a failure."

"Then let us try the air plan. If electricity won't go underground, we must try and get it to go through the air."

The new plan was to string the wire on poles, with an insulator to keep the current from the wood. Professor Henry, of the Smithsonian Institution, a man who was an expert in electricity, suggested a suitable insulator, and the work went rapidly on. To raise poles, put a glass bulb at their top, and string wires over them, was an easy and rapid process. And the signals passed perfectly. All the old trouble was at an end.

On the day of the nomination by the Baltimore convention the wire was only partly laid. It began at Washington, but was still miles from Baltimore. But the train from Baltimore that carried the news of the nomination to Washington carried also one of the telegraph experts. He left the train at the end of the wire, telegraphed the news to Washington, and when the train reached that city its passengers were utterly astounded to find that they brought stale news, that the story of the nomination was already spread through the capital. It was an overwhelming proof of the power of the electric telegraph, and Professor Morse sprang into fame. The wire was completed to Baltimore by May 24, 1844, and, as Morse had promised, Miss Ellsworth was given the honor of choosing the first message to be sent over it. She selected an appropriate passage of Scripture: "What hath God wrought?" With these significant words began the reign of that marvellous invention which has since then tied the ends of the world together and fairly annihilated space. So strange was its principle to most people that, as we are told, even so high a dignitary as John C. Spencer, Secretary of the Treasury, asked one of Morse's assistants how large a bundle could be sent over the wires, and if the postal mails could not be sent in that way.

While Morse was working on his telegraph system, others were working in Europe. While he was fighting Congress, inventors in England were experimenting with short lines, with the wire carried in buried pipes. But the system adopted there was one of signals by vibrating needles, and was so inferior to the Morse system that the latter is now used almost throughout the world.

Professor Morse no longer suffered from poverty. Telegraph companies were soon organized all over the country, his invention was adopted in Europe, and in a few years he was the happy possessor of a large fortune. Honors also were showered upon him. Yale College complimented him with the degree of LL.D., and tokens of recognition came to him from many other quarters, many of them from Europe, gold medals and insignia being presented him by several monarchs.

The telegraph was not the last of the Morse inventions, several others being made by him. He also took the first daguerreotypes in America, made a pump-machine for fire-engines, and laid the first telegraph under water. This was a short line, but he afterwards took great interest in the efforts of Cyrus W. Field to lay a submarine cable, and gave him important aid and advice in the project. He died in New York, April 2, 1872, having lived to see the telegraph working across the Atlantic.

CYRUS W. FIELD, THE DESIGNER OF THE ATLANTIC CABLE

THE work done by Morse in inventing the electric telegraph and stretching it over the land was but half the battle to be fought. He had made the continents a pathway for thought, but the ocean remained to be conquered also, a channel needed to be made through the depths of the seas for the passage of human thought, and the invader of this watery realm came in the person of Cyrus West Field.

This man of enterprise, who was born at Stockbridge, Massachusetts, November 30, 1819, was a retired merchant of thirty-five years of age when the movement of events first brought him into the field of telegraph invention. He was one of four brothers who became notable in various ways. One of these, David Dudley Field, became prominent in the law, and was president of a commission to digest the political, penal, and civil codes of law in New York. A second, Stephen J. Field, became Chief Justice of the Supreme Court of California, and afterwards an Associate Justice in the Supreme Court of the United States. A third, Henry M. Field, was prominent as a clergyman and author, and editor of *The New York Evangelist*. The fourth, by far the most famous of them all, is the one with whom we are specially concerned. He entered into business, made a fortune, and retired to enjoy it while still young.

This was at the time that the newest great discovery, the electric telegraph, was becoming widely known, being laid rapidly in all directions, and men had not yet ceased to wonder at its marvellous powers. In 1854 a number of enterprising persons became associated in an ambitious scheme. They undertook to build a telegraph line across the island of Newfoundland, and connect it with a line of fast steamers from the eastern side of that island, arguing that these could reach Ireland in five days, and the news of Europe be brought to America within a week.

These men had ideas, but they lacked cash. They wanted a man with money to help them. After trying to build the line and failing for want of funds, they looked around for a suitable man of wealth. Some of them knew of Mr. Field as a man who had built up a big business from a small beginning, was able, rich, and enterprising, and was out of business and with leisure to look into their scheme.

The plan was strongly laid before the retired merchant. He was assured it would be of great benefit to the country and be certain to pay. He promised to think of it, and as he sat in his library, slowly turning a globe and looking for the situation of Newfoundland and its distance from Ireland, the thought came to him: "Why not carry the line across the ocean?"

It was one of those illuminating thoughts which lie at the basis of most great enterprises. Field turned it over in his head, studied what had been done with the telegraph, and became daily more assured that it could be accomplished. It had some warrant in preceding efforts. Morse had suggested an Atlantic telegraph in 1842, before his first land line was laid, and in 1852 a submarine cable had been laid from Dover to Ostend, thus connecting England with the continent of Europe.

The idea conceived, Field lost no time in putting it in practice. In 1855 he obtained from the legislature of Newfoundland the sole right for fifty years to land telegraph cables, from either Europe or America, on that island. He was the man for the work, full of energy, enterprise, and enthusiasm. He formed a stock company at once, and followed this by organizing in London the "Atlantic Telegraph Company." His faith in the project was shown by his furnishing one-fourth of the capital himself. So devoted was he to the work that he crossed the ocean nearly thirty times before it was finally carried out.

The project called for great care in the preparation of the cable. It needed to be made strong and flexible and to be thoroughly insulated. A mere pin-hole in its entire length might let the electric current escape. The centre steel wire was wound round with small copper wires, and these were covered with several coatings of gutta-percha and Manila hemp. Gutta-percha is a non-conductor of electricity, and was intended to prevent the current from leaving the interior wires. Outside of all these, eighteen strands of iron wires were laid.

The submarine lines already laid served as examples. In addition to that between England and France, one was now working from Newfoundland to the mainland of America. These short ones were successful; why should not a longer one be? Field's enthusiasm induced some wealthy men to put money into the enterprise, and in 1857 a wire was ready and an expedition set out to lay it on the ocean bottom, ships being provided by the American and English governments. This first attempt proved a failure, as did a second one in the spring of the following year. But in August of that year a third trial was made and this time with success. For the first time in history the thoughts of man were sent in an instant of time under and across the ocean.

Those who lived in those days will remember the vast interest, the great excitement, it produced. There were celebrations on both sides of the water. Messages passed between President Buchanan and Queen Victoria, words of greeting and congratulation. They passed very slowly, but they passed. It took sixty-seven minutes to send the queen's message of ninety words. The current was distressingly feeble. It gradually failed and ceased to work. The sending of messages across the ocean was at an end.

Field now found himself in a quandary. These experiments had been very costly, and the capitalists began to think that there was enough of their money lying on the bottom of the ocean. They tied their purse strings, and the enterprising projector found money for a new cable very hard to get. " It worked once. It will work again," he argued. " It failed once, it may fail again," they answered. They had the best of the argument, for they had the money and the answer both.

Then came on the American Civil War, which put an end to the enterprise for four long years. But Cyrus Field did not despair. All through the war he kept at it, arguing, persuading, beseeching, and in time the money for a new and stronger cable came in. In August, 1865, the new cable was ready. It was much superior to that of seven years earlier. Two ships had been used in 1858, and the wires spliced in mid-ocean. Now only one, the huge " Great Eastern," was employed. On her decks the whole length of cable, 2300 miles, weighing 4000 tons, was laid, and she steamed away from Valentia, Ireland, on her difficult task. All went well until she was 1067 miles out, when by accident too much strain was put on the cable, it broke and sank, and failure had come again.

But the end was near at hand. With great difficulty Field raised more funds, had another cable made, lighter and stronger than the last one, and this time the "Great Eastern" made her journey without an accident, the shore end was safely landed at Trinity Bay, Newfoundland, messages passed freely from end to end, and one of the most wonderful of modern enterprises was safely accomplished. Then the ship went back to mid-ocean, grappled in the water's depths, two miles down, for the lost cable of the year before, caught it and brought it up, spliced it to the unlaid part, and set out again for Newfoundland. This, too, was landed, and two electric cables crossed the seas. Cyrus Field had not only achieved his great work, but had duplicated it.

The wires worked splendidly. Men began to talk across the ocean as they had formerly talked across the street. It was expensive at first, one hundred dollars being charged for twenty words of five letters each. But the rates soon went down, and now, instead of paying five dollars for a word, messages can be sent for twenty-five cents a word.

Mr. Field's success brought him the highest honor. Men no longer laughed at his enterprise as, years before, they had laughed at that of Morse, and, years earlier still, at that of Fulton. Congress voted him the thanks of the nation, and presented him a gold medal and other testimonials of honor and respect. The French Exposition, which was held soon afterwards, gave him its grand medal, and honors were showered upon him from other quarters. Success in his great enterprise had made him one of the conquering heroes of the world.

Mr. Field did not rest in his later years, but spent an active and useful life, taking part in various important business enterprises. In 1871 he went into a company which proposed to lay a cable across the Pacific by way of Hawaii and Japan to China. This was not done, but since then electric cables have been laid across that great ocean. He also took part in laying the street railways of New York, and engaged very actively in the building of the elevated railways of that city. He died in New York, July 12, 1892.

ELIAS HOWE, THE INVENTOR OF THE SEWING MACHINE

For centuries and tens of centuries the needle has been in use as woman's especial tool. From the remote stone age down to the present day the song of "Stitch! Stitch! Stitch!" has been sung, and only about sixty years ago did the whirr of the sewing-machine begin to serve as the chorus to this wearisome song. Then a poor inventor of Yankeeland set his wits to work, and when he ended the machine was devised whose merry music may be heard to-day in hundreds of thousands of homes.

Poor Elias Howe! The story of his life reads like a romance; but, like that of many inventors, it was a romance of poverty, misfortune, endless discouragements, stern perseverance, a clinging to one idea through the darkest of days, and, in the end, success. He would have been a far happier man if the fever of invention had not seized upon him, but millions of households would have been less happy if he, or some one like him, had not brought ease and rest to the fingers of the sewing-woman.

Elias Howe was born in Spencer, Massachusetts, July 19, 1819. He was born to poverty and hard work. Until he was sixteen years old he dug and delved on his father's farm and wrought in his mill. Then he went to Lowell and learned the machinist's trade, and from there to Cambridge—a frail, sickly fellow, barely able to earn a living on account of persistent ill health. Yet he married, and by the time he was twenty-three had a wife and three children to support. Then, one day, he happened to hear some men in the shop talking of what a useful thing a sewing-machine would be, and the true work of Elias Howe's life began. From that day on, the idea of inventing such a machine stirred in his mind and would not let him rest.

The idea was new only to him. Many had tried it before, but with no great success. The first invention dates back to 1755, when Charles F. Weisenthal, of England, patented a needle with an eye in the centre and pointed at both ends. Several other inventions were made, intended for embroidering, and some also for sewing shoes and gloves, but none of them making a firm, secure, and satisfactory stitch. The task of accomplishing this was left for Elias Howe.

From the time he heard the men talking in the shop Howe was haunted with the idea. In the evening, after his day's work was done, he would sit for hours in his humble home, watching his wife's busy fingers as her needle went in and out through the cloth, and thinking deeply as he sat. Up to this time, through all the ages, the hand of woman had been the one sewing machine, and his first idea was to make a machine that would work like the fingers of a seamstress. For a year he watched and worked, trying various devices, but in the end he gave this project up. He saw that a stitch of a different kind was needed.

His constant thought at length bore fruit. A single thread evidently would not do. It would not hold. If broken it would ravel out. All previous machines had used one thread, but to do work that would hold two threads were needed. He was now on the right track, that of the lock stitch. The idea came to him of using a needle with an eye near the point, passing through the cloth and making a loop in the thread, and a shuttle carrying another thread and darting backward and forward, carrying its thread through the loop and locking the stitch by the joint movements of needle and shuttle.

It was a happy idea. It contained the principle on which the sewing-machine of to-day is based. It it true that there are single thread sewing-machines now in use which make a stitch that is all right if the thread does not break; but it is all wrong if it does. The shuttle was Howe's great invention, and it is the life of the sewing machine.

But it is one thing to have an idea in the mind, and another thing to make it work in wood and metal. Feeble in health, empty in pocket, the young inventor had a difficult task before him. His father could not help him, for he was as poor as himself. Finally he found a friend who believed in his idea, and who had money. This was George Fisher, a Cambridge wood and coal dealer, who agreed to give Mr. Howe and his family a home and food and to furnish him with five hundred dollars for his experiments. For this he was to have a half interest in the invention, if one should be made.

At last poor Howe had the opportunity to work out his ideas. The garret of Fisher's house was his workshop, and there he toiled diligently day after day, his day often running far into the night. For a great part of the year he kept at it, planning and devising, trying various ways of making his needle and shuttle work, experimenting in a dozen directions. Finally, in April, 1845, he had it so far perfected that it would sew a seam, and in July he proved what it could do by making with his machine a suit of woolen clothes for himself and another for Mr. Fisher. Success was at length attained. Crude as the machine was, it contained the essential features of the splendid machines made to-day.

Howe's needle was a great invention, without which no sewing-machine would be available. So was his shuttle. The two together made the firmest of stitches. His needle at first worked horizontally, and the cloth was passed vertically through the machine. But it was not long before the needle was set to work vertically, and the cloth was laid upon the table of the machine, with devices to move it at proper speed under the needle. This done, victory was gained.

So far the difficulties had been workshop labor. Now the inventor had a fight with the world before him, and he found it a terrible one. The machine was completed, it was patented, it was offered to the tailoring trade, but nobody would buy it. Tailors looked at it, saw it work, said that it was no doubt very ingenious and might be useful—but they would not buy it. It was costly, and might soon get out of order. And if successful, think of the thousands of men and women it would throw out of work! In the end Mr. Fisher got tired of keeping Howe and his family for his interest in a machine that would not sell, and the older Mr. Howe was obliged to take them in. He was too poor to support them, and Elias got a place as railroad engineer, and the precious machine was banished to a corner. As for Fisher, in the end he grew to look so contemptuously on the invention that he was ready to sell his half interest in it for a small sum, and Howe succeeded in regaining possession of the whole.

As soon as he had saved a little money, Elias sent his

HEROES OF PROGRESS 163

brother Amasa to England with the model of his machine, to see if it could be introduced there. Amasa made some sort of arrangement with a corset-maker, and Elias, with new hope, set off with his wife and children for London, trusting to find a market for his wares. But it was the same story over again. Everywhere he met with discouragement and disappointment. The corset-maker did not treat him fairly, his money ran very low, and he was forced to send his wife and children back again to his father, staying himself in London in hope of better luck.

No luck came, his last dollar was spent, and in the end he had to pawn his model and patent papers for money enough to bring him home again. He landed in New York, and there received the distressing news that his wife was dying of consumption in Cambridge.

The poor fellow had not money enough to pay railroad fare, he was too weak to walk, and he had to stay where he was until some one sent him money enough to bring him home to his dying wife. He reached Cambridge barely in time to see her alive. Soon the spirit of the faithful wife and mother, whose busy needle had formed the inspiration for his machine, passed away and left him almost heart-broken.

It may well be that poor Howe wished he could follow her himself and give up the fight. It was now 1849. Several years had been spent in America and England in destitution and constant disappointment; his labor, his time, his talent, had gone for nothing; ill health had been his companion, death had removed his wife, he and his children were a charge upon his father, many of his friends thought that he had wasted his life in useless fancies; the outlook was enough to make him despair.

But there came a change in the tide of events. The inventor found friends ready to advance him money for a purpose next to be mentioned, and for the first time fortune began to smile on him. No doubt it was a bitter thought to him that the good wife who had shared his days of misery was not with him now that hope was rising in his sky.

The fact was that while he was in England his invention had been pirated in America, machines had been made on the principle discovered by him, and their makers, more fortunate than he, had found buyers for them. He came home to learn that his name was growing famous and his invention was fast coming into use. There were various inventors who had made improvements upon it, but all of them used his ideas in some form or other and were infringing upon his patent. He thereupon, aided by his friends, began a series of lawsuits against those who were using the ideas to which he had given years of his life, and especially against a Mr. Singer who was making money by selling an improvement upon his machine.

The battle in the courts was long and hard. The pirates fought fiercely. Among other things they unearthed a machine which had been worked upon by a Walter Hunt of New York about 1832, in which the lock-stitch was to be employed. But it was proved that this had been a dead failure, and in 1854 the courts decided in Howe's favor, ordering all the pirates to pay him a royalty on every machine they had made or should make. Thus, after ten years of desperate work, the inventor attained success.

He had opened a small factory in New York, but his royalties now began to pour money upon him much faster than his sales, and his total income from them amounted in time to over $2,000,000. He lived to see the machine to which he had given the best years of his life accepted as one of the world's greatest inventions, while honors were showered upon him. Among these were the Cross of the Legion of Honor, which came to him from France, and a gold medal from the French Exposition.

In 1861 he raised and equipped at his own expense a regiment for the Civil War, in which he served as a private until ill health compelled him to resign. His labors, his long anxiety and privation, his naturally frail constitution, were now telling upon him, and two years after the war, on the 3d of October, 1867, the famous inventor died.

CYRUS H. McCORMICK, THE BENEFACTOR OF THE FARMER

At Walnut Grove, Virginia, on February 15, 1809, was born a boy who lived to become one of the greatest benefactors of the farmer ever born in any land. This was Cyrus Hall McCormick, the inventor of the reaping machine. Such a machine had long been needed. Reaping by hand was slow and back-breaking work, and something was wanted that would cut and gather grain swiftly and economically. While young McCormick was a schoolboy, his father was trying to invent such a machine, but was making a very poor job of it. The boy spent much of his time on the plantation, helping in the fields or occupying himself in the saw and grist mills, the carpenter and blacksmith shops, which were on the plantation. All this interested him, for the spirit of invention was in his blood.

He showed this when only fifteen years old by making a light, easily-handled grain cradle, much better fitted to his weight than the heavy cradles then in use. Two years after this he produced a hill-side plough with the special feature that it was self-sharpening, a new feature in a plough. The boy's inventive powers were developing. He watched his father working upon the reaper, and when the latter gave it up in disgust, he asked permission to try his hand on it. "You would only waste your time," said the father. "The thing has been tried a hundred times, and no one has brought out anything worth talking about. A reaper is an impossibility."

Young McCormick did not think so. He was almost a man then, and his ideas were ripening. "All right," said his father at length. "There is my old failure. Take hold of it and see what you can do with it. Let us see if you are smarter than your father."

The boy took hold of the machine, studied it, investigated it, considered its difficulties, and found that, as his father had said, that particular reaper was impossible. But a different one might be made. Gradually he worked out in his active brain a new plan. There were several things to be done. The standing grain was to be held in a body and cut, and there must be a platform upon which it could fall and be taken care of.

He decided that the cutting must be done with a sort of shears, arranged in a series and acting right and left with what is called a reciprocating motion as the machine moved forward. There must be a reel to gather and hold the grain, the sharp-edged blades to cut it, and a platform upon which it could fall and be gathered into bundles or sheaves. These were the ideas; how they were to be applied was the problem.

The inventor went to work, experimenting, devising, thinking out point after point. Every part of the machine was made by his own hands, the cranks, the gears, the cutting blades, the gathering reels, the various other devices; he fitting them, putting them together, and finally sending his machine into the field to see what it could do. It did not work badly for a beginning. A man rode on the horse that drew the machine through the grain. Another man walked beside it to draw the swaths from the platform. No doubt the elder McCormick looked on with curious interest, but we do not know what he said.

In 1831—the inventor was then twenty-two years old—the first public trial of the machine was made. A number of experienced farmers looked on while it cut its way with considerable speed through several acres of oats. The next year it was tried in a wheat field, and harvested seventy-five acres. So far it was a success, but the farmers did not approve of it sufficiently to buy it, and McCormick set it aside for the time being, going into the iron-smelting business, in which he saw better promise of quick returns.

The panic of 1837 and the hard times that followed wrecked this enterprise, and the best he could do was to get out of the affair without money but free from debt. Then he turned back to the reaper, saw at once where it could be improved, tinkered with it for a time, then moved west with it, first to Cincinnati and afterwards to Chicago. Here he set up factories for the manufacture of the machine.

It was about 1840 that he got the reaper in what he thought satisfactory working order, and began to push it on the market. Buyers were found, the farmers saw the advantage of the new machine, and after he had gained a good business in this country he went abroad with the purpose of introducing his reapers into the fields of Europe. In 1851 he showed it at the World's Fair at London, where it was looked upon as the queer production of a Yankee crank. The newspapers and visitors made no end of fun of the odd-looking machine, which the London *Times* said seemed like a cross between an Astley chariot, a wheelbarrow, and a flying machine.

A few weeks later the laugh was on the other side.

COMBINED HARVESTER AND THRASHER

The reaper was tested in a number of English grain fields, in competition with some other machines, and left them all so far in the rear that there was an utter change of front, the McCormick reaper being voted the most important thing in the whole fair. The *Times* made atonement for its former ridicule by saying that the reaper was equal in value to the whole exhibition. Among all the agricultural implements shown, this alone received the great medal, and the lately ridiculed man was rewarded with the highest honors, as having done more for agriculture than any other man of the century. France matched England by honoring him with the Cross of the Legion of Honor. Some years later it bestowed the greater honor of making him an officer of the Legion of Honor and a member of the French Academy of Science.

McCormick was more than an inventor. He was a business man, which many inventors are not. While manufacturing and selling his reaper he kept on improving it till it become the wonderful machine of to-day, cutting grass and grain alike, gathering the grain into sheaves, binding them with twine, and laying them on the ground. And all this it does itself, without stopping, and with only one man to manage it, the man who drives the horses.

Before McCormick went to Europe he had gained a large business in America. In 1848 he took the great risk, for a man of moderate capital, of building seven hundred machines for the coming harvest. But they were all sold, and he could well smile at the comments of the London press in 1851. In 1880, after the business had been in operation more than thirty years, it was made into a joint-stock company, with Mr.

McCormick as president, and his brother, who had long been his partner, as vice-president.

Four years later, on May 13, 1884, Mr. McCormick died. At that time the company had a capital of three million dollars, and was turning out nearly fifty-five thousand machines a year, these being sold in all parts of the world. It is largely due to this great machine that the United States outstrips the world as a grain producer, and that the hay-harvest has grown to be one of the most valuable of our farm crops. Cyrus McCormick ranks among the greatest benefactors of mankind.

CHARLES GOODYEAR, THE PRINCE OF THE RUBBER INDUSTRY

The stories of Morse of the telegraph and Howe of the sewing-machine are remarkable examples of perseverance under difficulties that would crush a common man. The story of Charles Goodyear, which we have next to tell, is one of the same kind. No man ever kept up his spirit longer under trials and troubles than this great discoverer, winning success where thousands would have failed. The story of his life is that of the India-rubber industry. His labors in this took more than ten years of the prime of his life. For it he suffered poverty, imprisonment, and ridicule, and, though he produced one of the great modern industries, he failed to gain an adequate return in money for his great sacrifice. Fortune did not come to him as it did to Morse and Howe, and he had largely to be content with the satisfaction of helping mankind.

The sap of the India-rubber tree long held out a promising lure to inventors. It formed a waterproof material which could readily be moulded into almost any shape, and in the first half of the last century many companies were organized for the manufacture of shoes and other rubber goods. But there was one great difficulty, the rubber was fit for use in winter, but it would not bear the summer's heat, softening and becoming useless.

In the opinion of certain manufacturers of India-rubber life-preservers in 1834, the business was almost hopeless. They would make a large quantity of goods during the winter and sell them for good prices, but in the summer many of these melted down and were returned as ruined. The rubber would grow sticky in the sun and stiff in the cold. Many efforts had been made to overcome this by mixing other materials with it, but all in vain, and ruin seemed to stare all rubber manufacturers in the face. The man who saved them from this fate was Charles Goodyear, a merchant of Philadelphia, but a native of New Haven, Connecticut, in which city he was born on the 29th of December, 1800.

At the time mentioned he was engaged in the hardware business of A. Goodyear & Sons in the Quaker City. At this period a very large business had sprung up in the rubber trade, in spite of its disadvantages, and he grew interested in it as a possible source of profit. When in New York one day he bought one of the India-rubber life-preservers made by the Roxbury Rubber Co., the manufacturers above spoken of. Having the taste for invention of a true son of Connecticut, he took this home, examined it carefully, and fancied that he could improve upon it. He soon devised a plan, which he took to the Roxbury Company and asked them to adopt. They declined to do so, telling him the story of their difficulties in some such words as those above given.

"Your plan is a good one," he was told, "but business conditions will not let us take on new expenses. If you can only find some way to make India-rubber stand the heat of summer and the cold of winter, both our fortunes will be made. Anything less than that will be of no use to us."

Here was an idea, thrown out as a mere suggestion, but it was one that sank deep into Charles Goodyear's mind. But he was very poorly fitted to work it out. A chemical process was needed, and he knew almost nothing of chemistry. In fact, he had little education of any kind. Money was wanted, and he was scantily provided with that. The failure of some business houses about this time made his father's firm bankrupt, and he, as a member of the firm, was arrested and imprisoned for debt.

Those were the years in which a debtor could be put in prison, and during the several years following Goodyear spent much of his time in jail. He had a family, he was in poor health, he needed to do something that would make him a living, but he had grown so infatuated with the idea of discovering the secret of a marketable India-rubber that he could think of nothing else.

Rubber was abundant enough in those days, and he was able easily to get it even when in prison. He was constantly engaged in experiments with it, whether in prison or out. His friends, who aided him at first, soon grew tired of encouraging him in what they deemed his infatuation. His ignorance of chemistry was much against him, and though he explained his difficulty to the chemists of his city, none of them were able to help him.

If Charles Goodyear lacked money, there was one thing he had in abundance—perseverance. He never gave up. Persuasion, argument, ridicule, had no effect upon him. He tried endless experiments, made Indiarubber fabrics of various kinds, and, with a native taste for art, ornamented some of them. It was this that led to his first step towards success.

He had bronzed the surface of some rubber drapery, and, finding his bronze too heavy, poured aquafortis on it to eat some of it away. The acid did its work too well, removing all the bronze and discoloring the fabric, so that he threw it away as spoiled. Thinking over it some days later, he picked up the discarded piece and examined it again, and was delighted to find it much improved in quality, it bearing heat far better than any he had tried before. Here was something learned. He hastened to patent his new process, and, gaining some money, he engaged in the manufacture of rubber treated with aquafortis.

But his troubles were not yet at an end. People had grown sick of India-rubber, which had ruined many firms that had engaged in it, and no capitalists cared to touch it. As for Goodyear himself, many began to think that he had become so possessed with his idea that he was little better than a crazy man. His enthusiasm for his rubber was such that he wore whole suits made of it, coat, cap, shoes, and all, and made himself a walking advertisement. He talked of it so incessantly that people felt like running away from him. It was "rubber, rubber, rubber," all day long, till many voted him a nuisance.

All this time he was suffering from poverty, and the pawnbroker and he grew much too well acquainted. His family suffered as well, and want ruled in the Goodyear household. After a time he persuaded some of the members of the old Roxbury Company to invest in his new discovery, and a new factory was started, which for a time did a large business. Then it was found that the aquafortis hardened the surface only, and that the rest of the rubber would not bear the heat. At once the business fell off, the Roxbury men withdrew their funds, and the inventor sank into destitution again.

His friends now did their utmost to persuade him to give up his fruitless work. His wife and children did the same. But they advised and persuaded in vain. He would not yield. Through all he was working blindly, handicapped by his small knowledge of chemistry, and simply making chance experiments, but for all this he kept on. Luck came through an assistant of his who had tried the effect of mixing the gum with sulphur. This was a new process, not tried before by Goodyear, and he studied it thoroughly, working at it for months, but with very unsatisfactory results. Yet the end was near at hand. Chance helped him where science had failed. One day in 1839 a mass of gum and sulphur he had mixed happened to touch a red-hot stove. To his surprise and delight, its character was changed by the heat and it would not melt. He tried and tested it in every way he could think of, and always with the same result. He had penetrated the mystery. The great secret was his! All that was needed was to mix the gum with sulphur and expose it to great heat. It would afterwards stand both heat and cold.

For five years the indefatigable investigator had been steadily at work, in prison and out, in poverty and want, under every discouragement, enduring the ridicule of the public, the reproaches of friends and family, the insults of those who touched their heads significantly when they looked at him. He had at last won out, as the saying is; the great discovery of vulcanized rubber was his, and fortune at length seemed to lie in his path.

Yet it did not come quickly. Six years more of severe labor and hard trials were before him. He did not propose to act hastily again, as he had with his former discovery. He spent these years in new experiments, working out one thing after another, perfecting this point and that, and taking out a patent on everything achieved, until he had sixty patents in all, covering every step he had made.

Unfortunately, his patents were confined to America. Other parties secured in England and France the rights which should have been his, litigation was needed at home to protect his rights, and his profits from his valuable discovery were far smaller than they should have been. But honors came to him from many sources. From the Crystal Palace Exhibition of 1851 he received the Grand Council medal, and at the Paris Exposition of 1855 the emperor gave him the Grand Medal of Honor and the Cross of the Legion of Honor. But disease had attacked the discoverer. Returning to America in 1858, he went to work energetically to perfect his processes, but his ills had become chronic, and death came two years later, on July 1, 1860.

"He lived," says Parton, "to see his material applied to nearly five hundred uses, and to give employment, in England, Germany, France, and the United States, to sixty thousand persons. . . . Art, science and humanity are indebted to him for a material which serves the purposes of them all, and serves them as no other known material could."

DE WITT CLINTON, THE FATHER OF THE ERIE CANAL

In October, 1825, the close of the first quarter of the nineteenth century was made notable by a spectacular event. At Buffalo, on the western border of the State of New York, the sluice-way was opened that closed the mouth of the Erie Canal, and the waters of Lake Erie rushed into this vast excavation, much the greatest example of engineering work the country had then seen. This was before the days of the electric telegraph, and a novel system of telegraphing was adopted to convey the news to the eagerly awaiting people of New York City. A row of cannon, about five miles apart, was arranged along the canal, and these were fired in succession as fast as the sound traveled from one to the next in line, so that in a very short time the news was sent across the State and made its way from Buffalo to New York.

Then a triumphal barge was launched on the canal, carrying Governor Clinton, the great patron of the work, over the three hundred and sixty-three miles from Buffalo to Albany and thence down the Hudson River to New York, the people of the State gathering in multitudes to cheer him as he passed. He brought with him a keg of water from Lake Erie, which was poured with pomp and ceremony into the waters of New York Bay, thus accomplishing the marriage of the lake with the ocean. It was the final test of a great success, that which linked the Great Lakes with the Atlantic at the Hudson's mouth.

The canal was a work of the noblest economic importance. Before its opening it cost ten dollars and took three weeks to transport a barrel of flour overland from Buffalo to Albany. By way of the canal it could be sent through in a week, at a cost of thirty cents. To-day grain boats follow each other in one continuous line, day and night, along the canal, while a like procession of boats laden with merchandise traverses its waters in the opposite direction.

De Witt Clinton, to whose energy and enterprise our country owes this great achievement, was born at Little Britain, New York, March 2, 1769. He came from a distinguished colonial family, his grandfather being Colonel Charles Clinton and his father General James Clinton, a prominent officer in the French and Indian and the Revolutionary Wars. His uncle, George Clinton, was a member of the Continental Congress; voted for the Declaration of Independence, though military duties prevented him from being present to sign it; was the first governor of New York, and held that office for eighteen years; and was elected Vice-President of the United States under Jefferson in 1804, and again under Madison in 1808.

As may be seen from his ancestry, De Witt Clinton was born to a prominent position in New York, if he should prove capable of filling it. As it was, he showed himself an able statesman, and his whole life was spent in the public service. A boy patriot in the Revolution, he graduated at Columbia College in 1786, and studied law, though he afterwards had very little opportunity to practice it.

His public career began in or about 1790, as private secretary for his uncle, Governor George Clinton. Though then only twenty-one years of age, he quickly became active in public affairs. We are told that " the life of Clinton was from this moment one of political strife, into which he threw all the force of his ardent temperament and brilliant talents." In the course of some years he rose from one political position to another, entering the legislature in 1797, the State Senate in 1798, and being elected a Senator of the United States in 1801 or 1802. Politically, he was a member of the Anti-Federalist party, and shortly rose to be the leader of the Democratic party in New York.

As a member of the Senate Clinton showed himself an orator of commanding eloquence, his most notable speech being one on the navigation of the Mississippi River, the leading question of that day. In this he opposed a war with Spain, which country had closed that river against American shipping. Soon afterwards this question was settled amicably, President Jefferson purchasing the Mississippi and all the territory through which it ran, and making the whole of it a part of the United States.

In 1803 Mr. Clinton was elected Mayor of the city of New York, then a post of high importance, for the Mayor was President of the Council and Chief Judge of the Common Pleas and Criminal Courts. In the words of Professor Renfrew, " He was on all sides looked up to as the most rising man in the Union." He served as Mayor at successive intervals until 1814, the city growing prosperous under his administrations. Among the institutions fostered by him were the Historical Society, the Academy of Fine Arts, and the first orphan asylum of the city. He favored other institutions, and devoted much time and thought to the founding of free schools, public libraries, and other aids to the education of the people.

In the early years of the century he found his chief political rival in Aaron Burr, then one of the ablest and most unscrupulous politicians of the country. After the discredit of Burr, Daniel D. Tompkins, a man who excelled in gaining the favor of the people, became his competitor for control of the Democratic party. Clinton was deficient in the art of currying favor. A man of stately and often haughty bearing, with a hasty temper which at times got him into needless difficulties, he had only his fine powers as an orator and his many acts of kindness to depend upon. But these won him many friends, and in spite of all the harm his political enemies—the Tammany Party—could do him, there was not a poor man in New York but looked upon him as a friend, and he held the people's love till his death.

Clinton had the laudable ambition which has affected many worthy statesmen since his time, that of becoming President of the United States, and he had made himself so prominent that in 1812 he was a candidate against President Madison for the Presidency, gaining the electoral vote of nearly all the New England and Middle States. He was defeated by a vote of one hundred and twenty-eight to eighty-nine. He lost favor in a measure by his disagreement with the President about the War of 1812, though his opposition to it was solely on the basis that the country was ill prepared for such a war. The event proved that he was right in this.

For two of the years in which Clinton was Mayor, 1811–13, he was also Lieutenant-Governor of the State, and in 1817 he was elected Governor by an almost unanimous vote. The great question of the campaign was that of the projected Erie Canal, the need of which the State of New York was feeling more and more strongly as the years passed on and population increased. This was before the era of the railroads. Had they existed at that time, the canal would never have been made. But the growth of the lake trade, and the difficulty of carrying grain and merchandise in wagons over the whole length of the State, called for some cheaper and easier method, and the question of a canal grew prominent in the popular thought and talk.

The idea of excavating a canal from the lakes to the Hudson was not a new one. It had been germinating since early in the century. Seven commissioners had been appointed in 1809 to examine and survey a route for such a canal, and Mayor Clinton was one of these. The need of it grew more urgent as time went on, but the magnitude and great cost of the work stood in its way. In 1817 the canal was the great State question of the day, and Clinton stood as its candidate. In the spring of that year, largely through his influence, the legislature passed a bill authorizing the canal, and on the 4th of July, 1817, the great work which was to become his chief title to fame was begun.

It called for heavy taxation, many did not believe it possible, and a powerful party, called "Bucktails," arose, who denounced the project as visionary and ridiculous. "Clinton's big ditch" it was called in derision, and this title became a standing joke in the opposing newspapers. It was utterly absurd, they said, to think of digging a canal across three hundred and sixty miles of territory, through unbroken forests, over hills, against difficulties innumerable. It was incredible that boats could make their way from the lakes to the sea across such a country. But in spite of all this Clinton went on with the work.

In 1820 Clinton's old rival, Daniel D. Tompkins, was

on the opposition ticket, and though he was re-elected, his opponents gained majorities in both branches of legislature. The canal policy had been the great issue of the campaign, and the work became blocked by a refusal to vote money for its prosecution. In 1822 he declined to run for the office, and in 1824 his adversaries, who had come into power, removed him from the office of Canal Commissioner. This excited the indignation of the people, who regarded Clinton as the father of the canal, and in the election of that year he was made Governor again by a majority of 16,000, the largest that any candidate had ever received in the State.

Meanwhile the canal went on, slowly but surely, now halting, now hasting, in its career, its construction sustained throughout by the perseverance and energy of Governor Clinton. The task was an immense one, well calculated to frighten a sparse and poor population. For eight years it employed an army of laborers, who cut down forests, blasted a channel through rock, carried the bed up seemingly impassable hills by the aid of locks, conveyed it over rivers in aqueducts, keeping on indefatigably until 1825, when the last spadeful of earth was lifted, the sluices were opened, water was let into the " ditch," and Governor Clinton made his triumphal tour by water across the length of the State.

He could well be proud of it, for it was his. Without his far-seeing enterprise it might never have been possible to carry it to completion. Clinton was the hero of the day. Men who had called him a visionary idiot were now loud in his praises. Bonfires, fireworks, processions, and speeches were the order of the day, and when the victor appeared in

HEROES OF PROGRESS 183

New York with his keg of Lake Erie water, the whole city rose to do him honor and went wild with enthusiasm. In 1825 he was offered by President Adams the honorable post of Minister to England. This he declined, and the next year was re-elected Governor by a rousing majority. He was now the most popular man in the State. He lived to see the canal a great success, dying suddenly at Albany, in the Governor's chair, February 11, 1828.

Even to-day, with all the great engineering works of the age, the Erie Canal does not appear a small affair. It seemed stupendous in those days, when the country was young and poor, and when much of the state was an unbroken and largely unknown wilderness. It was a great credit to the foresight and indefatigable energy of De Witt Clinton, and has since been of immeasurable benefit to the State of New York. as it stands to-day, its length is given as 365½ miles; its width from 53 to 79 feet at the bottom and 70 to 98 at the top; its depth from 7½ to 9½ feet. Its total rise above sea-level is 656½ feet, this height being overcome by the use of numerous locks. Despite the rivalry of the railroad, no thought has arisen of abandoning "Clinton's big ditch." On the contrary, it is proposed to increase it in size so that it may carry ships instead of barges, and the people of the coming future may see grain-bearing vessels or steamers making their way along a deep and wide artificial river from end to end of the State of New York.

HORACE WELLS AND THE DISCOVERERS OF ANÆSTHESIA

On the 11th of December, 1844, one of the most important experiments in the history of the world was performed in the office of Dr. Horace Wells, a dentist of Hartford, Connecticut. Dr. Wells, as a patient, was trying a discovery of his own upon himself. His friend, Dr. Riggs, was the experimenter. Dr. Wells inhaled a quantity of nitrous oxide gas, went to sleep under its effect, and had a large, sound tooth drawn out without pain.

It was a wonderful, phenomenal operation. Never before in the history of the world had a surgical operation been performed without pain. Untold thousands of times in previous years legs and arms had been cut off, cancers cut out, and terrible operations of other kinds taken place, and in all cases the patient had to lie wide awake, often suffering frightful agony. Various things had been tried to reduce sensation, but as a rule they had done more harm than good, and surgeons were afraid to use them. To perform such an operation now without making the patient unconscious would be thought shameful and barbarous, and it seems strange to us that the first time it was successfully done was only sixty years ago. About the same time two other American scientists produced anæsthesia by other means, so that the great discovery seemed to come at once in several fields. We shall tell the story of these other two when we have told that of Dr. Wells.

HEROES OF PROGRESS 185

Horace Wells was born in Hartford, Vermont, January 21, 1815. His parents were well-to-do farmers. He was a handsome, active, intelligent boy, and he was given a good education. His father dying before his school life ended, he completed his education by aid of money earned by teaching in district and writing schools. As he grew up towards manhood he had serious thoughts of studying for the ministry, but chose the profession of dentistry instead, and at the age of nineteen went to Boston to study for it.

Not much can be said for the dentistry of that period. It was a relic of barbarism, with very little of art or skill in its practice. A movement to improve it had but recently begun. The first College of Dental Surgery in this country was founded in Baltimore in 1840, and young Wells did not find any very skillful professors in Boston in 1834. But he was quick and intelligent, made rapid progress in his profession, invented many instruments for himself, and was not long in practice before he was looked upon as one of the most expert of the dentists of Boston.

Among his inventions was a solder to fasten artificial teeth upon the plate, and to manufacture and use this he went into partnership with Dr. William Morton. Dr. Charles T. Jackson, a noted chemist of Boston, gave them a certificate of the purity and value of the solder, which was much superior to the imperfect substance then in use. Drs. Morton and Jackson were the other two discoverers of anæsthesia mentioned, and it is worthy of mention that these three benefactors of mankind came thus at one time into close association.

The firm of Wells & Morton did not succeed very well, and they soon separated, Morton staying in Boston, and Wells opening an office in Hartford, Connecticut. While here he gave much time to the thought that there might be some means of taking out teeth without pain. He was a student of chemistry, and from his knowledge of nitrous oxide gas thus learned he decided to try this substance. He studied its effect upon animals, and when satisfied that it would put them to sleep without danger, he decided to make an experiment upon a man—choosing himself as the man. It was this that led to the notable experiment we have described, in which his friend, Dr. Riggs, drew out one of his teeth with scarcely a trace of pain.

The most beneficial of discoveries had been made. He had given to mankind one of the greatest of blessings. As the poet and physician, Oliver Wendell Holmes, stated it, " The deepest furrow in the knotted brow of agony has been smoothed forever." But, like nearly all new discoveries, the world was slow to accept it. The innovation was too great and sudden. Some chemists and doctors wrote and spoke against it, and there were ministers who went so far as to denounce it on the ground that it was an impious meddling with the ways of the Creator, who had sent pain to the earth as a discipline and benefit to mankind. But it was soon in use by the dentists of Hartford, and in no great time made its way to all civilized lands.

Dr. Wells was a handsome and attractive man, thoughtful in face, cheerful and cordial in manner, his face lighting up in conversation in a bright, pleasant fashion. He was by nature sensitive, and did not make many new acquaintances, confining himself chiefly to the society of his special friends. Shortly after his discovery failing health obliged him to go to Europe for rest and recreation. Here he kept up his studies in colleges and hospitals. To pay his expenses abroad he imported and sold pictures, and also lectured on birds, whose habits he had studied lovingly in his early years.

After returning from Europe, he went to New York for the purpose of introducing anæsthetics in the hospitals there. Morton and Jackson had made known their discoveries by that time, and he tried them all, finally becoming convinced that chloroform, Dr. Jackson's discovery, was a better anæsthetic than his own. He began experimenting with it upon himself, not knowing its dangerous character, and continued these experiments till his mind was ruined by the perilous drug. He had not been a month in New York before, in an attack of insanity due to his unwise use of chloroform, he took his own life. He was just past his thirty-third year, dying January 24, 1848, a little more than three years after the date of his famous discovery.

On September 30, 1846, Dr. William T. G. Morton, of Boston, performed an experiment similar to that of Dr. Wells nearly two years before. The substance used by him was sulphuric ether. He had convinced himself of its safety by trying its effect upon himself, and now administered it to a patient, from whose jaws he drew a large, double-pronged tooth. To his delight, the patient felt no pain, remaining unconscious during the operation. Soon after he used it upon a patient at the Massachusetts Hospital. A tumor was removed from the jaw, a very painful operation in a state of consciousness, but the patient felt no pain. A second anæsthetic of unmeasured value had been given to mankind.

Dr. Morton was born in Charlton, Massachusetts, August 9, 1819. He entered the new dental college in

Baltimore in 1840, studied there and in Boston, and after graduating was for a time in partnership with his friend, Dr. Wells. The two men were alike in one thing: they were both active in improving the instruments of their profession, and both eager to discover some means of removing teeth without pain. It may well be that they had talked of the matter together when in partnership, and even begun their studies and experiments then. At any rate, we find Dr. Morton soon afterwards busy in seeking to discover some pain-killing substance. He tried stimulants, giving the patient liquor till he was intoxicated. He tried opium. He experimented with magnetism. All were of no avail.

One cause of his difficulty was that he knew very little about medicines or chemistry, and to overcome this he began to attend lectures in the Medical College at Boston. It was here he learned that small quantities of sulphuric ether could be breathed in without injury, and that it tended to produce unconsciousness. This led him to the successful experiment we have mentioned. Sulphuric ether was added to the list of pain-dispelling substances.

Dr. Morton's discovery was no sooner made known than it began to be used widely in private institutions and by the Government, without regard to his rights. He had patented it in the United States and England under the name of "Etheon," giving free right to its use in charitable institutions, but it was pirated on all sides without regard to his patent, and he found it impossible to obtain redress. There was a bitter dispute between him and Dr. Jackson, who claimed to have discovered before him that ether was an anæsthetic. When the French Academy of Sciences appointed a committee to investigate the merits of the two claimants, and adjudged a prize of twenty-five hundred francs to each, to Dr. Jackson as "the discoverer of etherization," and to Dr. Morton "for the application of this discovery to scientific operations," Morton refused to receive his award. Some years later, in 1852, the Monyton gold medal prize in medicine and surgery was awarded to him.

He continued to maintain his claim for years, appealing to Congress for his rights under his patent, though the struggle became so ruinous to his business that even his home was attached by the sheriff. A committee of physicians appointed by Congress reported that the merit of the discovery was his, and Congress subsequently made a like acknowledgment, but the appropriation voted upon for him was lost. In 1858 he won a lawsuit before the United States Court for an infringement upon his patent. But all this brought him in no money, the royalties were never paid, and the contest ruined him. He finally became a farmer, engaged in importing and raising fine cattle, and died July 15, 1868.

Coming now to the third discoverer of anæsthesia, Dr. Charles Thomas Jackson, we may say that he was born in Plymouth, Massachusetts, June 21, 1805, and became a noted chemist and geologist. He studied medicine at Harvard, graduating at twenty-four, but did not gain any special distinction as a doctor, his time and attention being given to mineralogy, geology, and chemistry, in which he became famous. He was geologist in succession for Maine, Rhode Island, and New Hampshire, taking an active part in studying the geological and mineral conditions of those States, as also of the wilderness of northwest New York. He had, shortly after graduating, spent several years studying in Paris, and investigating the geological conditions of several parts of Europe. His return was made on the ship "Sully," and among his fellow passengers was Professor S. F. B. Morse. It was Dr. Jackson who told him of the electrical experiments he had seen in Paris, and thus put in Morse's mind the idea which afterwards led to the invention of the electric telegraph.

It was not until after Drs. Wells and Morton had made public their discoveries that Jackson claimed to have made the discovery of anæsthetics many years before. He said that in the year 1834 he had found that chloroform dissolved in alcohol and put into an aching tooth would deaden the pain. He also studied other substances, especially sulphuric ether. Once in his experiments he breathed by accident chlorine gas into his lungs. This gave him so much pain that he inhaled the vapor of ether, hoping for relief. The relief was so quick and great that he made up his mind that a surgical operation might be performed without pain under the influence of ether. This was about the year 1846, the year of Morton's discovery. Dr. Jackson did not try ether on others, and he did not make his discovery about chloroform known till this time. But his scientific standing was so high that many took his word for it. Most of the physicians of Boston believed in his claim, and great honor was given him abroad, orders and decorations coming to him from the governments of France, Sweden, Prussia, Turkey, and Sardinia. The Academy of Sciences of France, as above stated, awarded him a prize of twenty-five hundred francs for his discovery.

Dr. Jackson had won a wide reputation as a geologist

and mineralogist, and had become very prominent as a chemist, making important practical studies upon the cotton and tobacco plants and other American products. His bitter contest with Dr. Morton, however, over what he looked upon as the most important of his discoveries, was a severe strain upon him, and this, combined with his devotion to difficult studies and experiments, may have been the cause of the mental failure which came upon him in his later years. The last seven years of his life were passed in an asylum for the insane. He died August 29, 1880.

The controversy which arose between the three discoverers of anæsthesia made life unhappy for all of them. It was mainly due to the combative disposition of Dr. Morton, and his determination to assert his rights. Of them all, so far as public announcement of their discoveries was made, Dr. Wells stood first, and to him belongs the honor of first making known to the world a means of deadening pain in surgical operations. But this is a matter of minor importance, and the echoes of the hot controversy over their respective claims has long since died away.

The discoveries came so close together in time that they may be looked upon as a threefold one, Dr. Wells being given the credit of discovering the pain-deadening powers of nitrous oxide, Dr. Jackson of those of chloroform, and Drs. Morton and Jackson simultaneously of those of sulphuric ether. This, however, we may say, that all these discoverers were Americans, natives of New England, and that to our country is due, among its many valuable discoveries, the supreme one of saving man from the agonies of mortal pain.

WILLIAM LLOYD GARRISON, THE GREAT EMANCIPATOR

On the 10th of December, 1805, at Newburyport, Massachusetts, was born one of the great leaders in the train of events that brought on the Civil War. As great a leader on the opposite side was John C. Calhoun, the story of whose life we have given. An impressive scene, well worth painting, was that in which, after the capture of Charleston by the Union army, William Lloyd Garrison, the bitter foe of slavery, stood beside the grave of Calhoun, its persistent advocate. These two men, one for, the other against, the institution of slavery, had done their utmost in bringing about the war which led to its fall, and strange and deep must have been the thoughts of Garrison as he gazed upon the grave of his former opponent.

William Lloyd Garrison, as a boy, had to make his own way in the world. His father was dead, his mother poor. At the age of nine he began to work in a shoemaker's shop; but he gave this up when the opportunity came for an education, which he paid for by sawing wood and doing odd jobs when out of school. Before he was fifteen his school life ended and he settled down to work.

After trying several things, he became an apprentice to the printer's trade. At this he not only became a good workman, but, like Franklin before him, began to write articles, which were printed without his name and attracted flattering attention. He was only twenty-one when he started a paper of his own, and after this

HEROES OF PROGRESS 193

failed he was made editor of *The National Philanthropist*, a Boston paper devoted to reform, and one of the first to take up the temperance cause.

Reform was in Garrison's blood. The whole current of his thoughts ran that way. A year later we find him at Bennington, Vermont, editing a little paper that advocated peace, temperance, and anti-slavery. All this was pioneer work; he was educating himself in the school of reform. His real work began in 1829, when he went to Baltimore and became editor of an insignificant newspaper called *The Genius of Universal Emancipation*.

This was published by a mild little Quaker named Benjamin Lundy. It advocated the gradual emancipation of slaves, but had so little sting in it that few paid any attention to its diatribes. Lundy did not like this. He wanted more vitality in his paper. He had read some of Garrison's articles, and judged they were the stuff he needed. So he trudged on foot from Baltimore to Bennington,—there were no railroads then,— called on Garrison, and asked him to go to Baltimore and edit his paper.

The new editor's touch gave it life. The wasp had found a sting. No one now thought the paper harmless. Instead of gradual emancipation, it demanded immediate and unconditional emancipation; it denounced slaveholders and slave-dealers, and this in a city in which slaves were held. Every week it had a column on the horrors of the slave system, describing many things the editor had seen or heard of in Baltimore itself. One slave called on him and showed his back bleeding from twenty-seven lash cuts. He had been thus dealt with for loading a wagon in a way that did not please his overseer.

As may be imagined, *The Genius* now created a sensation. Garrison's fiery editorials were like so many bomb-shells thrown among the Baltimore slave-holders. He was sued for libel, found guilty, and fined fifty dollars and costs. As he was not able to pay the fine he was sent to jail. His imprisonment was not severe. Friends were allowed to visit him, among them John G. Whittier, the anti-slavery poet. After about a month and a half Arthur Tappan, a New York merchant with views like his own, paid the fine, and he was set free.

Garrison's imprisonment made a great stir. It was a flagrant interference with the liberty of the press. Even some Southerners, Henry Clay among them, strongly objected to it. But Garrison saw that Baltimore was not the city for his work, and he went north again, delivering there a course of lectures against slavery.

His lectures were not well received. The anti-slavery cause was then exceedingly weak, even in New England, the mass of people being opposed to any interference with the institution. At Newburyport, his native town, and at Boston, the churches were closed against him. His lecture in Boston was delivered in the hall of a society of infidels. They cared nothing for emancipation, but they cared a great deal for freedom of speech.

Garrison, finding his voice muzzled, turned again to his pen. He started a small paper called *The Liberator*, the first number of which appeared on January 1, 1831. That was an eventful day in the history of slavery, for with that first number of *The Liberator* began a fierce campaign which was not to end while a slave remained in the land.

It was an enterprise which needed courage and intrepidity. Garrison had not a dollar in the world. His friend, Isaac Knapp, who became his partner, had little more. They worked as type-setters on *The Christian Examiner,* and took their pay in the use of the type and presses of *The Examiner.* All the work on *The Liberator* was done after the regular day's work was finished, by Garrison and Knapp. In the first number they said they would publish the paper as long as they had bread and water to live on, and for a time they did live on little more than bread and milk.

The Liberator soon made itself felt. In its opening address Garrison said: " I will be as harsh as truth and as uncompromising as justice. On this subject I do not wish to think or speak or write with moderation. I am in earnest—I will not equivocate—I will not excuse—I will not retreat a single inch—and I will be heard!" And he was heard. Some abolitionists soon supplied a little money, a small office was taken, he and his partner worked, ate, and slept there, and *The Liberator* was launched on its stormy sea.

The new paper speedily made a sensation. Never had the slave system been so vigorously assailed. Emancipation of the slaves, without delay, without conditions, without compensation, was its doctrine. Slavery was an utter wrong and sin, and it was the duty of every Christian and every man to fight it with all his might. Such sentiments, strongly expressed week after week, were not long in raising a breeze. *The Liberator* soon found readers, alike among friends and foes. It met with much opposition in the North, where the great bulk of the people were at that time in sympathy with the slave-holders. In the South it aroused a torrent of rage.

It had at this time only a small circulation, and

even if the slaves had happened to see it, they could not have read it. But there was a pictorial heading with its story for all, the picture of an auction where " slaves, horses, and other cattle " were offered for sale, and a whipping post, where a slave was being flogged. Back of them was the Capitol at Washington, on its dome a flag with the word " Liberty " upon it.

Editorials in the Southern papers hotly denounced Garrison. Threats of lynching were made. The law was appealed to to prevent *The Liberator* from circulating in the South. The grand jury of North Carolina indicted Garrison for publishing " a paper of seditious tendency," and the Assembly of Georgia offered a reward of five thousand dollars to any one who would bring him to Georgia, prosecute and convict him.

Garrison's response to this was to found an anti-slavery society in New England. In 1833 this society sent him to England, where he spoke so vigorously about American institutions that on his return he was accused of libeling this country. A mob threatened the *Liberator* office. The Mayor of Boston was called upon to suppress it, as an agent of mischief. A meeting which Garrison attended in New York to found an anti-slavery society was driven from the hall by a mob. Going from there to Philadelphia, he founded in that city the American Anti-Slavery Society.

The most perilous moment in Garrison's life came in 1835, in consequence of the arrival in Boston of George Thompson, a noted English lecturer against slavery. His arrival and his attempt to speak led to a riot, not of the rabble, but largely made up of " men of property and standing," who were determined " to put a stop to the impudent, bullying conduct of the foreign vagrant, Thompson, and his associates in mischief."

A meeting of the Ladies' Anti-Slavery Society, at which Thompson was expected to speak, was raided by this mob of the genteel of Boston. Luckily for Thompson, he was not there. But Garrison was, and the rioters laid violent hands on him, pulled him from the hall, tore the clothes from his back and dragged him through the streets with a rope around his body. Their rage would probably have ended in a lynching if Mayor Lyman had not rescued their victim and sent him to prison as the safest place he could think of.

This was not the only time in which Garrison was threatened and molested in Boston, but nothing stopped him in his work. *The Liberator* continued to appear, and not for a moment did it change its tone. Its effect was great. The anti-slavery cause grew. The societies he had formed began to flourish. In all they did he was the leader, his name was on all lips, the growing army of emancipation hailed him as its general, almost as its martyr.

In 1840 he went to England again, to attend there the World's Anti-Slavery Convention. Others from America came, among them Lucretia Mott, Elizabeth Cady Stanton, and other women delegates. But England was innately conservative, and all women were refused admission to the hall. As a consequence Garrison, the most distinguished abolitionist in the convention, refused to enter. Some years after this he was made president of the American Anti-Slavery Society, and held that position for twenty-two years, giving it up only when slavery had ceased to exist.

The Liberator hammered away persistently at the fetters of the slave, and they began to yield before its blows. It even opposed the Union of the States, with slavery as one of its institutions, saying that such a Union was "a covenant with death and an agreement with hell." He came at length to the conviction that slavery could be abolished only by a dissolution of the Union. He did not then see clearly what was coming, that an attempt to dissolve the Union would be made and would fail, but that slavery would perish in its failure.

The Civil War came. *The Liberator* was still published. Its former tone of denunciation now became a tone of appeal to the President, a demand for freedom. When emancipation was decreed it became a hearty supporter of President Lincoln. In April, 1865, Garrison was one of the party that went to Charleston to raise the Union flag over the ruins of Fort Sumter, from which it had been pulled down four years before. It was on this occasion that he stood in brooding silence over Calhoun's grave. Both these men had fought strongly for what they thought the right. The one whose cause had fallen did not live to see the end; the other survived to behold the triumph of his cause.

Soon after this the last number of *The Liberator* appeared. It had finished its work, and its mission was at an end. About the same time a welcome tribute was made to the editor, in a purse of thirty thousand dollars, to which many distinguished men had contributed as a mark of their deep appreciation of his services in the cause of human freedom.

The remainder of Garrison's life was passed peacefully. Part of it was spent in Europe, where he was received with high respect. In America he was paid the highest attention. He was a frequent writer for periodicals on political and other subjects, and was especially interested in all matters affecting the black race. He died in New York City on May 24, 1879.

WENDELL PHILLIPS, SILVER-TONGUED ORATOR AND REFORMER

NEXT to William Lloyd Garrison, Wendell Phillips was the most forceful opponent of the system of human slavery in the United States. He was not a born reformer, like Garrison. He did not leap into the saddle from the start. The feeling of hatred to slavery grew in him stage by stage, though when it was fully developed he was the mate of Garrison in his detestation of the system. These two men did not stand alone—there were many who thought as they did; but for years they bore the brunt of the fray, keeping the fight alive till the mass of the people of the North joined their ranks.

Wendell Phillips was born in Boston, November 29, 1811. He was not born to poverty, like Garrison, his father being a man of wealth and distinction, of sense and judgment. His wise motto in training his children was, "Ask no man to do anything that you are not able to do for yourself." Inspired by the spirit of this saying, his son Wendell sought to train his hands in work, and it is said that by the time he grew up there was hardly any trade in New England that he did not know something about.

He began his education in Boston's famous old Latin School, and from there went to Harvard College, where he graduated in 1831. John Lothrop Motley, the historian, graduated in the same class, and they had the reputation of being two of the handsomest and most elegant young men in Boston, with a place ready for them in the best society. Each had been born with a silver spoon in his mouth, to apply the old saying, but each found something better to do in life than chew upon that spoon. There was work to do in the world, and they were the kind of men to take their full share of it.

After his graduation Phillips entered upon a course of legal study in the Cambridge Law School, and at the age of twenty-three was admitted to practice in the Boston courts. This took place in the period when the country first began to be stirred up upon the question of the abolition of slavery. For several years William Lloyd Garrison had been thundering away against slavery in the columns of *The Liberator,* and a band of devoted men and women were gathering round him, ardent pioneers in the cause of the liberty of the slave; but the great mass of the people held themselves aloof.

At first Phillips took little interest in this subject. He had early shown himself an orator of unusual powers, but he was concerned as yet with his profession, which probably occupied most of his time and thoughts. He had his social duties also, as a young man occupying a position in Boston's best society. While the demands of the former occupied his business, those of the latter occupied his leisure, hours, and the handsome and attractive young lawyer and orator had very likely little time for thoughts of reform. But he was soon to be awakened.

What first set him to thinking strongly upon the socially tabooed subject of anti-slavery was the attack upon Garrison in October, 1835, by the mob of " gentlemen of property and standing." He doubtless looked upon this act as a shameful outrage, and was brought by it into sympathy with the reformers, for in the next year, 1834, he became a member of the American Anti-Slavery Society. He went farther than this in his newly-developed opposition to slavery: he relinquished the practice of the law, being unwilling to act under an oath to support the Constitution of the United States while it recognized the institution of slavery.

Though he took this decided step, he did not become active in the advocacy of the new cause until an event occurred that stirred him to the depths of his soul. The anti-slavery sentiment was growing all through the North, but the great mass of the people were on the side of the slave-holders, the abolitionists were few, and their leaders were widely insulted and threatened. The hostile feeling grew to tragic heights in 1837, when Elijah P. Lovejoy, publisher of an abolition paper at Alton, Illinois, was attacked in his office by a pro-slavery mob and murdered while defending his press.

This murder sent a wave of horror throughout the land. It made abolitionists of hundreds who had been lukewarm before. In Boston Dr. Channing called a meeting of indignation at Faneuil Hall, which was attended by many who had been indifferent or even opposed to the reform movement, but were not ready to countenance murder. Speeches were made denouncing the murderers, and all seemed of one mind about the crime, until Mr. Austin, Attorney-General of the State, rose and made a vigorous speech on the other side, saying in the course of his remarks that Lovejoy had died as the fool dieth, and comparing the mob at Alton with the men who threw the tea into Boston harbor.

There were many in the audience ready to applaud these sentiments, and when Wendell Phillips, known to be an abolitionist, arose to reply, hisses came from the more violent. He was not the man to be cowed by a hiss. He began with these stinging words:

"When I heard the gentleman lay down principles that placed the murderers of Alton side by side with Otis and Hancock, with Quincy and Adams, I thought these pictured lips"—pointing to their portraits, which hung upon the walls—"would have broken into voice to rebuke the recreant American, the slanderer of the dead!"

There were no more hisses. Those words, vibrant with the feeling that moved the speaker's heart, took the throng captive. They remembered what brought them there, indignation against the ruffianly band that had murdered an American citizen while defending one of America's cherished institutions, the freedom of the press. All listened with bated breath as Phillips, in a burst of indignant and powerful eloquence, rebuked the sordid spirit of those who dared to defend a crime against the liberty of speech and the rights of humanity. Rarely had so eloquent a speech been heard within those walls, and no doubt it had a strong effect upon his hearers. Dr. Channing often afterwards spoke of it as "morally sublime."

From that time on there were no half-way measures with Wendell Phillips, no dallying with his subject. He gave his whole heart and soul, his wealth, his profession, his place in society, for the cause he had made his own. The moneyed aristocracy of Boston closed its doors against him, but he never faltered. He made himself poor by his generous aid to the cause, and devoted to it the greater part of the money he made by lecturing. He even refused to vote or to call himself a citizen of the United States so long as its Constitution recognized the slave system. His powers of oratory were so marked that he drew large audiences wherever he appeared, and to hear Wendell Phillips became an event in any one's life. The money his lectures brought him he scarcely regarded as his own so long as the anti-slavery cause stood in need.

Garrison was an older man than Phillips. He was the great anti-slavery pioneer, and the younger man looked up to him as his chief. The one with pen, the other with voice, ardently advocated the cause of the slave, and they exerted a powerful influence in converting the host of the northern people into opponents of human slavery. Like Garrison, Phillips believed that a dissolution of the Union would be the most effectual means of gaining freedom for the slaves, and what he thought he did not hesitate to say. He gave his life and strength to the great work he had made his own, and kept at it with the energy of a giant until the war came and the cause was won.

During the war Phillips condemned the administration as dilatory in the cause of emancipation, and he opposed Lincoln's re-election. After the war was closed Garrison wished to disband the American Anti-Slavery Society, of which he had been president for more than thirty years; but Phillips would not listen to this. It must keep together until the negro was given the right of suffrage, he said. He succeeded Garrison as its president, and kept this position till 1870, when, its work fully done, the society disbanded.

Emancipation of the slave was Phillips's one great thought, but it was not his only thought. There was scarcely any reform he did not work for. The cause of women's rights enlisted his heartiest sympathy. He was an earnest advocate of the rights of the Indians, who had been robbed and oppressed. The frequent sufferings of the working class stirred his noble soul. He became an ardent supporter of temperance, and even of State prohibition of strong drink, and was nominated for Governor of Massachusetts on the Prohibition ticket in 1870. He also was strongly enlisted in the Greenback movement—the issue of an irredeemable paper money by the Government.

On all these subjects his voice was heard, and for many years he lectured also to admiring audiences on topics of history and literature. He could always command a large audience, whatever his subject, for the fame of the " Silver-Tongued Orator " was almost world-wide.

A gentleman always, was Wendell Phillips, manly, dignified, courteous, winning the respect of all with whom he came in contact, while his unyielding devotion to the cause he had made his own in time elicited the admiration even of his opponents. Never had there been a sturdier reformer or a nobler character. The power of steady, persistent agitation which he displayed he acknowledged he had learned from the example of Daniel O'Connell. He had learned it well.

In 1881 Harvard College, which had always held aloof from her noble son in consequence of his unstinted denunciation of what he held to be public evils, so far relaxed as to invite him to make the address on the centennial anniversary of the Phi Beta Kappa Society. It was a distinct and valued triumph to the veteran agitator. His voice was last heard in public on December 28, 1883, and on the 2d of the following February he died.

CHARLES SUMNER, THE CHAMPION OF POLITICAL HONOR

IN Boston, on the 6th of January, 1811, was born Charles Sumner, one who in his later years was to play a very prominent part in that era of agitation when the Union itself was in danger of overthrow. As he grew up he began early to show an ambitious desire for learning. Alert in mind, studious by nature, he wanted to know all there was to know. His father was a lawyer, learned in his profession, but with little power of making money, and he wished to confine his son to practical studies, those that would help him to earn a living and do his share towards supporting the family. So he was put to study the common school branches.

This did not satisfy little Charles. He had heard that an educated man must know Latin and Greek, so, saving his pennies, he bought a second-hand Latin grammar and a Latin reader. These he studied in spare moments when out of school, and his father was utterly surprised one day to hear his son quote Latin. Finding what the boy was at, he thought it a shame to check such an ambition, and he let him enter the Latin and Greek classes in the school. When he was eleven his father sent him to the Boston Latin School, where his quickness and anxiety to learn greatly pleased his teachers. As for his schoolmates, while somewhat too much of a bookworm for them, he made friends of them by his kindly disposition.

No one could say that young Sumner was the brightest boy in the school. He was never a wonder in that way. Many of the boys left him behind in the classes. But he lived among school-books; he was always at them; he loved reading as much as the other boys loved playing, and when it came to general knowledge he was ahead of them all. Bright and quick and with a good memory, he stored his mind with facts. He loved history above all, reading it slowly and carefully, with maps spread before him, so that he impressed it on his mind in a way that made it stay. Many years after, when he was one of the leading legislators of the land, the knowledge of history gained in these early days was always ready for his use. He not only read many books, but he talked much with older people, if he found they could tell him anything new. Of course a boy like this had not much time for the play-field, and the only sport he cared for was swimming.

He remained in the Latin School for five years, expecting then to leave it and go to work instead of to college. But luckily his father at this time was made a county sheriff, in which position he earned more money, so at sixteen the studious boy was sent to Harvard College.

Here was the chance he had longed for. He studied hard and was a model college boy, except in the field of sport, for which he seemed to have no time or inclination. Every pleasure he took he tried to make in some way profitable. Thus he won high rank in his classes, especially in history and the languages. As for mathematics, he had no taste nor talent for them, so he paid little attention to this class of studies.

He graduated in 1830, and then entered the Law School, where he made the same satisfactory record as a student, and also as a refined and courteous classmate. His studies in the law went beyond the demands of his teachers, and he needed only a little practice in a Boston law office to gain admission to the bar. He was then twenty-three years of age.

It cannot be said that Charles Sumner made a good lawyer. His tastes did not run that way. He was engaged in some important cases, but he was not successful as a legal orator, and did not get a paying practice. He liked better to lecture on the law and to write for law journals. He edited *The American Jurist*, wrote three volumes of law books, called "Sumner's Reports;" and occasionally lectured to the Harvard students in place of the regular professors.

After three years of this, Mr. Sumner went to Europe, where he spent three more years in study. Thus he added much to his knowledge, and he also became acquainted with many prominent men, about whom he had much to say in his letters. These were published after his death, and contain many graphic sketches and lively anecdotes, showing that he was a quick observer.

But Sumner was never a favorite in society. He was greatly esteemed for his learning, sincerity, and earnestness, his stainless character and cheerful and kindly disposition, but he lacked the elements of wit, humor, and playful fancy, and was quite unfitted for the social small talk on which the wheels of society run. No doubt the Boston circles of that day voted him erudite but heavy, courteous but not stimulating.

The year of 1840 found the roving lawyer back again in Boston, where he took up his practice once more, though he liked its drudgery even less than before. He was much fonder of discussion and lecturing, and he became one of the regular teachers in the Law School.

Up to this time Sumner had taken little part in politics, but now was a time when it was next to impossible for thoughtful men to keep out of the political field. The slavery agitation was becoming bitter, and the country gradually dividing into two hostile camps. Boston had for years been the centre of the anti-slavery agitation, and Sumner's father had been a bold speaker against the slave system at an early date. Now the agitation had spread throughout the North, and numbers of ardent speakers were keeping it alive. It was impossible for a man of active public spirit to keep out of the fray, and Sumner threw his strength in favor of the cause which his father had sustained.

Up to 1845 the name of Charles Sumner was little known beyond the precincts of Boston, and there he was simply regarded as a law lecturer of wide information. But on the 4th of July of that year he made a public oration on "The True Grandeur of Nations" which was intently listened to by a large audience, and when published was read far and wide, even attracting a great deal of attention in Europe. It was simply an ardent denunciation of war, as the deadly foe of true greatness in nations, but its able arguments for the cause of peace, and its forcible and polished language, gave it a compelling power. From that time people began to speak of Charles Sumner as one of the coming men.

Sumner had hitherto voted with the Whigs, the party of Henry Clay and Webster, but in 1848, when those who opposed the extension of slavery into the territories organized the Free-Soil party, he joined their ranks. He did not believe, like Wendell Phillips, that the Constitution supported slavery, but he looked upon it as a sectional institution that could be dealt with politically and restricted by law until it would gradually dwindle and die away.

The efforts to widen its territory, therefore, called him into the political field, and he strongly combated them, making speeches against the annexation of Texas and on similar subjects. He had now become so well known as an able public speaker that the Free-Soil party made him one of its first candidates for Congress. He was easily defeated by his Whig opponent, but in 1851, when Webster left the Senate to become Secretary of State, Sumner was elected to succeed him in this elevated post of duty, being supported by the combined Free-Soil and Democratic members of the legislature of Massachusetts. He had now found the true field for his energies, and he was kept in the Senate during the remainder of his life.

When he entered the Senate Sumner stood alone in his attitude as an uncompromising opponent of slavery. The speeches he made, elaborately prepared and bristling with facts and arguments, were notable for the boldness of their denunciation of the slave system, and excited universal attention, winning him support and admiration on the one side, and bitter hostility on the other.

During the first year of his term he took his stand as a firm opponent of the Fugitive Slave Bill, an act which made it lawful for United States officers to arrest runaway slaves wherever found in the Northern States. The passage of this bill, and the attempts to enforce it, greatly increased the anti-slavery sentiment in the North, and was one of the leading steps towards the Civil War.

But the event that brought Sumner into startling prominence and had a far deeper effect upon the North than any speech could have had was an act of violence which took place in 1856. It was an outcome of the Kansas-Nebraska discussion, in which Sumner was one of the leading speakers. On the 19th and 20th of May, 1856, he made an exhaustive and splendid oration in favor of admitting Kansas into the Union, and in denunciation of the growing power and arrogance of slavery. It led to what was almost a tragedy.

The boldness and vigor of Sumner's language excited many of the Southern members of Congress to a high pitch of rage, and one of the representatives from South Carolina, Preston S. Brooks by name, entered the Senate chamber after the close of the session of May 22, intent on violence. He found Sumner sitting alone at his desk, busily engaged. Treacherously approaching from behind, Brooks struck him fiercely on the head with a heavy cane, the force of the blow being such as to knock him over, stunned. The cowardly assailant continued his attack, striking blow after blow, until he was stopped by two men who ran in from an ante-room.

They were barely in time to save the Senator's life, for he was so nearly slain that for several days he was in imminent peril of death. Even after he began to grow better, his injuries were so severe that he was obliged to go abroad for treatment, and it was nearly four years before he was able to return to his place in the Senate. He never fully recovered from the effects of the dastardly assault.

During these years his vacant chair spoke for him more eloquently than any words of his own could have done. It was a constant reminder to the advocates of freedom of the violence of the animosity with which they had to contend. The conduct of South Carolina added to this feeling, for, on the resignation of Brooks in consequence of the censure of the House, he was re-elected and sent back. He died in Washington eight months after the date of his assault.

It was near the close of Buchanan's term that Sumner appeared in his old place in the Senate and resumed his former position as leader of the anti-slavery forces in that body. In June, 1860, he made a speech on the question of the admission of Kansas, in which he spoke with his old strength against the slave customs of the South. It was published under the title of "The Barbarism of Slavery," and had a telling effect.

While not agreeing with Lincoln in his views on the slavery question, he was his warm friend and supported him firmly in the coming election. Lincoln afterwards so frequently took counsel with Sumner, and so respected his wisdom and judgment, that he was looked upon in the light of a Minister of State outside the Cabinet. He was urgent for the emancipation of the slaves, and after the war equally urgent in seeking to gain for them full civil and political equality with the whites. He also secured the organization of the Freedmen's Bureau, to look after the needs of the hosts of poor and ignorant blacks who had been set free by the war. At the same time he was influential in having the seceded States readmitted to the Union upon fair and just principles.

During Grant's term as President, he and Sumner

more than once came into conflict. When Grant sought to make the republic of San Domingo a part of the United States in 1871 Sumner fought bitterly against it, on the ground that the consent of the people of San Domingo had not been obtained. He carried the public strongly with him in his opposition, and the bill was killed. His continued censure on the policy of Grant's administration, and the strong feeling that ensued, led him in 1872 to oppose Grant's re-election and to support Horace Greeley as a candidate. On the other hand, Grant removed Motley the historian, Sumner's warm friend, from the post of Minister to Great Britain, and at last forced Sumner out of the chairmanship of the Committee on Foreign Affairs, which he had held for years.

Sumner's breach with the administration did not lose him the esteem with which he was very widely regarded, and the breach was slowly closing when death came to put an end to all animosities. He died on the 11th of March, 1874, his old hurt in the Senate chamber having a share in bringing on the illness that carried him off.

Sumner was a man of great force and strength of will. When sure of the justice of his position nothing could change him. He was never a party man, but from first to last independent in his views. He was never the man to submit to any one's dictation, and he lacked the powers of persuasion and the dexterity in management that raise men to leadership. No one dared accuse him of dishonesty or trickery of any sort, his nature being too open to admit of misconstruction, and Longfellow, his intimate friend, spoke of him as the whitest soul he had ever known.

During his more than twenty years in the Senate

HEROES OF PROGRESS

his influence over the people of his way of thinking was immense. No hope of favor or popularity could make him swerve from any course which he deemed right, and even if he took the unpopular side of a question, his rectitude and the strength of his arguments often brought the people to look upon it with favor. No man that ever sat in the Congress of the United States left it with a cleaner record for courage, consistency, and integrity than Charles Sumner.

HORACE MANN, THE PROMOTER OF PUBLIC EDUCATION

THERE have been noble men who have aided the cause of American progress in many fields, and not the least among these are the men who have promoted the cause of education. Many such might be named, but chief among these stands the noble figure of Horace Mann, who in a large measure was the father of the improved public school system, as it exists to-day. There were schools for the everyday people before Horace Mann, such as they were, but the education to be had in them was of the most meagre sort. A very bright student might make some progress, but those of duller minds learned very little. The school books were few and were bad at that, while as for the teachers Horace Mann says of his own that "they were very good people, but very poor teachers."

As for Mann himself, who first set public education in America upon its feet, he had the greatest difficulty in getting any education at all. Born in Franklin, Massachusetts, May 4, 1796, he was the son of a poor farmer. Poverty surrounded him during childhood and boyhood, and his days were taken up with hard work. We are told that " it was the misfortune of his family that it belonged to the smallest district, had the poorest schoolhouse, and employed the cheapest teachers, in a town which was itself small and poor." What little chance for schooling there was did him no great good, for up to the age of fifteen he was only able to attend school eight or ten weeks in a year.

His health as a boy was injured by hard work. He had no time for recreation, and, his father dying when he was thirteen, he had to work harder than ever for the support of his mother and the family. From childhood he was eager for books, but there were few of them to be had. When he was still little he got some books by braiding straw, and he managed to read some of the books in a very small library in the town of Franklin, but as he grew older he had to work such long hours that he could find time for study only by losing sleep.

Thus it went with the boy until he was twenty years of age, and it looked as if he might have to go through life with what little knowledge he could pick up by desultory reading. But his desire for learning was too great for that, and in 1816 he succeeded in entering Brown University, having learned a little about Latin and Greek and some of the principles of English and grammar from a wandering schoolmaster. Poverty still troubled him, symptoms of consumption had developed, he had to cook and support himself while at college, his studies were interfered with in various ways, but he studied with the energy of desperation, and graduated with high honors in 1819. Choosing the law as a profession, he began its study in 1821 and in 1823 was admitted to the Massachusetts bar.

Thus the poor farmer's son had made his way with the greatest difficulty upward through poverty to a profession in which ability would bring him support. This ability he had. He developed a power of strong and forcible eloquence, which gave him much influence over juries and brought him continued success. But there was more than this, his integrity and high-mindedness contributing greatly to his success. When he began to practise he firmly resolved never to take the unjust side of any cause, and his sincerity and honesty of purpose made themselves felt by all before whom be pleaded. It is said that of all the contested cases in which he took part he won four out of every five.

An able lawyer, an eloquent orator, a highly respected citizen, a man of noble character and elevated motives, Mr. Mann was soon called upon for public duties. He was elected to the legislature of Massachusetts in 1827, and there soon became noted as an ardent advocate of temperance and education. Six years later he was elected to the State Senate. Year by year his influence grew until he became one of the most notable figures in the legislative halls, many of the steps of progress made by Massachusetts during this time being instigated and carried through by him. One of these was the asylum at Worcester for the care of the insane poor wholly or partly by the State. It was one of the first of the kind in this country, such patients formerly being sent to the almshouse.

His great service, however, was in the cause of education, during the eleven years in which he held the position of Secretary of the State Board of Education. This body was organized in 1837, its purpose being to revise and reorganize the common school system of the State. To this duty Mann gave all his time and energies, resigning for it his law practice and his Senatorial duties. He worked at it almost day and night, devoting fifteen hours daily to its demands, holding teachers' conventions, delivering lectures, and keeping up an enormous correspondence. He had the whole country, not Massachusetts alone, in his mind. The school system sadly needed reform, and Horace Mann came as its reformer. He labored diligently to improve the schools, wrote abundantly on the subject, told how poorly conducted were the educational systems of this country, and aroused a new interest in education on every side. The school-system needed an evangel, and he was the one demanded. By his efforts the State gained better schoolhouses, better books, and better teachers, and trustees and parents were aroused to do more for the cause of education than they had ever thought of doing.

The school laws, under his influence, were revised and made better, and the whole system by which children were taught was changed. In 1843 he made a visit to Europe to inspect the schools there and see if they presented any advantages that could be adopted at home. In furtherance of his purpose he published a periodical, *The Common School Journal*, in which his views on education were set forth, and also published a series of "Annual Reports" of such value that they have been called "a classic on the subject." His seventh report told of what he saw in Europe, and of how superior the schools of Prussia were to those of Massachusetts.

Having completed his work in his native State, and given the cause of public education throughout the country a boom such as it never had before, Mr. Mann gave up his secretaryship in 1848, to enter Congress as the successor of John Quincy Adams, who had just died. There he took the rôle which Adams had long sustained, that of opposition to the extension of slavery. His first speech had to do with the duty of Congress to exclude slavery from the Territories. In one of his speeches he expressed his opinion in these decided and, in a measure, prophetic words:

"Interference with slavery will excite civil commotion in the South. Still, it is best to interfere. Now is the time to see if the Union is a rope of sand or a band of steel. Dark clouds overhang the future; and that is not all, they are full of lightning. I really think if we insist on passing the Wilmot Proviso [a measure to limit the extension of slavery] that the South would rebel. But I would pass it, rebellion or not. I consider no evil so great as that of the extension of slavery."

Mr. Mann did not forget his favorite subject while in Congress. He tried to induce the Government to establish a Bureau of Education in Washington. It was years later before this was done. In 1853, after he had served two terms in the House, a double honor was offered him: he was nominated for Governor of Massachusetts, and was also asked to become the first president of Antioch College, at Yellow Springs, Ohio. He failed to be elected Governor, and accepted the college presidency. It was in the line of his life-work, and he threw himself into its duties with all his old ardor. The school was a new one, intended for the combined education of men and women—a novel conception at that time. It was in need of a hard-working president, careful management, and good support, and these he brought it. His earnestness was deep, his work engrossing, and after seven years of faithful attention to duty his health completely broke down. The college year had not long closed after his last term before death came to him, on August 2, 1859. Mann's important work in life was the great reform in the school system of Massachusetts, and the influence this produced upon the system of public education throughout the country, and he is still looked upon as the great school reformer of America.

LUCRETIA MOTT, THE QUAKERESS ADVOCATE OF REFORM

OF late years hosts of women have come forward in favor of reforms of many kinds, but a century ago such a thing was almost unthought of in America. Women's sphere was held to be the parlor or the kitchen, and the pioneers in the struggle for women's rights were met with ridicule or with sharp censure. It needed great strength of character in those days for a woman to come out as a supporter of any cause not directly connected with household affairs, and it is interesting that one of the first to do so in this country was a small, slight, sweet-faced Friend, mild and gentle in nature, who seemed unfitted to indulge in anything needing courage and energy.

The woman in question was Lucretia Mott, one of the ablest members of the Anti-Slavery Society in Philadelphia, and among the first in this country to take an open stand against the system of slave-holding.

We are apt to look upon William Lloyd Garrison as the pioneer of the active advocates of freedom for the slaves, but long before his name had been heard Miss Lucretia Coffin, a young lady from New England at a Friends' School in New York State, was speaking warmly against slavery in her narrow circle of influence. Her feeling against the slave system early displayed itself, and so strongly that she felt it her duty not to use anything made by slave labor, and while still a schoolgirl she did not hesitate to speak her mind openly and freely on this tabooed subject.

Miss Coffin was born on the island of Nantucket, January 3, 1793. When nineteen years of age, after some experience as a teacher, she married William Mott of New York. Her parents were at that time living in Philadelphia, and there she and her husband went to reside, and there they spent the remainder of their lives. This was in 1812, the year the second war with Great Britain began. The horrors of this war were a source of deep sorrow to the peace-loving mind of the young Quakeress, and probably had their share in strengthening her sense of indignation against wrong or injustice of any kind.

Shortly after the war ended, Mrs. Mott began to speak in public, her voice being first mildly raised in the meeting-house which she and her people attended. Among the Friends it was quite common for women to speak in meeting, and she soon became one of their favorite speakers. Her slender, small figure, her delicate and charming face, at once tender and strong; her soft grey eyes, that glowed as if they were black when she was much moved; the sweetness of her voice, the convincing earnestness of her manner, all tended to give her power over her audiences, while her fine powers of intellect and cultivated mind added weight and force to all she said.

Earnestness made her eloquent, her hearers were charmed, and her influence became so marked that she began to travel around the country, speaking of the Quaker meeting-houses, dwelling upon the peace-loving principles of the Friends, and pointing out the evils of slavery, intemperance, and strife or injustice in any form.

A schism took place in the Society of Friends in 1827, as a result of the preaching of Elias Hicks, a

"ROADSIDE," THE HOME OF LUCRETIA MOTT

speaker of great power and influence, who advocated Unitarian doctrines in the meetings of the society. The result was its division into Orthodox and Unitarian branches, Mr. and Mrs. Mott joining the Hicksites, as those who accepted the doctrines of Elias Hicks were called. Accepting the Unitarian view strongly, she felt it her duty to work for it, and during the remainder of her life was one of the ablest and most influential speakers of this branch of the Society of Friends.

Soon after this the feeling of opposition to the slave system, which she had long taught in the meetings of her people, began to win public advocates, the Garrison campaign was opened, and on every side the friends of freedom for the slave were coming out openly. New England formed its anti-slavery society, and in 1833 a national society was formed in Philadelphia. In organizing this Lucretia Mott took one of the most active parts and she became president of the Female Anti-Slavery Society, founded the same year. It was a work with which she had been warmly in sympathy since girlhood, and she entered upon the duties involved with the earnestness of conviction, working in her quiet and modest but convincing way.

Six years later, when a World's Anti-Slavery Convention was held in London, Mr. and Mrs. Mott were among the American delegates, in company with other men and women who had made themselves leaders in the cause. They went to London full of enthusiasm, but on arriving there found themselves in face of a deep-seated prejudice which was many centuries old.

For women to take any part in public affairs, or in any way to place themselves on an equal footing with men in questions of importance, was looked upon as out of all sense and reason. It was improper; women should keep within their sphere; they should stay at home and make themselves pretty and entertaining; to mingle in public matters robbed woman of her sweetest charm—such was the type of the arguments that were used, and when these women delegates from America came to attend the meetings of the society they found the doors shut against them.

They were indignant at this treatment, and so were some of the men who had come out with them. William Lloyd Garrison was among these, and he was so vexed with this example of British conservatism that he refused to attend any meetings to which his fair friends were not admitted. Thus the convention shut out not only the women, but the most famous abolitionist among the men of the world. Among the English women excluded were such well known persons as Elizabeth Fry, Amelia Opie, and Mary Howitt.

To soften the indignity of this refusal, a social entertainment, called a breakfast, was got up for the delegates, and to this the women were invited. The company that came to the breakfast was a distinguished one, many of the guests being men of high rank and prominence. Among them were a number of those who had voted against admitting women to the convention, and their surprise was almost consternation when a small, sweet-faced, soft-spoken woman rose and began to address them with a gentle dignity that carried much force with it. It was Mrs. Mott, who chose this way of saying what she had proposed to say before the convention.

To many of the Englishmen present this seemed unwomanly boldness, but her manner was so soft and sweet, her face and expression so attractive, her words so earnest and eloquent, her advocacy of freedom for all, black and white alike, so warm and logical, that their displeasure soon vanished and they found themselves listening with pleasure and admiration. If the vote had been taken after that address there would have been little question as to the admission of the women delegates, but as it was, Mrs. Mott succeeded in expressing her views before the members of the society and doing her duty as a member of the convention to which she had been sent.

At home, during the long agitation on the subject of slavery, Mrs. Mott continued to support the cause of human freedom with all her earnest enthusiasm. It was a work that exposed its advocates to obloquy and even to peril. Those opposed to it were often violent. Attacks were made on the abolitionists, their meetings were broken up, their members threatened and abused, and one of their meeting halls in Philadelphia was set on fire and burned. The fervent believers walked in an atmosphere of danger, but quiet Mrs. Mott had the courage of her convictions and let no fear of violence deter her in her work for the enslaved. When brickbats were flying or rioters swarming around the hall, she retained her calm demeanor and sought to dispel the apprehensions of those present.

It is said that on one occasion, when a violent mob threatened a meeting to which she was going, this delicate little lady, with the courage of wisdom, asked in her soft voice for the protection of the burly leader of the mob. Astonished by the request and disarmed by her appeal to his chivalry, the loud-voiced bully took her under his care, escorted her to the hall, and saw that she had safe entrance within. The story does not say that he was greeted with the cheers of his fellows, but no one ventured to interfere with the lady under his charge, if any had thoughts of so doing.

Mrs. Mott did not confine herself to the anti-slavery cause. She was as firm an advocate of the right of women to be put on an equality with men in the eyes of the law, and to have an equal voice with men in choosing the representatives of the people. In 1848 there was held at Genesee Falls, New York, the first convention ever called together in which the rights of woman to the ballot and the equality with man under the law were the subjects discussed.

The convention and all who took part in it were ridiculed from end to end of the country, and almost the entire press broke out in a chorus of sharp criticism and satirical comment on the coming together of the strong-minded. Yet all that was said did not prevent a body of earnest women, and some men who believed in their cause, from meeting and debating the subject. William Mott, who was as earnest for reform as his wife, presided, and Mrs. Mott was one of the ablest and most earnest of the speakers. Despite the roar of laughter and the torrent of ridicule and abuse with which the movement was hailed, the little band of reformers kept on fighting their battle in their own way, growing and spreading, winning tolerance first and afterwards slowly gaining the rights for which they so earnestly labored.

Mrs. Mott was long one of the earnest workers in this new cause, as also in the temperance crusade and the question of women's wages. Her voice was raised wherever needed, and she lived to see much of what she had worked for achieved. The war came and the slaves were set free. Her work in this field was at an end. And the cause of Women's Rights had outlived the era of ridicule and won toleration and respect from many who had once derided it. The ideas of its champions became endorsed by a large body in the community, and by the time Mrs. Mott had become an old lady she had seen some of them accepted and others with fair promise of final success. Her last public appearance was at the suffrage convention in New York in her eighty-sixth year.

The noble character and constancy of purpose of Lucretia Mott added greatly to the effect of her eloquence and ability. As a speaker, a simple, earnest, unaffected manner and clearness and propriety of expression gave force to her words. Her high moral qualities, her developed intelligence, the beauty and consistency of her character, won her respect and admiration even from the opponents of her views. And none could say that she kept herself in public to the neglect of her home duties, for she was a model housekeeper, keeping her home in order and comfort, and holding throughout the love and admiration of her husband, who was mutually in close sympathy with her.

Mrs. Mott was a guardian angel to the poor of her vicinity. She attended them in sickness, sympathized with them in their troubles, gave them aid where needed, and did it all in a way to win their deepest gratitude. They lost a good and charitable friend when she died, November 11, 1880.

ELIZABETH CADY STANTON, THE WOMEN'S RIGHTS PIONEER

The first meeting devoted to the rights of women that history records was held in the village of Seneca Falls, New York, in 1848, and chief among those to whom this meeting was due must be named that ardent advocate of the rights of her sex, Elizabeth Cady Stanton. This meeting was a notable event in the history of one half the human race, the weaker half in physical strength. It issued the earliest Declaration of Independence in the battle for the freedom of women. With it began a fight which has never since ceased. In this conflict many victories have been won, and there can be little doubt that the women reformers will win in the end all they have asked for.

It was not social rights that these women demanded. Those they had. Society was their acknowledged field. What they asked for were legal and political rights. They wished to become the equals of man in all property and personal laws, and they wished to have the right to vote, to be made man's equal in choosing those who were to govern and make laws for the nation. This is what an ardent host of women had been seeking for more than half a century and Mrs. Stanton was a leader among those who first set the ball rolling. This being the case, a sketch of the life of this able woman belongs to our work.

Elizabeth Cady was born at Johnstown, New York, November 12, 1815. Her father, Judge Daniel Cady, was a well known and much respected man in that town, long an able lawyer and afterwards a judge in Fulton County, in which Johnstown is situated. The little girl, as she grew up, delighted to be in her father's office, to listen to what was said there, and to chatter away in her own style when she had a chance. She was bright and quick, and would sit silent in her corner listening to those who came to see her father on business, and taking in with much intelligence what they said. When women came in and began to talk about how unjust the laws were towards them, the little girl listened more eagerly still. If they spoke angrily she grew angry for them, and if they complained sadly her sympathetic soul grew sad also.

Outside the office she had often been hurt to see how much attention was given to boys and how little to girls, and to find that girls did not "count for much" when their brothers were about. All this was a source of much mortification to the child, who could not see what made a boy better than a girl, and why he should have a better education and a superior chance in life. She resolved that she would show that she was the equal of any boy and had as much courage and ability as they had.

Little Elizabeth had four sisters and one brother, and her father seemed to regard the latter more highly than all five of his girls. When his son died he could not be consoled, though he had all these girls left. "I wish you were a boy," he said with a sigh to Elizabeth. "Then I will be a boy and will do all my brother did," she replied. She looked on courage and learning as the points of boyish superiority, and she resolved to show she had these by learning to manage a horse and by studying Greek.

Determined that none of the boys should be ahead of

her, she studied mathematics, Latin, and Greek, branches then usually thought beyond the scope of girls, and showed her ability by winning a Greek Testament as a prize for scholarship. No doubt her young heart swelled with joy at this triumph over the boys of her class. She afterwards graduated at the head of her class in the academy of Johnstown.

So far she had kept her word, but here her course was stayed. There was not a college in the country at that time that would take girl students, and her indignation and vexation were great to find that boys who had been much below her in the academy could go to college, while she, because she happened to be a girl, was kept out.

This seemed to her very unfair. And when she remembered what she had heard in her father's office about the injustice of the laws towards women she grew to feel very bitter about the one-sided way in which the world was managed. No doubt she made up her mind even in those early days to fight against this injustice, for the fight which she afterwards began she never gave up while she lived. As for education, she managed to get a fair share of it outside of college halls, partly in a young lady's seminary, but more by a course of home study after her school life was ended.

She early began to take an interest in the affairs of the country, and became very earnest in the cause of reform, no matter what its field. In 1839 she married Henry B. Stanton, at that time an eloquent and popular lecturer on the subject of anti-slavery, one of the reforms of which she had become an earnest advocate.

Mr. Stanton was sent to London in 1840, as a delegate to the World's Anti-Slavery Convention, and his wife went with him, not as a delegate, but as a companion and warm sympathizer. She was not one of those women who were excluded from the meetings of the convention by the votes of its members, but she was in close touch with those who were, and very likely her indignation was again aroused by this treatment of women as if they were inferior to men.

One pleasant thing came to Mrs. Stanton through this visit to London: she made the acquaintance of the sweet and charming Lucretia Mott, this growing into an intimate friendship which lasted through Mrs. Mott's life. They were doubtless in warm sympathy in many of their views, and especially in that to which Mrs. Stanton's thoughts were most strongly turned, the unjust laws and customs regarding women.

When she returned to America she had evidently made up her mind to devote her life to the cause of women, and resist, in all the forms it had taken, the ancient and obstinate tyranny against her sex. She was by no means alone in this. There were many of the same way of thinking. We may name Lucretia Mott, Susan B. Anthony, and Lucy Stone as well-known examples. But Mrs. Stanton was the most active and energetic in the work of calling together and organizing the advocates of Women's Rights, and it was very largely due to her that in July, 1848, the first Women's Rights convention in the world's history was called together at Seneca Falls.

What the members of this convention had in mind was to begin a contest to make women the equals of men before the law. Mrs. Stanton went farther than them all, demanding that they should include the suffrage for women among the rights they demanded.

This radical suggestion met with vigorous opposition. At first Mrs. Stanton stood almost alone in it, being supported only by one other delegate, Frederick Douglass. Her husband strongly objected to it as unwise and injudicious. Lucretia Mott did the same. Susan B. Anthony, whose activity in the cause began later, at first looked upon the demand for the ballot as ridiculous. Mrs Stanton and Douglass, her one supporter, were in face of a hard fight.

But she was in dead earnest, and she did what she had never done before: she stated her views in public, and with a power of oratory she did not know she possessed. Douglass, an able and eloquent speaker, strongly supported her, and between them they won vote after vote, until Mrs. Stanton had carried all her resolutions, including that in favor of woman suffrage.

The report of what was done in this convention excited great attention throughout the country. To demand the suffrage for women! It was preposterous! Anything so utterly absurd had never been heard of before. Such was the tone of most of the papers that deigned to consider it seriously, but the bulk of the newspapers looked upon it as only a matter for laughter and editorial humor.

This reception had a discouraging effect upon many, but not upon Mrs. Stanton. She set to work vigorously using her new-found powers of oratory and lecuring in all directions. Two years later Susan B. Anthony, who had ridiculed the demand for the ballot on first hearing of it, changed her views, joined Mrs. Stanton as a friend and fellow-worker, and the two devoted their lives to the advocacy of the cause.

In 1866 Mrs. Stanton, then residing in New York City, offered herself as a candidate for Congress to the 8th district voters. Out of 23,000 votes cast she got just 24. In 1868 she, with Miss Anthony and others, started *The Revolution,* the pioneer Women's Rights journal. She was one of its editors for the few years before failure met it. It was finally merged in *The Liberal Christian,* a Unitarian paper. She afterwards lectured for many years in her chosen field. A ready and happy speaker, her labors went far to advance the interests of the cause she had at heart. In addition, she, with others, compiled a voluminous " History of Woman Suffrage" (three volumes of 1000 pages each), made up of documentary evidence and biographical sketches. In 1883, being on a visit to Europe, she held conferences with John Bright and others upon her favorite topic.

The social and political reforms advocated by Mrs. Stanton made remarkable progress during the more than fifty years which she devoted to them. The property rights of women have been placed on a level with those of men in some States, and have everywhere advanced in the direction of equal treatment of the sexes. As regards the demand for the ballot, the work in which she was the pioneer, its success has been very encouraging. To-day women have the full right of voting in four of the States, and in many others can vote in school-board elections and other local matters. And it has spread to other lands, especially to Australia, in which women vote on equal terms with men.

Mrs. Stanton had the unique distinction of being able to look back to the day in which she stood alone among her sex as an advocate of woman suffrage, her only supporter being a man of negro race, Frederick Douglass, and living to see it adopted in four of the American States and in island realms afar. She was a conqueror in her life's fight when death came to her, October 26, 1902.

SUSAN B. ANTHONY, THE OLD GUARD OF WOMAN SUFFRAGE

The cause of the political rights of women has had no more strenuous and unyielding advocate than Susan Brownell Anthony, a woman who for more than fifty years rarely let a day go by without doing something to advance her favorite reforms. Among these woman suffrage stood first, but there was no modern movement for the good of woman or of humanity in general to which this veteran agitator did not lend her aid. And when Miss Anthony came to the aid of any cause it was with heart and soul.

Born in South Adams, Massachusetts, February 15, 1820, of Quaker ancestry, Miss Anthony received an excellent education from her father, who was a cotton manufacturer. She was yet in early childhood when her father removed to Washington County, New York, where her early studies were in a small school held in his house.

Her education was completed in a Philadelphia school, and at the age of seventeen, her father having failed in business, she entered upon her life duties as a teacher, glad to be able to earn her own living and relieve her father.

There was one thing, however, that the youthful teacher protested against from the start: the low wages paid, and the discrimination in favor of men. She had certainly some reason to complain of under-pay, in view of the fact that she received but a dollar and a half per week, in addition to the not very enticing privilege of "boarding around." The frequent change of diet and domicile arising from this custom of the times must have been anything but agreeable to a high spirited woman.

What principally roused Miss Anthony's indignation at this time was to see men whom she felt to be much inferior to her in education and ability as teachers receiving three times her salary. It was this injustice, as she deemed it, that led her first to lift her voice in public. This was at a meeting of the New York State Teachers' Association, where some of the men were deploring the fact that their profession was not held to be as honorable and influential as those of the lawyer, the doctor, and the minister.

During a pause in the debate Miss Anthony rose and, to the horror of many of them, began to speak. In those days for a woman to venture to offer her views in a meeting of men, or, for that matter, in any meeting, was looked upon as an event utterly out of woman's sphere. The fair rebel against the conventionalities did not sin greatly. Her speech was not a long one, but what there was of it was telling and pithy. She said:

"Do you not see that as long as society says that a woman has not brains enough to be a lawyer, a doctor, or a minister, but has ample brains to be a teacher, every man of you who condescends to teach school tacitly acknowledges before all Israel and the sun that he hasn't any more brains than a woman?"

With this brief but knotty sentence she sat down, leaving it to them to digest. For years afterwards she strove in the association to bring women's wages and positions as teachers up to those of men, and she succeeded in greatly improving the standing of women in this respect.

Miss Anthonys' career as a teacher continued until 1852, but several years before it ended she began to take an active part in reform movements as a public speaker. Her first appearance in public was about 1846, in the temperance agitation. At that time the popular prejudice against women taking part in public work was very strong, but Miss Anthony was one of those valiant souls that do not hesitate to cross the Rubicon of custom and prejudice, and she dared criticism by a bold ventilation of her views before some women's meetings. She was helping to break down the wall that stood between woman and the public platform.

Two years later, as stated in our sketch of Elizabeth Cady Stanton, a Women's Rights convention was held at Seneca Falls, New York, where a resolution was proposed and carried demanding the right of suffrage for women. When word of this action came to Miss Anthony's ears she spoke of it as ridiculous. It was a new thought, to which she had to become accustomed, but two years later we find her in full acceptance of it, convinced that only through the use of the ballot could woman succeed in gaining an equality in industrial and legal conditions with man.

By this time she was becoming widely known as a lecturer on social topics and an organizer of temperance societies, and in 1851 she called a State convention of women at Albany, to urge upon the public the wrongs and to demand the rights of her sex. From this time forward she was a friend and co-worker of Mrs. Stanton and became regarded as one of the most ardent and able advocates of the various reforms which she took in hand.

There were at that time more insistent questions before the public than that of women's rights. First among these was that of the freedom of the slave, in which she took part with her accustomed ardor and blunt plainness of speech. To this she gave much of her time after 1856, while not forgetting the other subjects to which she had devoted herself. One of these was to secure for women admission to temperance and educational conventions on equal terms with men. In this she succeeded. The fence of exclusion was slowly giving way before her assaults.

During the Civil War Miss Anthony was very active, lecturing from city to city upon the vital questions of the day. She joined others in forming the Loyal Women's League, and in association with Mrs. Stanton sent petitions through the country to develop a public opinion in favor of abolishing slavery as a war measure. The duty of decreeing universal emancipation was strongly urged by her upon President Lincoln and Congress.

By this time Miss Anthony had gained much facility as a public speaker. She never indulged in flowers of speech and rarely rose to eloquence, but was fluent and earnest, direct and business-like, always talking to the point, always sincere, and usually convincing. Her energy was untiring, her good humor inexhaustible, and she was always quick to see and to seize an opportunity.

The war ended, a promising opening for the women suffragists appeared, in the settlement of the many problems that arose. Among these was the question of negro suffrage. In Kansas in 1867 two amendments to the State constitution were proposed, one giving the right to vote to negroes, the other to women. Many Republican leaders favored the former but fought shy of the latter. Miss Anthony and other orators took an active part in the contest, but when it came to a vote of the people both amendments were rejected, the negroes getting a larger vote in their favor than the women.

An unfortunate enterprise was undertaken about this time, in the publication of *The Revolution,* a paper devoted to the cause of women. Miss Anthony was active in founding this, was one of its editors, and when it failed after a brief career of two and a half years, she was left with a debt of $10,000. This she paid, principal and interest, from the proceeds of her lectures.

She continued her work with indefatigable ardor, and in the decade from 1870 to 1880 spoke five or six times a week, in all the Northern and many of the Southern cities, the rights of women being her unceasing theme. She took advantage of every opportunity to deliver impromptu speeches on this subject. Thus once, when ice-bound on the Mississippi in a steamboat, she broke the monotony by organizing a meeting in the cabin and addressing the passengers on her favorite topic. Like the woman's cruse of oil, she never ran dry on the theme of woman's rights. Mrs. Stanton said she never knew her to be taken by surprise but on one occasion, when she was asked to speak to the inmates of a lunatic asylum. This was too much even for the ardor of Susan B. Anthony.

In 1872, having been registered as a citizen at Rochester, N. Y., and wishing to test her right to the suffrage, she voted at the national election. For this she was arrested, tried, and fined, the judge directing the jury to bring in a verdict of guilty and refusing a new trial. Under the advice of her counsel, she gave bonds to prevent being imprisoned. This she always afterwards regretted, as it prevented her taking the case to the United States Supreme Court. Her purpose was to test the validity of the Fourteenth Amendment to the Constitution. As to the $100 fine, it still remains unpaid.

The unceasing agitation kept up by Miss Anthony was not without its effect. Gradually the people of the country grew accustomed to the idea of woman suffrage, it gained a large support among men, and became established, in greater or less measure, in many of the States. In 1880 she made a plea before the Committee on the Judiciary, of which Senator Edmunds has said that her arguments were unanswerable, and were marshalled as skilfully as any lawyer could have done. For years she sought to rouse the people of this country to demand the adoption of a sixteenth amendment to the Constitution, making woman suffrage a part of the fundamental law of the country.

Miss Anthony said that her work was like subsoil plowing. Through the many reforms brought about by her in the condition of women she was simply preparing the way for a more successful cultivation and a more liberal harvest. One of her larger labors was the "History of Woman Suffrage," edited by her in conjunction with Mrs. Stanton and Matilda J. Gage, which embraces three bulky volumes of 1000 pages each.

Miss Anthony attained her eighty-sixth year of age without losing her ardor in the cause. Her life's work had won her a reputation as wide as civilization, while the honor in which she was held was indicated by the refusal of the Empress of Germany to remain seated in her presence when a party of American suffragists visited the German court. The empress was unwilling to seem to put herself on a higher level of rank than this plain American woman, whom she regarded as having won a station of honor above that of the throne. Miss Anthony died, ripe in years and in the world's respect, on the 13th of March, 1906.

DOROTHEA DIX, THE SAVIOR OF THE INSANE

THE treatment of the insane in the past centuries was a frightful example of "man's inhumanity to man." Their condition was pitiable in the extreme. No one had a conception of the proper way of dealing with these unfortunates, and they were treated more like wild beasts in a menagerie than human beings; iron cages, chains, clubs, and starvation being used as methods of restraint, while their medical care was crude and barbarous, purging, bleeding, and emetics being usually employed. It was ignorance rather than malice that led to this merciless treatment. When in 1792 Pinel in France declared that such methods were barbarous and fit only to make bad worse, no one was ready to believe him. And when he proved that mercy was tenfold better than severity, it came as a new revelation. About the same time a similar system began to make its way in England. The system of restraint by straitjackets, etc., was continued till later, and in the United States the old methods held their own until well into the nineteenth century. The change to a more merciful treatment of these unfortunates was largely brought about by the efforts of one woman, a philanthropist of the highest type.

This woman, Dorothea Lynde Dix, was born April 4, 1802, in Hampden, Maine, the daughter of an itinerant physician, who died while she was quite young. She had her own way to make, and at fourteen years of age was teaching a child-school. In 1821 she taught an older school, and in 1831 opened a select school for young ladies in Boston. Frail and delicate, she broke down completely in 1836. Fortunately, she had inherited an estate which made her independent. She now went to Europe for her health, spending a year or two there.

During her period of teaching she had given much time to the care and instruction of the neglected inmates of the State's prison at Charlestown, and on her return from Europe became deeply interested in the condition of the paupers, prisoners, and lunatics, especially the latter, of Massachusetts. She was not alone in this. Others were awakening to the sorry condition of these unfortunates, and the benevolent Dr. Channing gave her much aid and encouragement in the investigation which she undertook.

Her inquiry into the condition of the insane in the State roused at once her pity and indignation; her deepest sympathies were awakened, and she began an investigation of the subject which had the merit of being thorough and untiring. Practical in character, she made a complete study of the question as it existed in other lands, and in 1841 began her earnest investigation of the methods of dealing with the insane in America. What she discovered was heart-breaking to one of her sympathetic nature.

At that time there were very few insane asylums in the country. Lunatics were placed with the paupers in almshouses and the prisoners in jail, all being herded indiscriminately together, and treated with brutal inhumanity. Filth prevailed, fires were lacking in bitter weather, there was no separation of the innocent, the guilty, and the insane, and fetters were used for the restraint of those who might easily have been managed by kindness.

Miss Dix's investigation led to a memorial to the legislature of Massachusetts, in which she vividly depicted the state of affairs and earnestly called for an amelioration of the horrors she had found. Her memorial revealed a shocking condition of things, the result of neglect and indifference. The methods of mediæval times had by no means died out even in intellectual Massachusetts, ignorance of the true condition of the almshouses and prisons having much to do with it. Miss Dix was determined that the plea of ignorance should no longer prevail. Her memorial was full of disquieting facts and earnest appeals. We can here quote only one of its most startling passages: " I proceed, gentlemen, to call your attention to the present state of insane persons confined within the commonwealth; in cages, closets, cellars, stalls, pens; chained, naked, beaten with rods, and lashed into obedience."

This general statement was borne out by detailed accounts of the horrible things she had seen in many instances. As a mild example may be mentioned the recital of one almshouse keeper, who said that one of his insane inmates had been troublesome and disposed to run away, but was now satisfied and docile. His docility proved to be due to an iron ring round his neck and a chain fastening him to the wall.

The memorial was a revelation to the legislature. A bill for measures of relief was quickly introduced and carried by a large majority, and with that memorial began the era of wise and merciful treatment of the insane in Massachusetts. By two years of hard work Miss Dix had set in train a regeneration of the condition of paupers and lunatics in that old commonwealth.

Her researches in Massachusetts carried her over the borders of other States, in which she found like conditions prevailing, and her inquiry was gradually extended until it covered the whole United States. She traversed the entire country east of the Rocky Mountains, made investigations everywhere, and found the same sickening conditions which Massachusetts had revealed. At that time very few States had any public asylum for the insane, and an important field of her labors was to have these established. Her first success in this was in New Jersey, an asylum being founded in Trenton in 1845 as a result of her earnest representations. This was but the beginning; many other States followed, and the herding of the indigent and the insane together in almshouses began to be a thing of the past.

Miss Dix spared no efforts in her indefatigable labors. She went from legislature to legislature, interviewing members, pleading, demanding, repeating the results of her inquiries, winning votes, everywhere commanding respect and attention, everywhere gaining favorable legislation. And this was not alone in the United States, for more than once she crossed the ocean and found conditions still existing in Europe that badly needed improvement. In Italy she appealed to the Pope in aid of the ill-treated insane.

The plea of State poverty was one of the difficulties she met at home, and this she sought to overcome by an appeal to Congress. Large grants of the public lands were being made for the endowment of schools, and she begged for a similar grant in aid of her lifework. Her first application was made in 1848, when she asked for 5,000,000 acres. She later on increased this demand to 12,250,000 acres, 10,000,000 being for the benefit of the insane and the remainder for the deaf and dumb.

It was a difficult task she had undertaken. Congress was then occupied with exciting questions that threatened to lead to civil war, and it was hard to enlist its attention to an act of pure beneficence. Year after year Miss Dix kept up the struggle, only to meet defeat and disappointment. More than once her bill was passed by the Senate but killed in the House. Again, the House supported it and the Senate defeated it. Not until 1854 did she succeed in getting a favorable vote from both houses.

It was with the highest gratification that she heard of her success, her triumph. The unfortunates for whom she had so long worked and pleaded would now be amply cared for, and the disgrace on the nation, which had so long existed, come to an end. Her heart was filled with joy, and congratulations poured in upon her. Alas! the bill had the President still to pass, and her heart sank into the depths when President Pierce, moved by a spasm of constitutionalism, vetoed the bill, on the ground of its being alien to the Constitution.

Miss Dix was defeated. It was hopeless to seek to revive the measure during the years of excitement that followed, but she continued her work with success among the States until the outbreak of the Civil War rendered useless all labors in this direction.

She now sought Washington and offered her services in a new rôle of benevolence, as a nurse for wounded soldiers. In this the zeal and ability in management she displayed were such that on the 10th of July, 1861, Secretary Cameron appointed her Superintendent of Women Nurses. As such she established excellent regulations, which were strictly carried out, but not without controversies with others in authority. Miss Dix had a somewhat autocratic manner, which was likely to cause offence and lead to opposition, but her instincts were all for good. She continued her service till the end of the war, carefully inspecting the hospitals, overseeing the work of the nurses, and maintaining a high state of discipline among them. For this she accepted no salary, and provided amply for the health of those working under her.

The war ended, Miss Dix returned to her labors in behalf of the insane and kept them up until advancing age reduced her powers. She resided at Trenton, N. J., the seat of the first asylum instituted through her efforts, and died there July 18, 1887.

GEORGE PEABODY, THE BANKER PHILANTHROPIST

On more than one occasion men of wealth have come to the aid of this country when in need, and won fame by their patriotism. We have spoken of two of them, Robert Morris, the financier of the Revolution, and Stephen Girard, who bought the unmarketable Government securities in the war of 1812, and relieved the authorities in a great emergency. There is a third, less known, though not less patriotic, to be named—George Peabody, who used his wealth to sustain his country in the dark days of the panic of 1837.

Gloomy times were those. A black cloud hung over the nation. The business of the country was prostrated and the nation itself in disgrace, for it was unable to pay its debts. Money was needed for government purposes, but the credit of the United States was at a very low ebb. There was no money to be borrowed at home, and foreign capitalists were not eager to loan their funds, except at ruinous rates.

At that time there was an American merchant, George Peabody by name, settled in London, where he had done a large business and grown very rich. He had begun his business life in Baltimore, and when Maryland asked him for help in her low state of finances, Mr. Peabody did not hesitate. He showed his faith in his country by buying American bonds freely, at good prices. It was at a loss he did this, for the securities could have been had at lower rates, but Pea-

245

body's example was contagious, the other London capitalists having faith in his judgment. They began to buy bonds, too, and the crisis was passed. When the trouble was over, he declined to accept any reward for his valuable services.

This was a case in which Mr. Peabody was in no danger of losing his money, but he looked for no profit and was ready to face a possible loss. He afterwards gave such large sums for useful purposes, and was so benevolent, that he is looked upon as one of the noblest of philanthropists. It is for this reason that we feel called upon to tell the story of his life.

George Peabody was born at South Danvers (now known as Peabody), Massachusetts, February 18, 1795. He came from a good New England family, that included patriots and thinkers among its members, but not capitalists until he came. His father was poor. His education was scanty. He was taken from school and put at work in a grocery store at eleven years of age. Here he stayed for four years, getting some idea of how to do business, and showing some ability in that field. After a short experience in another store, he left South Danvers to take a place in his uncle's establishment at Georgetown, District of Columbia.

He was there in 1812, when the war with England broke out. Early in that war a British fleet came sailing up the Chesapeake and the Potomac, threatening the city of Washington, and the young merchant's clerk joined the band that prepared to defend the city. But the ships were only making a feint, and soon sailed away, and Peabody went back to the store.

Young as he was, he showed much of the business skill which was to make him rich in later days. He was shrewd enough to see one thing: the business was conducted in such a way that there was danger of his being held responsible for his uncle's debts. In fact, it was carried on for a time under his name. This induced him to give up his position and look around for another place. It soon came. A Mr. Riggs of Baltimore, a wealthy merchant, who had seen a good deal of young Peabody and knew that he was bright and trusty, offered to make him his manager in a dry-goods store in Baltimore, he supplying the capital and Peabody handling the business. This was a splendid offer for a boy of nineteen, and he lost no time in taking it. Mr. Riggs knew what he was about. The boy was alert and careful in business, with sound judgment, knowing when to make a deal and when to avoid one, when to spend and when to save. He had abundance of energy, he was industrious, honest, courteous, and had no bad habits. He was the man to command success and was soon made a full partner, the firm being named Riggs & Peabody.

The judgment of Mr. Riggs was fully justified. The business grew rapidly, branches were established in other cities, and before twenty years had elapsed both partners were very rich. Mr. Peabody had often crossed the ocean to buy goods for the firm, and in 1837 he decided to settle in London and carry on an English branch of the business. A quick interchange of goods was established between the two countries, money made rapidly at both ends, and large sums began to be left by customers in Peabody's hands, to be drawn upon when needed.

In this way he was unintentionally led into the banking business, and in 1843 the firm name was changed to George Peabody & Co., and banking made its principal business, the house dealing very largely in American securities. In this way he became one of the richest men of the time, his bank being looked upon as one of the strongest in London and immense sums of money intrusted to its care.

As for Mr. Peabody himself, he was a fine-looking but plainly-dressed man, generous and open-hearted, courteous and obliging. Americans in London always found a genial greeting at his office, and it became their common resort. He remained unmarried, living modestly in his bachelor apartments, but entertaining generously at his club. When the Fourth of July came around he did not forget that he was an American patriot, and for many years gave a grand dinner in honor of the day, to which distinguished guests of both countries were invited.

George Peabody was one of those warm-hearted, broad-minded souls who feel that riches are a gift from heaven to be used for the good of the world; their mission is one of duty to be done, not of hoards to be laid away. Giving, in his mind, stood side by side with getting; his nature was broadly charitable; he did not wait until death to dispose of his great wealth, but wisely gave it during his life, while he could see that it was well administered and that his purposes were faithfully carried out.

He began his career by giving. When a boy, with a very small salary, his earnings went to the needs of his mother and sisters. He had always a warm heart for those at home, and from the time he was twenty-four he took all the care of their support upon himself. Later, when his wealth began to grow enormous, he looked around for other places where he might do good. Being a bachelor, he had no family of his own to care for, and, with a broad Christian benevolence, he felt like making the world his family and using his wealth so that it would do the greatest good.

Mr. Peabody was wise enough to know that giving money for the direct support of the poor is a form of charity that may lead to more harm than good. It is apt to encourage improvidence, idleness, and a disposition to depend upon help rather than work, and the effect of caring for the poor in this way is often only to increase the number of the poor. He looked around to see where he could make his money do help without hurt, where it could benefit mankind by improving their conditions or, by aiding their education, put them in a way to take care of themselves.

His two greatest gifts were made for this purpose. But before stating what they were, there are some smaller examples of his public spirit to mention. In 1851, when the great World's Fair in London was being held, our Government had not much money to spare, and Congress was not willing to supply any funds for the American exhibit. Seeing this, Mr. Peabody generously offered to bear all the expense and to see that his native country was fitly represented. As a result there was a valuable American display, and the inventors and producers of the United States went home with many prizes and awards of honor. It was the first occasion in which the world was made to see the great things that America could do, and George Peabody gave it the opportunity.

In 1852 he gave ten thousand dollars to pay the expenses of the celebrated expedition of Dr. Kane to the Arctic Seas in search of Sir John Franklin, who had gone there years before and failed to return. In the same year his native town of Danvers celebrated its hundredth birthday, and he honored the occasion by sending it twenty thousand dollars for an institute and a library. This was only a beginning. He kept adding to it until the sum was more than two hundred thousand dollars.

In 1857 Mr. Peabody had been away from the United States for twenty years, heaping up wealth in his foreign domicile. He thought it time to see his home country again, and paid a visit to the United States, going to Danvers and Georgetown and Baltimore, and recalling his old memories in those places. For many years he had been thinking over a plan for benefiting Baltimore by a great educational institution, and had carefully laid out plans for it. He wanted it to be one that would grow and keep up with all demands upon it.

This splendid institution he saw well under way before he left America. It is called the Peabody Institute, and includes a large free library, an academy of music, an art gallery, and rooms for the Maryland Historical Society, which he helped also with money. To this institution he gave over a million dollars, supplying the money from time to time as his plans unfolded and the institute developed.

A greater gift was that which he made soon after to the city of London, for it was one which reached down to the needs of the suffering poor of that mighty city. Mr. Peabody had long seen in what miserable homes they lived and the dirt and degradation which surrounded them. To provide these hard-working and poorly paid people with comfortable homes and healthful surroundings was one of the best ways of helping them, and this he was among the first to see. The industrial home which he built, and the opportunities for education and recreation he provided, cost him in all about two and a half millions of dollars. It was a splendid benefaction and was gratefully received. Queen Victoria offered to make him a baronet, but Mr. Peabody was a true American and would accept no title. Then she had her portrait painted on ivory and set in jewels, and presented it to him as a token of her deep feeling for his charity to her people. This was deposited by him in the institute at South Danvers.

His greatest gift was for the education of the poor of the South. The Southern Education Fund, as this is called, was a gratuity of $3,500.000. It has been of immense benefit in the advancement of education in that section of our country, in which education was then greatly neglected, and it is of as much service to-day as when it was given.

These are not all of Mr. Peabody's gifts. There were many smaller ones. Harvard and Yale Colleges each received $150.000, and smaller sums, for churches, institutes, libraries, and colleges, were given to a number of American towns. His total gifts amounted to about eight and a-half million dollars, and when he died he left five millions to be divided among his relatives and friends.

He did not wait till death to dispose of his money; he gave it during his life, and was careful to see that his instructions were carried out. As a consequence, his gifts have not gone astray in their objects, but are still doing good. When he died, on the 4th of November, 1869, his body was laid in state in Westminster Abbey, and was then brought to this country in a royal man-of-war. Here it was received with the highest respect and buried with national honors.

While so generous to the public, Mr. Peabody was abstemious in his personal habits. He had to live with close economy in his youth, and he never changed from this. His habits were very simple, and he might often be seen making his dinner on a mutton chop at a table laden with viands, at his cost, for his friends. He dressed neatly but plainly, did not indulge in jewelry, and disliked display of any kind. In business methods he was very exact, and while giving away millions, would demand the last penny in the fulfilling of a contract. When the conductor of an English railway train charged him a shilling too much for his fare, he complained and had the man discharged. " It was not that I could not afford to pay the shilling," he explained, " but the man was cheating many travelers to whom the swindle would be oppressive."

PETER COOPER, THE BENEFACTOR OF THE UNEDUCATED

THE city of New York owes a deep debt of gratitude to Peter Cooper, one of its most generous and far-seeing philanthropists, who gave thirty years of his life to planning and developing the Cooper Institute, his noble educational gift to the metropolitan city. His father had named him, not after some insignificant Peter in the family, but after the Apostle Peter, and trusted that this boy would prove worthy of his godfather. He believed devotedly that his son would "come to something," and his faith was not misapplied.

Peter Cooper was born in New York, February 12, 1791. His father was a poor hatter, and the boy had to begin helping him as soon as he was tall enough to reach above the table and pull the hair out of rabbit skins. He kept at this till he knew all about the making of beaver hats, the common head-gear of that day. He badly wanted an education, he was not very old when he saw the advantages of learning, but all the schooling his father was able or willing to give him was half of every day for one year. That was all the school education he ever received.

The boy worked at hat-making till he was seventeen. Then his father went out of that business and into the brewing of beer, at which his son continued to work. Peter did not like this occupation, and as his father was willing to have him try something else, he became an apprentice to a coach-builder. He kept at this till he was of age, learned the business thoroughly, and proved himself so diligent and efficient that his late master offered to build him a shop and set him up in business. This was an excellent offer, but the young man would not accept it. It would leave him with a debt to pay, and of debt he had already a horror, perhaps from his father's experience, so he declined the kind offer.

The young coach-builder had three trades at his fingers' ends, but he had only a smattering of book-learning, and his loss in this respect he felt sorely. While he was an apprentice he bought some books and tried to teach himself. But good school books were not then very plentiful, and those he bought were so learned that he could not half understand them. There were no evening schools to help him, but after a time he found a teacher who was willing to give him lessons in the evening for small pay. His difficulty led the boy to a resolution that had much to do with shaping his future life. He said to himself:

"If ever I prosper in business so as to acquire more property than I need, I will try to found an institution in New York wherein apprentice-boys and young mechanics shall have a chance to get knowledge in the evening." This was a noble purpose, that stayed by him until it was realized.

Young Cooper was not long idle. He got a job that fitted in with none of his three trades. This was in a shop where machines were made for shearing cloth. He got good wages at this and saved all he could, and when a chance opened to buy cheaply the rights to make the shearing-machines in New York he had cash enough for the purchase. This was about the time of the second war with Great Britain, and when the young

HEROES OF PROGRESS 255

man was not much over twenty-one years old. He had done very well for a beginner, and he did very well in his new enterprise. Always careful, energetic, and enterprising, and with native business tact, he made money from the start, and on one large transaction cleared five hundred dollars in profits.

This seemed like a good lift for the young manufacturer, but he did not look upon it in that way. While he was going ahead his father had been going behind and getting deeper into debt, and the affectionate son used the five hundred dollars to pay his father's debts. This some might consider not business-like. But it was laudable; it showed a strong moral fibre in the young man; it was something that stood higher than business success.

Peter Cooper was a good deal of an inventor, and made an improvement in the machines that helped their sale, so that he built up quite a large and prosperous business. But after the war ended the demand for shearing machines fell off, and he looked around for something that would pay better. There happened to be a little grocery store for sale at some distance above the town of that day. Fields and vacant lots surrounded it. As he wanted to change his business, he bought this place and moved his home to the store—for he was married by this time. He was now twenty-three years of age.

It is an interesting fact that the little store stood just where the great Cooper Institute now stands. The young merchant was looking far forward. The city was fast growing, and would in time grow round this spot, so that the land which he bought at a cheap price would become very valuable. But he had his future evening school already in his mind, and fancied that some day the plot of ground would become a good central spot for the building he proposed to erect.

There was one thing that must be said for Peter Cooper; he was a born man of business. Everything he touched paid. He knew nothing about the grocery trade, but he soon had his store on a paying basis. And the money he made in this, and that he had made in the machine shop, enabled him after some years to buy out a glue factory and to pay down in cash every penny of the price. At the same time he was supporting his father and his two sisters and paying his brother's way in a medical school. He had made himself the good angel of the family.

The glue factory, like everything he handled, proved profitable, and grew to be one of the most important in the country. He made isinglass as well as glue, and went into other lines of business, and bought all the pieces of land he could find for sale around his grocery store plot, until in time he owned the whole block on Astor Place, where Third and Fourth Avenues now meet. It was thus he got together the ground on which his evening school for boys was to be built.

In 1828 there was much land speculation in Baltimore. The Baltimore and Ohio Railroad, the first important one in the country, was then being built, and many thought it would bring business prosperity to that city. Peter Cooper evidently thought so. He was now getting to be quite a capitalist, and concluded that Baltimore property would be a good investment, so he bought three thousand acres of land within the city limits, paying for it one hundred and fifty thousand dollars. This was only thirty-five dollars an acre, seemingly a very small price for city territory, but it soon began to seem as if he had paid too much, for the building of the road came to an end. All the money invested had been used, and the stockholders would not put in any more. They were afraid of losing what they had already paid in.

This was not to Peter Cooper's liking. He was now a large holder of Baltimore property, and wanted to make it profitable. So he asked the stockholders to wait a while and he would see if he could do something to help their road. He would build them a steam-engine suited to run upon it.

At that time there was not a locomotive in this country except one or two that had been imported from England. And there were not many in that country, for the locomotive was a new thing even there. George Stephenson had only lately invented his improved engine. But Cooper, as we have said, had the inventive faculty, and he set himself to building a steam engine adapted to the new railroad. He succeeded in this. His locomotive was the first ever built in this country, but it was a good one. It was in some ways better than those that had been built in England.

He said about it: "This locomotive was built to show that cars could be drawn around short curves, beyond anything believed possible. Its success proved that railroads could be built in a country scarce of capital and with immense stretches of very rough country to pass, in order to connect commerce centres, without the deep cuts, the tunneling and leveling, which short curves might avoid."

A queer little concern it was, this first American engine. To-day it would look like a toy, but in those days it seemed a wonder. It did what its builder said it would do, and saved the railroad company from failure. But it did not add any new value to

Cooper's Baltimore land. To make this pay something else was needed, and he decided to build a rolling-mill upon it. Nothing lay idle very long in his hands. He built his mill. The establishment was called the Canton Iron Works, and soon became prosperous. Great improvements were made in the blast furnace, and the mill and the land both brought him in money. The works were afterwards removed to Trenton, N. J., and for many years were a source of great profit to Mr. Cooper. And in New York he was making not only isinglass and glue, but also oil, prepared chalk, and Paris white; was grinding white lead, and preparing skins for making buckskin leather. His energies reached in many directions, and money was flowing faster and faster into his coffers.

We may be sure that a man as full of public spirit as he would not let his spare cash lie idle. He wanted to help wherever he could, and was active in nearly every work of public benefit going on. He helped Governor Clinton in the Erie Canal project, and invented an endless chain arrangement for pulling the boats along. He aided in the building of telegraph lines, and for many years was president of the New York, Newfoundland, and London Telegraph Company. He served in public offices in New York City, and his interest in education was shown in the work he did for the improvement of the common schools.

All these years Mr. Cooper had his cherished project in mind, considering its character, developing its purposes, adding to its site. By 1854 he felt himself ready to begin the work which had been his boyhood's dream, but which unfolded in his mind much beyond a simple night-school for poor apprentices. To know just to what his plans had grown, one must see the Cooper Institute as it stands to-day, on the spot where the little grocery store of its builder once stood. His final purpose, as declared by him, was that it should be " forever devoted to the improvement and instruction of the inhabitants of the United States in practical science and art."

He gave to it a great deal of money and a great deal of thought and work. He haunted the building, watching every step of its progress, taking hold himself where needed, altering and adding to it wherever he could see a chance of making it better. As it stands to-day it is the most complete free school of its kind in the country, with every convenience for students and everything necessary for them to gain an education in the practical needs of life. Over two thousand pupils attend it every year, coming from all parts of the United States, and no man ever built himself a nobler monument than Peter Cooper.

For almost thirty years his hale and hearty figure and kindly face were to be seen by the students, while his interest in their pursuits gave them zest in their work. The warm-hearted philanthropist lived to a ripe old age, during which his hands never ceased in good work. He had passed the great age of ninety-two when he died on April 4, 1883.

ABRAHAM LINCOLN, THE EMANCI-PATOR OF THE SLAVE

In a miserable frontier hut, the son of miserably poor pa 'ents, was born on the 12th of February, 1809, a boy who fifty-four years later was to sign the grand decree of emancipation that gave liberty to the slaves of the United States. An offspring of the wilderness, a child of poverty, a boy who had to win his way by the sternest labor, to gain an education against the severest obstacles, he developed qualities sure to make him a great man,—simple-minded honor, noble instincts, earnest devotion to life's duties, and a practical ability and unusual power of expression which enabled him to win his way with men.

The story of this man, Abraham Lincoln, has often been told. But he holds a high station in the ranks of the heroes of progress, and an outline sketch of his life must be given here. In the words of Emerson, " He was a man who grew according to his need; his mind mastered the problem of the day, and as the problem grew so did his apprehension of it. By his courage, his justice, his even temper, his fertile counsel, his humanity, he stood a heroic figure in the centre of a heroic epoch. He is the true history of the American people in his time; the pulse of twenty million people throbbed in his heart, and the thoughts of their mind were uttered by his tongue."

Lincoln was a self-made man in every respect. Born at the bottom of the pit of poverty, he climbed his own way up. Born on a stony and weedy hillside, at a

Copyright, 1900, by McClure, Phillips & Co.

ROCK SPRING FARM, KENTUCKY, WHERE ABRAHAM LINCOLN WAS BORN
(From a photograph taken in September, 1895. The cabin in which Lincoln was born is seen to the right, in the background)

place called Nolin's Creek, in Kentucky, in a house without windows or floor; taken to as sorry a house in Indiana while quite young; doomed to hard labor from childhood; he early manifested a desire for knowledge that nothing could check and that forced its way through all impediments. His scanty school education taught him little more than how to read and write, and he had to depend upon himself for the rest. His stepmother, a good woman, helped him all she could and taught him all she was able, and on this slender foundation the ambitious student built nobly.

The frontier settlement he lived in had few books, but he borrowed all he could and read them thoroughly. He read in the evening by the light of the log fire, wrote on a shingle when paper was not to be had, and worked out questions in arithmetic on the back of a wooden shovel, scraping off the figures when it was full and beginning again. The first book he owned, a "Life of Washington," he had borrowed from a farmer and kept it in a place where it got soaked with rain. He took the ruined book to the farmer and asked how he should pay for it. The farmer's price was "to pull fodder" for the cattle for three days. In this way little Abraham earned his book, which he dried, pressed out, and valued as a great prize.

A boy like this cannot be kept in ignorance. "Abe Lincoln," as he was called, grew up to be the best informed and the strongest young man in the whole district. He was tall and sinewy; not a man in the neighborhood could beat him at wood-splitting, at wrestling, running, or any athletic sport. In addition to this he was kind and helpful, bright and willing, good-natured and fun-loving, ready to do anything for anybody, and the prime favorite of all the district. As a young man he kept everybody laughing. He had a store of amusing stories and was an adept in telling them. He could make a speech also, and his book learning grew to be wonderful to the uneducated farmers around. He had not read many books, but he had read them well.

Such was Abraham Lincoln as a boy and young man. As he grew older he made river trips down the Ohio and Mississippi to New Orleans, served as a store clerk, and then set up a store of his own in which he showed very little business ability, attending to his books instead of to his customers. Yet the people admired him so that after a time they elected him to the legislature. He was at that period living in Illinois, and in the legislature of this frontier State he served four terms, making his mark by the clear good sense and breadth of view of the speeches he made, so that he came to be considered one of the leading Whigs of the State.

While thus engaged, he became a surveyor, got hold of some law books and studied them, was admitted to the bar in 1836, and began to practice in 1837, when twenty-six years of age. He had traveled up a long distance from the poor boy of the log cabin of his childhood. And by this time he had developed some strong ideas. During his visit to New Orleans he had seen some things that gave him an earnest dislike to slavery, and his sentiments on this subject he expressed vigorously in the legislature in 1837. At that time anti-slavery views were very unpopular in any part of the United States, and some extreme pro-slavery resolutions were passed by the Democratic majority in the House. Against these he and another member entered a protest, saying that " they believed that the institution of slavery was founded in injustice and bad policy."

That was Lincoln's first public statement about slavery, of which he was afterwards to become one of the greatest opponents. While he was in New Orleans on his Mississippi trip he chanced to see an auction where negroes were bought and sold. The scene stirred his feelings deeply, and on leaving he said in stern accents to his companion, " If I ever get a chance to hit that institution, *I'll hit it hard.*" He kept his word in later days.

There are many stories showing what a genial, kind, helpful man Lincoln was in his early life. All round where he lived people grew to depend on him. His tenderness of heart was such that he could not bear to see even an animal in distress. There is one story telling how he waded an icy river to rescue a worthless pet dog that had been left behind and could not get across. A second story tells of his seeing a pig mired in a ditch. As he was dressed in his best, he rode on. But he could not get poor piggy out of his mind, and after going a mile or two he turned back and pulled the animal out of the ditch without regard to his fine clothes.

Lincoln's law office was opened in Springfield, which he had helped to make the capital of the State. His knowledge of the law was not great. In studying it he had sometimes walked miles to borrow a law book, and doubtless lacked many which he should have read. But he knew how to talk strongly and to the point, which helped him with juries, and he had the reputation of not taking any case which he did not believe to be just. He was known to refuse profitable cases which he thought unjust, even when the law favored them. This integrity helped him, and he built up quite a business in the law.

Regarding young Lincoln's honesty, it may be said that when he sold out his store on credit, the man who bought it ran away, leaving debts for which he felt himself responsible and all of which he paid, though it took him many years to do so. His first public position had been as postmaster at New Salem, where there was so little business that he fairly kept his office in his hat, handing out the letters when he met the parties they were addressed to. The office was soon discontinued, no settlement being made, so that the postmaster owed the government some eighteen dollars. Several years passed before this was claimed, and in these years Lincoln had often been obliged to borrow money to keep things going. But when at length a postal agent came for a settlement the honest young postmaster brought out an old blue sock from which he poured the money in the very coins in which it had been received. No needs of his own had been met from that sacred store.

There was nothing going on in which young Abe Lincoln did not take a hand. He had been farm-hand, wood-chopper, boatman, clerk, storekeeper, postmaster, surveyor, lawyer, and legislator. For a time he was even a soldier, serving as captain of militia in the "Black Hawk War," though he saw no fighting. But there was nothing as yet to show that he would ever be known beyond his own district or State, though he had gained a powerful influence among his neighbors, was becoming one of the prominent Whigs of Illinois, and was several times a candidate for Presidential elector. The leading politicians of that State had a way of dividing the offices among them, and in 1846 it was Lincoln's turn to be sent to Congress. He was accordingly elected and served one term. While he did not distinguish himself in Washington, the party leaders saw that there was some good wood in the ungainly Congressman from the frontiers.

For a number of years after that Lincoln devoted himself to the law. The biggest fee he ever got was in 1853. He defended the Illinois Central Railroad in a suit for taxes and won his case, for which he sent in a bill for two thousand dollars. This the company refused to pay, whereupon Lincoln, on the advice of some fellow lawyers, sued for five thousand dollars, and the railroad company had to pay him this amount.

At this time, only seven years before his election to the Presidency, few outside his own district looked upon Abraham Lincoln as a man of any great merit or ability. He was simply a country lawyer and politician who had seen some service in legislature and Congress, was a ready and telling speaker, but was not known outside his State. It was not till the time of the repeal of the Missouri Compromise, in 1854, that his opportunity came. This radical act of the pro-slavery party thoroughly awakened him. He had been opposed to slavery ever since his visit to New Orleans, and now roused himself to "hit it hard." An able and popular orator, he took strong ground against the extension of the slave system, denounced its acts of encroachment bitterly, and became the leader of the Whigs in the debate which Senator Douglas, the Democratic champion, had started in favor of "Squatter Sovereignty," or the right of the people of each Territory to decide whether it should be admitted as a slave or a free State.

Douglas was an able and powerful speaker, the

"Little Giant" of the Democrats of the West. Many thought that Lincoln, whose reputation as yet was largely local, would be quite overweighted when pitted against this skilled and vigorous debator, who was immensely popular throughout the State. Their first great battle took place in October, 1854, at Springfield, during the State Fair. Douglas spoke first, making one of his best speeches to an enthusiastic throng of people. His friends thought he had demolished his opponent, and were ready to carry him on their shoulders.

The next day Lincoln took the stand, a tall, awkward, unprepossessing figure, with plain, homely face. Few expected much from him, but he astonished his hearers with an extraordinary burst of oratory and width of argument. He had never shown himself so great and able. The doctrines of Douglas were overthrown by his logical criticisms. As a friendly editor said, "The Nebraska bill was shivered, and like a tree of the forest was torn and rent asunder by the hot bolts of truth. At the conclusion of this speech every man and child felt that it was unanswerable."

It was in 1858 that Lincoln did the work that was to make him President. In the four years that had elapsed since his first contest with Douglas he had grown rapidly in political importance and made himself the unquestioned leader of the Illinois Republicans—the new party which had succeeded the Whigs. It was the time for the election of a United States Senator, and Lincoln was the choice of his party as opposed to Douglas, who was seeking a re-election.

The debate that followed was the opening of the door for Abraham Lincoln. It spread his reputation from Illinois through the whole country. He showed himself not alone a skillful orator, but a great political manager, one who was ready to sacrifice the hopes of the present for the assurance of the future. He pressed Douglas to declare himself upon an important point. His friends said that Douglas would answer his question in a way to insure his election. Lincoln replied: "I am after larger game. If Douglas so answers, he can never be President, and the battle of 1860 is worth a hundred of this." He was right. Douglas took a position that lost him his friends in the South and robbed him of their support two years later.

In this debate Lincoln took his stand in a way that gave him a continental reputation. He read to his friends a part of his speech and they opposed it bitterly, declaring that if he said those things it might ruin all his political future. Lincoln answered sturdily: "It is *true,* and I will deliver it as written. I would rather be defeated with those expressions in my speech held up and discussed before the people than be victorious without them."

What he said was this: "A house divided against itself cannot stand. I believe this government cannot endure permanently half slave and half free. I do not expect the Union to be dissolved; I do not expect the house to fall; but I expect it will cease to be divided. It will become all one thing or all the other."

This was a new and startling way of putting it. It set the country to thinking and talking, and the name of the man who could thus put the whole question in a nutshell became more widely known. Douglas defeated him for the Senate, but this he expected and did not care for. He had said, "I am after larger game."

During ten years Lincoln had been making himself the leader of his party in Illinois; now he began to be talked of all over the country. In 1860, at the invitation of Horace Greeley, he made an address at the Cooper Institute in New York, before an audience of the best citizens of the metropolis. They had heard of this eloquent Westerner, and were curious to hear him, though many expected only something of the nature of a grandiloquent stump speech, fitted for a prairie audience. The calm, clear, scholarly, logical address they heard surprised and electrified them. They had listened to nothing equal to it in force and dignity since the days of Webster. All New England wanted to hear the prairie orator, and everywhere he enlisted the deepest attention and warmest conviction. The character of his oratory was well expressed by one hearer, who praised him for "the clearness of your statements, the unanswerable style of your reasoning, and especially your illustrations, which were romance and pathos, fun and logic, all welded together."

In 1856 some of his friends had spoken of Lincoln for Vice-President, and even for President; but this was mere local admiration. In 1860 Seward seemed the man of the convention, but Lincoln had won the West, and it proved too strong for the East. Lincoln was nominated on the third ballot amid a most generous burst of enthusiasm. He was the man of the West, the rail-splitter of the prairies and forests, and a display of some fence rails of his own splitting by his friends helped immensely in rousing the excitement that carried the convention.

From this time on the life of Lincoln is the history of the Civil War. All readers know of his triumphant election, of the secession of the Southern States in consequence, of the danger to Lincoln's life in his journey to Washington, and of the need of protection during his inauguration, there being men in Washington who had sworn he should never take his seat. They know also of his wisdom, his judgment, his shrewdness, and his devotion to the best interests of the country.

He had said in 1858, " This country cannot endure permanently half slave and half free. It will become all one thing or the other." Three years afterwards the war that was to make it " one thing or the other " began, and in less than two years more the act to make it " one thing " was consummated in Lincoln's Proclamation of Emancipation, that set the slave free.

There was fighting still to be done, much of it, but step by step the freedom of the slave came nearer and surer, and early in 1865 the war ended in victory for the North, and the great work of Lincoln's life was achieved. In 1864 he was a second time elected President, and on the 4th of March, 1865, in his second inaugural address, spoke those famous words, so full of the character of the man: " With malice towards none, with charity for all, with firmness in the right, as God gives us to see the right, let us strive on to finish the work we are in."

In a little more than a month later the work, so far as it was the work of the sword, was finished, in the surrender of General Lee at Appomattox; and in less than a week later, on the 15th of April, 1865, Lincoln's career ended in the deed of an assassin, who was moved by an insane fury which few men in the South would have sustained even in that day of heated feeling. The time came when the South suffered bitterly for this act of horror, which had carried away its best friend.

WILLIAM H. SEWARD, THE WAR-TIME SECRETARY OF STATE

SHALL we picture a tragic scene that took place in Washington in April, 1865, just after the close of the dreadful Civil War? There came then a night of horror. An assassin shot down the noble President Lincoln as, happy at the end of his great work, he sat in quiet enjoyment in his box at the theatre. The same dreadful night other assassins entered the house of the Secretary of State, forced themselves into the room where he lay ill in bed, and attacked him with tigerish fury, stabbing him in the face and body. Only the courage of the old soldier who served as his nurse saved his life, and for days it was doubtful if he would recover.

Fortune alone saved William H. Seward from suffering the fate of his great chief. He had played as active a part in the drama of insurrection and won the hatred of the rebellious element as much as Lincoln himself. It is our purpose here to give some of the incidents in the life of this able and prominent man, who so nearly became a victim of the band of assassins that murdered the President.

William Henry Seward was at this time well advanced in years, having been born in the town of Florida, New York, on May 16, 1801, almost at the beginning of the century. The boy must have been difficult to manage, for he began his career in life by running away from college and seeking far-off

Georgia, where he undertook to act as principal of an academy at a salary of eight hundred dollars a year. This was a daring escapade for a boy of seventeen. It was due to a dispute with his father about tailor's bills and other such college matters. The young rebel, however, surrendered when he heard that his mother was in sore distress about his behavior. He gave up his position to a friend and went back to his studies.

After graduating at Union College, Seward studied law and opened an office in the town of Auburn. This town he made his home throughout his later life. It happened that here lived a Miss Frances A. Miller, with whom the young lawyer had fallen in love, and whom he married as soon as he had business enough to make the venture and set up a home of his own.

The young lawyer was not long in practice before he became active in politics. He had been brought up a Democrat, but he soon joined the Anti-Masons, then the Whigs, and in later years came to be a leader of the Republicans. In 1830 he became intimate with Thurlow Weed, then the most prominent figure in New York politics, and the two formed a political partnership which for many years ruled the politics of the State and had much to do with the politics of the nation. It was known as the Whig firm of Weed & Seward. In later years, when Horace Greeley joined in, it became what Greeley called the firm of Seward, Weed & Greeley. Seward's name now came first.

In 1830 Seward was elected to the State Senate by the Anti-Masonic party. When the next election for Governor came round this party had vanished and the Whig party had been formed. It nominated Seward for Governor, but he was defeated and went back to his law business. In 1836, however, he was elected Governor. This position he held for six years, and then retired to private life, declining to run for a third term.

By this time Seward had taken a decided stand on the slavery question. He made a visit with his wife to the Natural Bridge of Virginia in 1835, and saw things while in that State that made him a foe of the slave-holding system. While Governor, he plainly showed his enmity to this system. Three black sailors were wanted by the Governor of Virginia on the charge of having helped a slave to escape, but he refused to give them up, saying that what they were charged with was not a crime in New York. He also had the law repealed by which a slave-holder travelling with his slaves could hold them for nine months in the State of New York.

One thing he did is of interest as taking a stand against an old but evil New York custom. For many years the celebration of New Year's day in New York City had been an occasion for social visits at which punch and wine were set out for the guests. The Governor in 1842 substituted cold water and lemonade for these strong drinks. This was not in consequence of his own tastes, but he felt that it was his duty to throw his influence on the side of the growing temperance sentiment.

On returning to the law, Seward soon became very successful, and gained a large practice in patent law cases, of which he had previously known very little. While active in the law, he did not give up his hold on politics. He, Weed, and Greeley were the active powers in New York politics, the causes they favored were the winning ones, the State offices were theirs to

HEROES OF PROGRESS

dispose of, and they earned for New York the title of the "Empire State" by making it the arbiter in two Presidential elections. Seward supported Henry Clay for President, opposed the annexation of Texas, and in 1848 used all his influence in favor of the election of President Taylor. Shortly after this he was himself elected to the United States Senate and took his seat in that great body of legislators.

He had won a reputation in his own State, and soon made himself prominent in the Senate, placing himself in the ranks of the most vigorous opponents of the system of slavery. Seward was not a specially attractive man personally. He is pictured to us as a slender, hook-nosed, grey-eyed, homely man, with red hair, a harsh and unpleasant voice, and a very awkward manner. But his speeches were at once graceful in delivery and strong in thought, his style clear and pure, and when Seward rose to speak the Senators sat still to listen. With all his defects of personality, he had the power to hold an audience. He was never addicted to coarse efforts at satire or buffoonery, but he had a keen, dry humor, delightful and telling, which still makes his speeches agreeable reading.

In the Senate he distinguished himself by certain striking phrases which took hold of the public fancy and became campaign cries in later political contests. Thus, in the debate on the admission of California to the Union, he said: "The Constitution devotes the national domain to the Union, to justice, to defence, to welfare, and to liberty. But there is a higher law than the Constitution, which regulates our authority over the domain, and devotes it to the same noble purposes."

This speech was widely read and much talked of,

and its phrase, "a higher law," took hold strongly upon the popular mind. It was everywhere repeated, and the doctrine of the "higher law" became one of the potent influences of the times. Another phrase which struck the public fancy was that of the "irrepressible conflict," which could end only by making the country all free or all slave. He had in some degree the gift of prophecy.

Seward as a Senator made himself one of the great forces of the time. He was one of the organizers of the Republican party, and a strenuous opponent throughout of the spread of slavery into the territories. As such he had a marked share in bringing on the "irrepressible conflict" which he foresaw, and in 1860 was so plainly the leader of the Republican party that he was widely looked upon as the logical candidate for the Presidency. He fully expected it himself, and was bitterly disappointed when the voice of the convention was given for Abraham Lincoln. Several causes led to this—local prejudice, personal enmity to Seward, the question of availability, and, perhaps strongest of all, the opposition of his old associate, Horace Greeley, who preferred Lincoln, and threw the powerful influence of the *Tribune* in his favor.

However deeply Seward may have been disappointed, he did not let it openly appear, but worked earnestly for the success of his party, aiding the election of Lincoln by a series of powerful speeches which vigorously presented the anti-slavery side of the contest. After Lincoln's election, he did his utmost to check treasonable designs in Buchanan's cabinet, and made a very able speech against disunion.

It was the prominence of Seward and his declared policy that induced President Lincoln to select him as his Secretary of State, and thus gave him the opportunity to make himself famous by his wise and skillful management of the foreign affairs of the country during the trying period of the Civil War. Various questions arose that demanded the highest statesmanship in the Secretary, in some of which a man of less discretion than Seward might have plunged the country into a foreign war.

It must be said that in all these questions President Lincoln had a voice, and often a controlling one. It is matter of common opinion that when Seward accepted the position of Secretary of State he looked upon himself as the virtual master of affairs. He had a degree of contempt for the awkward, uncultured, inexperienced man who had been put in the Presidential chair, and expected to pose as the "power behind the throne," who would be able to manage and control the new man from the West, keeping him from doing harm.

He soon found himself mistaken. In his first attempts to handle Lincoln he found himself "up against a stone wall." He was taught that Lincoln had a mind and a will of his own, and knew precisely where he was and what he was doing. He was willing to take advice, but preferred to make his final decisions for himself, and Seward soon fell into his true place, that of the President's adviser. He had enough to do in managing Europe during the Civil War. Urgent and perilous question arose, some of them with no precedent to aid in their settlement, but Seward rose in the level of his duties, and showed himself as great in the Cabinet as he had been in the Senate. It has been said that during the four years of war "his brain was pitted against all Europe and always won." Perhaps this is an exaggerated view, but he certainly showed himself a statesman of unusual acuteness and ability.

The most critical question with which he had to deal was that of the seizure by an American war-vessel of two Confederate commissioners from the English mail-steamer "Trent," and the bringing them into a Northern port as prisoners of war. The authorities of Great Britain were furious and made more than threats of war, for they sent troops and war-ships to Canada and demanded in harsh terms that the commissioners should be given up to them. They were turning the tables on us, for in 1812 the United States had declared war against Great Britain for a similar affront, though a far more aggravated one.

What was Seward to do? The whole North was in a flame of patriotism. Everywhere Captain Wilkes was praised for seizing the commissioners, and the administration was called on to sustain his act. Seward had a very awkward affair to handle, but he handled it very judiciously. The United States had never admitted the right of search of vessels on the high seas, and on this basis the administration admitted that Captain Wilkes had done wrong, and agreed to give up the men. But it took the opportunity to rap England shrewdly on the knuckles and remind that country that it had done the same thing hundreds of times before the War of 1812, and had never acknowledged that it had no right to do so.

As for the people of the North, they did not accept placidly this settlement of the case. There was a wide feeling that Great Britain had taken an unfair advantage of this country by threatening it when its hands were tied by a war at home. The show of unfriendliness was not soon forgotten. It was only one case among many. The result was a bitter feeling against the British nation that took years to die away.

We have already told how, soon after the war ended, President Lincoln was murdered and his great Secretary narrowly escaped death. Seward continued as Secretary of State under President Johnson, the remainder of his career being marked by two important events. While Great Britain had taken advantage of the trouble in America in one way, France did so in another, Napoleon III. taking the opportunity to invade Mexico and put a monarch of his own choice upon the throne. Seward protested against this at the time, and as soon as the war was over he plainly advised the French emperor to take his troops away from Mexico if he did not want them driven out by our Civil War veterns. Napoleon III. meekly obeyed orders. He saw that he had made a mistake.

The other event was the purchase of Alaska from Russia. By this purchase our country obtained for a few millions of dollars a territory which has already been worth hundreds of millions of dollars to us. Mr. Seward was throughout an earnest, honest, and upright man. He was always ready to help the poor or the unfortunate, and to do his duty by his clients, and he took the side of danger boldly when, in 1846, he defended two negro murderers against whom a bitter mob spirit had been aroused. He at that time, moved by the feeling against him, expressed the hope that some one might carve on his tombstone the words, "He was faithful." These are the words to be seen on his tomb in Auburn Cemetery, where he was interred after his death on the 10th of October, 1872.

JAMES G. BLAINE, THE PLUMED KNIGHT OF REPUBLICANISM

It was a memorable scene that took place in the Republican National Convention of 1876, when Robert G. Ingersoll, an orator of skill and power, rose to present the name of James G. Blaine as a candidate for the Presidency. Referring to Blaine's brilliant attack on those who had accused him of wrongdoing, the orator said:

"Like an armed warrior, like a plumed knight, James G. Blaine marched down the halls of the American Congress and threw his shining lance full and fair against the brazen forehead of the defamers of his country and the maligners of his honor. For the Republican party to desert this gallant leader now is as though an army should desert their general upon the field of battle."

From this speech Blaine became known as the "Plumed Knight," a title of honor that clung to him as long as he lived. At that time he had been in Congress for thirteen years, having entered it in 1863, in the very heat of the Civil War.

Blaine was a Pennsylvanian by birth, though for most of his life he was a citizen of Maine. He was long known as the "Man from Maine," as Henry Clay, the Virginian, with whom he was often compared, was known as the "Man from Kentucky." But Blaine's birthplace was in Washington County, Pennsylvania, where he was born on January 31, 1830, and lived until his days of manhood.

When about eleven years of age young Blaine was sent to the home of his uncle, Thomas Ewing, then Secretary of the Treasury, at Lancaster, Ohio. William T. Sherman, the great general of later times, had lived with Mr. Ewing a few years before. His house was frequented by statesmen and politicians, and during the year or two that the boy stayed there the conversation he heard must have been excellent early training for his future career. He returned home in 1843, and entered Washington College, where he made a good mark as a scholar, always showing up well in his classes.

He preferred logic and mathematics, though history and literature were favorite studies, and his memory was so fine that it is said he could repeat from recollection many of the chapters in " Plutarch's Lives." As another example of his retentive memory, it is said that when anxious to be elected president of the literary society of the college, he made himself familiar with the whole of " Cushing's Manual " in one evening, that he might know the rules of order in acting as president. He early made himself a leader among the college boys, and in debate he stood at their head. The great power which he was afterwards to show as an orator was thus early displayed.

Blaine's first position in life was as a teacher in the Western Military Institute, at Blue Lick Springs, Kentucky. Here he did very well as a young teacher, making himself highly popular with the boys, with whom he was friendly and confidential from the first. He knew the whole of them by name, and knew also in what each of them was weak or strong. He is said to have been at this time a thin, handsome, earnest young man, with the same fascinating manners that remained with him throughout his life.

At this place Blaine met a young lady from Maine, named Harriet Stanwood, whom he soon afterwards married. He returned to Pennsylvania in 1851, when twenty-one years of age, and there obtained a position as teacher of science and literature in the Institution for the Blind at Philadelphia.

For two years he remained there, engaged in teaching the blind, and then, at the solicitation of his wife, who wished to return to her native State, he left Pennsylvania for Maine. He made Augusta his home, and from teaching turned to oratory and editorship, as fields better fitted to win him a successful career. He became in 1854 part owner of a newspaper, the *Kennebec Journal,* on which he served as editor, writing in a trenchant style that soon made itself felt. The *Journal* was one of the organs of the Whig party, and already had considerable influence. Its new editor speedily added to this, and in a few years became a leading spirit in Maine politics.

When the Whig party went to pieces, Blaine took an active part in organizing in Maine the new Republican party. He entered into this with the energy of youth and conviction. His life in Kentucky had made him an enemy of the slave system, and he engaged ardently in the conflict between freedom and slavery, which was now growing intense. His clear discussion of this vital subject added greatly to the influence of his paper and his personal standing in the party.

He had not yet become widely known as a public speaker, but was soon to make his mark. In 1856 the new Republican party held its first national convention at Philadelphia. Blaine, as one of the party leaders in Maine, was sent as a delegate, and on his return reported the proceedings of the convention at a public meeting. It was his first appearance before a large audience, and he began to speak in a timid and hesitating way. But as he warmed up he grew confident and broke out into fervid speech, and before he ended had proved his native power in oratory and won himself a sure place upon the rostrum.

He began the real work of his life, that in which he was to become eminent, in 1858, as a member of the legislature of Maine. Here he soon distinguished himself as a hard worker and fine speaker, and during two of his three years there served as Speaker of the House, doing so in an impartial and dignified manner that won him great popularity in the State.

The second national convention of the Republican party, that memorable Chicago meeting which nominated Abraham Lincoln for the Presidency, was held in 1860, and as before Mr. Blaine attended it as a delegate. On his return he plunged ardently into the campaign for Lincoln's election, speaking with such warm eloquence that he was called for on all sides. "Send us Blaine!" was the appeal of every committee that wanted a speaker. He had changed his place of residence to Portland and became editor of the *Portland Advertiser*.

Blaine was growing too important to be buried in a State legislature, and in 1862 he was elected to Congress, in which he was to remain during much of his later life. A believer in Lincoln, and his earnest supporter, he became a confidential friend and adviser of the great War President, worked vigorously for his re-election in 1864, and was a sincere mourner of him after his terrible death.

He continued a member of the House during the stormy reconstruction period following the Civil War, and was one of the most prominent among those in opposition to President Johnson. An expert in political matters and management, and a ready and fearless debater, he worked his way steadily to positions on important committees, and became a prominent factor in all the important legislation of the time. Brilliant and impulsive, with a wonderful memory of persons, facts, and faces, he was rapidly surging to the head, and when Thaddeus Stevens died took his place as the Republican leader of the House. In 1869, after Schuyler Colfax, the Speaker, was made Vice-President, Blaine was chosen Speaker, and highly distinguished himself in this capacity by his thorough knowledge of parliamentary rules, his firmness, quickness, and impressive manner in the chair.

He was looked upon as one of the great speakers of the House, always courteous and fair and especially rapid in the discharge of his duties. It was one of the sights of the times for visitors to see the rapidity and accuracy with which Speaker Blaine counted a standing House for the ayes and noes. He continued in this post for three terms, but in 1875 the Democrats gained a majority in the House for the first time after 1860, and his career as Speaker came to an end.

During the period of his Speakership the long dominance of the Republican party had brought many men of doubtful integrity to the front, and various scandals were developed within Grant's second term. This was the period of the "Credit Mobilier," the "Whisky Ring," and other frauds, and in the investigation that followed there was hardly a man in Congress who was not accused of being in some way implicated in these shady transactions. Blaine was too prominent to escape. Several charges were brought against him, the severest being that he had been bribed with a gift of Little Rock and Fort Smith Railroad bonds. All these charges he disproved in an indignant speech on the floor of the House, in which he showed that he had bought and paid for the bonds and had lost $20,000 by the transaction. After showing the falsity of the charge against him, he exclaimed:

"Having now noticed the two charges that have been so extensively circulated, I shall refrain from calling the attention of the House to any others that may be invented. To quote the language of another, 'I do not propose to make my public life a perpetual and uncomfortable flea-hunt, in the vain effort to run down stories which have no basis in truth, which are usually anonymous, and whose total refutation brings no punishment to those who have been guilty of originating them.'"

This was the speech to which Ingersoll referred when he spoke of Blaine as a "plumed knight" in the Republican National Convention of 1876. But the charges hurt him before the convention, and Hayes was nominated by 384 votes, Blaine receiving 351. On every ballot but the last he had received the highest number of votes, though not a majority of all the candidates. In the same year Blaine was appointed by the Governor of Maine to the United States Senate to fill a vacancy, and in the subsequent meeting of the legislature was unanimously elected. While this was a great compliment, the Senate was not well suited to his energetic and vehement type of oratory, yet he continued to debate party questions urgently and to perform diligent committee work.

When the nominating convention of 1880 came round Blaine was again a leading candidate, but General

Grant and John Sherman were also strongly sustained, and a deadlock ensued which was only broken by the selection of a "dark horse" candidate in General Garfield, who was nominated in spite of his earnest protests. On taking his seat, the new President at once called upon Blaine to fill the chief place in his Cabinet as Secretary of State.

It was a position for which he was well fitted, but the assassin's bullet that struck down the President made his term in this office very brief. While the lamented Garfield lay slowly dying, Blaine performed all the duties of his office. When the sad drama closed at the grave of Garfield in Cleveland, Blaine was much the worse for his arduous duties. He remained in the Cabinet long enough to invite all the American republics to join in a Peace Congress at Washington, but soon after resigned and retired to private life.

On the 27th of February, 1882, he delivered in the hall of the House of Representatives one of the greatest orations of his life, his pathetic eulogy of the late President, before an audience of the most distinguished character. He was listened to with breathless attention as he bore touching tribute to the virtues and abilities of his dead friend, and ended with a passage of sublime beauty which held the audience spellbound with approval and admiration. A solemn hush fell upon the assembly as these impressive words were spoken, and all present felt that they had listened to one of the greatest oratorical efforts of history.

When, in 1884, another national convention was held, it was the general feeling that Blaine's nomination was a sure conclusion. So it proved; he was triumphantly nominated, and the convention adjourned. He had risen from the humble station of an obscure editorship to the choice of one of the great parties of the country, the party which had been triumphant in every Presidential election since 1860. Blaine had every reason to look for election. His position was in a measure like that of Henry Clay in 1844, but a far more virulent personal attack was made upon him than any one thought of bringing against Clay. In the end, however, a trivial incident led to his defeat. In the last week of the campaign he was visited at his hotel in New York by a delegation of clergymen, of whom the Rev. Dr. Burchard was the spokesman. The latter, after some appropriate words, made the glaring mistake of his life, saying: " We are Republicans, and don't propose to leave our party and identify ourselves with the party whose antecedents have been Rum, Romanism, and Rebellion."

This alliteration of the " three R's " defeated Blaine. The Democrats took quick advantage of it, circulating widely the scandal that Blaine was a declared enemy of the Roman Catholic Church. The effect was fatal. Enough votes were lost in New York State to give a Democratic majority of about one thousand votes. Elsewhere the election was so close as to give New York the casting vote, and thus, because an insignificant clergyman pleased himself by getting off what he thought a telling phrase, Blaine's hopes of the Presidency went down in defeat.

During the administration of President Cleveland Mr. Blaine remained in private life, part of his time being spent in European travel, part in literary work. It was during this interval that he wrote his highly valuable " Twenty Years in Congress," a work which admirably supplements Benton's " Thirty Years' View." He made up his mind not to run again for the Presidency, and in 1888 positively declined a nomination. As a consequence, Benjamin Harrison was nominated, and Blaine resumed under him his old office of Secretary of State. One of the most important things done by him was to bring about that meeting of the American republics which he had worked for in 1881. This conference, called the Pan American, was held in 1889, and was an important step in the interest of American unity. Illness obliged him to resign from the Cabinet in 1892, and he died January 27, 1893.

Thus passed away one of America's greatest legislators. Chauncey M. Depew has said of him: "He will stand in our history as the ablest parliamentarian and most skilful debater of our Congressional history. He had an unusual combination of boundless audacity with infinite tact. No man during his active career disputed with him his hold upon the popular imagination and his leadership of his party. He has left no successor who possesses, in any degree such as he possessed it, the affection and the confidence of his followers."

HORACE GREELEY, THE PREMIER OF AMERICAN EDITORS

THE United States has been a nest of able editors, who have lifted the art of the journalist to so high a level that the American newspaper has no equal in the world in enterprise and picturesque presentation of news. There are many who have helped to make it what it is, America's greatest lever of progress. Beginning with Benjamin Franklin, editors of genius have been numerous. Lack of space prevents us from mentioning many who became famous in this field, and we must confine ourselves to Horace Greeley, the ablest and the most widely known of them all.

No one who saw Horace Greeley as a boy could have dreamed that this awkward and backward lad, with his tow-colored hair, his shabby and ill-fitting clothes, his piping and whining voice, could ever become a man of note. But his face bore the marks of intellect, and no one could talk with him long without discovering that he had an alert and intelligent mind, amply supplied with facts, for he had read every book upon which he could lay his hands and had a memory which retained all of value that came into it. He was a thinker, too, that was evident; not alone a man of facts, but of original opinions as well. Such was the boy who was destined to make himself the most famous figure in American journalism.

Horace Greeley was born at Amherst, New Hamshire, February 3, 1811. His father was a poor farmer, who moved to Vermont in 1821, and in 1830 to a farm of wild, new-cleared land in western Pennsylvania, building a log-cabin there, but finding it so hard to make a living that Horace felt obliged to set out and shift for himself.

He had learned the art of printing at East Poultney, Vermont, and worked there from 1826 to 1830, picking up during this time some valuable knowledge of party politics. His opportunities for education had been poor. Some of the leading men of the town, seeing his quickness of mind and thirst for knowledge, offered to pay his expenses through college, but his parents refused. They either were not willing to accept what might look like charity or could not spare his help as a bread-winner. But in spite of this the boy managed to learn a good deal at home, which he added to by such chances as presented themselves in a little country printing office. Certainly, while there was little in his pocket, when he set out late in 1830 to seek his fortune in the world, there was much in his mind.

Let us follow the boy in his wanderings. A tall and awkward youth, ill fitted with homespun clothes, lacking attractiveness of appearance and grace of address, his chances seemed poor. Luckily for him, one of the men on the Erie *Gazette* had been laid off for some reason, and young Greeley found there an opening awaiting him. He soon proved that he knew well how to set type, and showed excellent qualities of character that brought everybody in the office to look on him with respect. But in seven months the absent hand came back and there was no longer room for his substitute, so Greely had to set out on his travels again.

He had worked hard and lived cheaply, but not for his own benefit, for he kept only fifteen dollars of his wages, and sent all that was left—about one hundred and twenty dollars—to help his father in his needs. From Erie he made his way to New York, several hundred miles distant, travelling now on foot and now by canal, and spending so little on the way that when, one summer day in 1831, he walked into the great city, ten of his fifteen dollars were left.

He knew nobody in New York, and his shabby, awkward, and retiring aspect was not calculated to help him to a place. Getting a very cheap boarding house, he set out to look for work. Nobody would have him. All printing offices were full, or doubt was felt of the ability of this tow-haired country lad, who knew nothing of the art of pushing himself.

A week passed and he began to despair. Then his landlord, who liked the youth, spoke to a friend about him and of his fruitless search for work. The friend replied: "Tell him to try No. 85 Chatham Street; they want printers there." The next morning Horace was on hand before the doors were opened, and fell into conversation with one of the first men who came. This man afterwards said, "I saw that he was an honest, good young man, and, being a Vermonter myself, I determined to help him if I could."

Horace's new acquaintance spoke in his favor to the foreman; the latter looked him over doubtfully, not believing that a country-trained typesetter could be fit for the difficult work they were engaged on, a polyglot Testament; finally he agreed to give him a chance. The new hand worked steadily all day, and at night showed the foreman a printer's proof of his work. It proved to be the best day's work—in quantity and correctness—done in the office that day, and Horace was definitely engaged.

He worked for more than a year in this office. The wages were not high, and the bulk of it went to his father to help him in paying for his farm. But the young printer saved a little for himself. He was ambitious. He had no idea of keeping at the bottom of affairs. Those were the days in which the old style of newspaper was passing away and the modern newspaper coming into being, and Greeley, feeling that he had the ability to edit and conduct a paper, grew anxious to branch out into that broad field of enterprise.

He began his editorial career by joining Francis Storey in issuing the *Morning Post,* the first daily penny paper ever published. It was very ably handled, but the innovation did not take and the paper lived only a few weeks. Its ambitious editor saved some more money and was soon in the saddle again. The next year, 1834, he founded, as head of the firm of Greeley & Co., the *New Yorker,* a weekly literary paper, and at that time the best of its kind in the country. And Horace Greeley had most to do with making it such.

The next year another of the aspiring New York newspaper men, James Gordon Bennett, recognizing the ability that lay behind the *New Yorker,* came to its editor and asked him to join in a new enterprise, a one-cent paper to be called the *Herald.* Greeley knew Bennett to be a clever and progressive journalist, but his experience with the *Morning Post* had made him cautious. " How much money have you?" he asked. " Five hundred dollars," was the answer. " It isn't enough. I won't go in with you, for I don't think you can succeed."

Everybody knows that the *Herald* did succeed, despite the handful of money with which it was started, but Greeley did well in keeping out of it, for it is not likely that his views and those of Bennett would have agreed. He was a man born to be at the head of a great journal, not to drive in an ill-matched team.

Greeley kept on with the *New Yorker*. It was not profitable, but it kept afloat for seven years. During one year, 1838-39, he also edited the *Jeffersonian*, a weekly Whig paper, and in 1840 started the *Log Cabin*, a spirited little weekly which supported Harrison for President, was ably handled, and became so popular as to gain a circulation of over 80,000. It was an ephemeral sheet, issued for the campaign in the interest of Thurlow Weed, but it gave Greeley a great reputation in all parts of the country as an able writer and a zealous politician.

Politically, Greeley had cast his lot with the Whigs, and was a strenuous advocate of their views and those of the succeeding Republicans throughout his life. So far his business ambition had led him into several journalistic enterprises which had brought him into notice but not made him money. The *Herald*, which he had refused to take part in, was becoming a notable success. The *Sun* was also in the field and making its way. Greeley felt that it was time he was launching out with the paper he had long held in mind. He had married in 1836 a Miss Cheney, of North Carolina. Years and family cares were creeping upon him. Delay was dangerous, and in the last number of the *Log Cabin* he announced that a new daily paper, Whig in politics, was about to appear. On April 10, 1841, the *Daily Tribune* was launched, as a one-cent newspaper, with Horace Greeley as its editor and proprietor, Henry J. Raymond, afterwards editor of the New York

Times, as its sub-editor. It was fortunate in obtaining for business manager Thomas McElrath, an able and experienced financier. Greeley himself lacked financial judgment, and much of the success of the *Tribune* was due to Mr. McElrath.

It was Greeley's fixed purpose, while working for the success of his party, to make his paper one that should be an intellectual and moral aid to its readers. It was to sail in a channel of its own on the sea of public opinion, with his hand steadily at the helm. The first edition of five thousand copies could hardly be given away, but there was a new tone in the paper that quickly attracted attention, readers came to it rapidly, and before two months an edition of eleven thousand was called for, while its four columns of advertisements had increased to thirteen. It was a quick and big success, and began from the very start that career of journalistic good fortune which it has since maintained.

Its purpose was not like that of the *Herald.* The latter set out to mirror in its columns the world's daily events. The *Tribune* had a different aim. It was to be a storehouse of opinions, a moulder of thought, a leader of the public mind, and in this field Horace Greeley proved himself unsurpassed. His views on political subjects came to be looked for and read with avidity, and its scope spread out to cover science, literature, the drama, and all the fields of thought. Himself possessed of excellent literary taste, he drew to the *Tribune* many of the best editors, reporters, and critics to be had, and thousands came to look for it daily as their exponent of opinion on all subjects of interest.

Its moral tone was kept as high as its intellectual. It warmly supported all projects of reform and philanthropy. One of its great aims was to promote the good and prevent the bad. Every movement designed to aid the struggling poor was earnestly seconded. The various "isms" of the day were supported in its columns, despite the ridicule which its rivals cast upon it. Temperance, women's rights, abolition of capital punishment, the uplifting of the poor, were among Greeley's "isms," and he supported every movement which seemed to him to tend towards right and justice.

But, first and foremost, the *Tribune* was a political paper. While the Whig party lasted it fought its battles strongly and shrewdly, Greeley himself claiming to be the junior partner of the great Whig firm of politicians, " Seward, Weed, and Greeley." The Republican party owed its existence largely to the powerful influence of the *Tribune*. It fought slavery with all its strength until slavery ended, and from its origin remained one of the ablest advocates of a protective tariff.

Mr. Greeley was elected to Congress in 1848, and during his life filled various political offices. But it was not in these fields he shone. His best field of effort was in the editorial columns of his paper, in which for many years he continued to mould and direct the opinions of his readers. In 1850 he published " Hints towards Reforms," made up of lectures delivered at various times and places, a work which led Parton to say: " His subject is ever the same; the object of his public life is single. It is the *Emancipation of Labor*, its emancipation from ignorance, vice, servitude, and poverty."

At the end of the Civil War he was in favor of universal amnesty and universal suffrage, and in 1867 he offered himself as bail for Jefferson Davis, then in prison, an act for which many of his own party severely condemned him. But Greeley deprecated revenge on the defeated; he was always governed by his conceptions of right, and never hesitated, for fear of adverse criticism, in adopting the course which appealed to him as the just one.

Aside from the immense labors of his editorial pen, he was the author of two works, " The American Conflict," a history, from his point of view, of the Civil War, and " Recollections of a Busy Life," a work of much biographical interest.

The *Tribune,* begun as a small, one-cent sheet, grew in size and price as time went on. Important as it was, the *Weekly Tribune* was perhaps still more important, from its able summing up of events and its fine literary merit. The circulation of these papers was by no means local. They made their way into all parts of the land, and to-day their great influence persists. Though Greeley has gone, his spirit prevails in their pages.

That Greeley was always wise or correct, not even his strongest partisan would maintain. No man ever is. But he had the courage to sustain any view which he thought right, and to support an unpopular cause which appealed to him, no matter what his political friends might say. No doubt he made many mistakes; no doubt haste or strong feeling often led him astray. But he meant right through all; he was not working from the point of view of the office-seekers, but to secure the best good of his fellow-men; whether right or wrong, he discussed all the questions of the day with a vigor and intelligence that made his opinions always of value, and the high moral purpose that always moved him won him the respect and esteem of many of his political opponents.

The close of Greeley's career was a sad one. He, the champion of Republicanism, permitted his name to be used as the Democratic candidate for President in 1872, in a hopeless contest against General Grant. That he would be defeated was almost a foregone conclusion. But what hurt him more than defeat was the accusation, by friends and enemies alike, that he was disloyal to his party and unprincipled in his act, and that, moved by his ambition to be President, he had committed dishonorable offences. To the depression caused by this came that due to the severe illness and death of his wife. The two combined seem to have sapped his vitality, and shortly after the announcement of his defeat he died, on November 29, 1872.

"It was not the Presidential defeat, but the cruel impeachment of his integrity by old friends, that wounded his spirit past all healing." His death changed the current of opinion. Many who had blamed him now mourned him, and it became apparent how deep a hold he had taken upon the admiration and esteem of the American people. He had made a great mark as a journalist—few have reached his level in this—and he had also made as great a mark as a moralist. To quote again, he was "one whose name will live long after many writers and statesmen of greater pretensions are forgotten."

JOHN ERICSSON, THE INVENTOR OF THE "MONITOR"

Our great men have not all been of American birth. Europe has sent us many men who became among the best of American citizens and the ablest and most useful dwellers upon our soil. One of these, a man of high distinction in the field of invention, was John Ericsson, born in Langbanshyttan, Sweden, July 31, 1803. He came to America in 1839, when thirty-six years of age, after having spent thirteen years in England, where he built in 1829 a locomotive that ran thirty miles an hour, and about 1833 exhibited a caloric engine. His most important work there was the application of the screw or propeller to steam navigation, an invention which in time fairly drove the paddle-wheel from the seas. When he reached the shores of America it was as a distinguished inventor. He was to spend here fifty years of his life, engaged in similar labors of many kinds.

It was the invention of the propeller, now almost universally used on steam vessels, that brought Ericsson to America. He offered this to England, but the British Admiralty, with the blindness which that body has often shown, would have nothing to do with the new-fangled notion, and the disgusted Swede crossed the ocean in search of a more wide-awake government.

He found the Americans far more open to new ideas, and was quickly set to work in building a warship, the steamer "Princeton," called by some one "a gimcrack of sundry inventions." It was the first steam vessel

BATTLE OF THE MONITOR AND THE MERRIMAC

that had her engines and boilers entirely below the water line, and the first in which the screw-propeller took the place of Fulton's paddle-wheels. The "Princeton" had many other new contrivances, connected with her furnaces, her guns, her smoke-stack, etc., and proved a great success in her trial trip. The propeller in especial attracted the attention of engineers, and before many years made a revolution in steam-ship building.

Unfortunately, Ericsson's new ship, despite its good beginning, had a sad ending. The first display of its powers was hardly over when a terrible accident happened to a distinguished party that was visiting it. The "Peacemaker," one of its great guns, burst in firing and scattered its iron fragments among the guests. Two of the Secretaries of President Tyler's Cabinet, a commodore, and several other persons were killed by the explosion.

This accident proved for the time fatal to Ericsson's credit with the Government. The gun that burst was an experiment in large cannon with which he had nothing to do, but it put an end to his government work for many years. It was not until the Civil War began that his abilities were again called into service. The idea of protecting warships with iron bars or plates had now been devised, and the South was prompt to make use of this idea, raising the sunken "Merrimac" in Norfolk harbor with the purpose of covering it with iron.

Ericsson, ever fertile in new schemes, devised a plan of his own, of a vessel that not only should be iron-clad, but should be sunk so deeply in the water as to leave only its gun turrets as a mark for hostile shot. The Government badly needed a powerful type of war-vessel, but did not take kindly to Ericsson's scheme, and he had great difficulty in obtaining an order from the Navy Department. It came at length, however, and he began work on his afterward-famous " Monitor," the " cheesebox on a raft " as it was derisively termed.

When he fairly began work on it haste was needed, for it was known that the " Merrimac " was being rapidly changed into an iron-clad, and the fear was felt that it might do immense damage unless a vessel of equal strength was ready to meet it. Not only the fleet in Hampton Roads might be destroyed, but the Potomac might be entered and Washington bombarded by this dreaded monster. As a result, work was pressed on the " Monitor," it was begun and finished within one hundred days, and it steamed its way down to Hampton Roads, reaching there on the night of the 8th of March, 1862, shortly after the " Merrimac " had appeared and made havoc among the wooden vessels of the fleet.

All readers of American history know what followed, of the terrible battle between the iron monsters, and of the withdrawal of the " Merrimac," leaving the little " Monitor " master of the field. After that Ericsson was kept busy building monitors, as all vessels of this type have since been called, and the era of the iron-clad warship was fairly inaugurated. To him is due the credit of building the first successful vessel of this kind.

Ericsson had now reached a high standing as an inventor. His propeller and his iron-clad were both great conceptions. In addition he spent many years upon a caloric engine, in which hot air was to take the place of steam. His caloric ship, the " Ericsson," made a successful trip from New York to Washington in 1851. It cost him and others large sums of money, but it mainly served to prove that hot-air engines of large size were much less powerful than those worked by steam. Yet the caloric engine is very useful where a small amount of power is needed, and many of them are in use at the present day.

Captain Ericsson gave much of his time in later years to inventing torpedoes and other devices for submarine warfare. In 1881 the "Destroyer," a vessel which was to fire projectiles containing 300 pounds of gun cotton into an enemy's vessel below the armor line, was tried, but its success was not sufficient to satisfy the Navy Department. In his later years he gave much of his time and ingenuity to the building of a solar motor, for use on the great sandy plains of rainless regions, where the sun gives out vast stores of heat which might be made of service to man. He died before he had perfected this machine, but since his death solar motors of much usefulness have been made. They are in use in Southern California and other hot and dry regions.

As may be seen, Captain Ericsson was an inventor of great versatility and fine powers. We have spoken here only of his most important inventions, but he made many others. In the thirteen years he spent in England, before coming to the United States, his inventions were numerous, most of them having something to do with power engines. One of these, which was quite a novelty, was the first steam fire-engine ever tried. This was used, to the great surprise of the Londoners, on a fire at the Argyle Rooms in 1829. As was said at the time, it was "the first time that fire was ever put out by the mechanical power of fire."

The inventions and improvements made by Captain Ericsson were far too numerous to be mentioned here. His studies and experiments added largely to the world's knowledge of the proper use of steam and other power agents. The old house on Beech Street, New York, where he lived and worked for many years, was the home of many inventions and experiments, to which he gave most of his time every day. His work was honored and his fame spread all over the world, and many were the learned and honorary titles conferred upon him by the governments and the scientific bodies of Europe and America. He died in New York, March 8, 1889.

THOMAS A. EDISON, THE WIZARD OF INVENTION

THERE are men to whom the idea of invention comes from seeing some great need. There are others with whom the faculty of invention is born, and who could scarcely take up a tea-cup without thinking of inventing a better handle for it. Such a one was the clever and enterprising little lad who, eager to experiment in telegraphy, made a line of stove wire, with bottles for insulators, wound the wire for his electro-magnets with rags, and tried to obtain electricity for his current by rubbing the cat's back. The effort was a failure but it showed the trend of his mind and the ingenuity of his ideas.

This boy, Thomas Alva Edison, born at Milan, Ohio, February 11, 1854, was the son of a poor man, a village jack-of-all-trades, who soon afterwards moved to Port Huron, Michigan. He could not, or would not, give his son any regular schooling, the boy's school-life being only two months long. What else he learned was given him by his mother at home, or gained through his insatiable thirst for knowledge. What can we think of a boy who was reading the histories of Gibbon and Hume at ten years of age, and poring over books of chemistry before he could pronounce the long names he found there? Before he was fifteen he had read all the important works in the Detroit public library and made a serious attempt to read the whole library through. Nothing could keep a boy like that from gaining an education.

Young Edison had to begin work early. At twelve years of age he was a newsboy on the Grand Trunk Railway. With some of the money he earned he began experimenting with chemistry, setting up a laboratory in an empty corner of the baggage car. One day, in his absence, a bottle of phosphorus which he had was upset and broken, setting the car on fire. When the baggage-master found out what was the trouble he kicked the apparatus out of the car and gave the youthful chemist a warm piece of his mind.

Later on, while he was still railroading, a Chicago publisher gave him a lot of worn-out type, and the enterprising boy was soon publishing, with several assistants, a paper of his own, called *The Grand Trunk Herald,* devoted to railroad items. It was the first of its kind ever known. The Civil War was now going on, and one day the alert newsboy persuaded a telegraph operator at Chicago to send word of the great battle of Shiloh to the principal stations along the road. Edison loaded himself up with papers and found crowds at every station eager to buy them at a high price, netting a splendid profit on his venture.

This was his first introduction to the advantages of telegraphy. He now wanted to know something about that, as he did about everything else, and soon got his opportunity by saving the child of a telegraph operator from being killed by a railroad train. The father, grateful to the boy, taught him the art of sending messages, and Edison, in his usual fashion of experimenting, soon had wires and batteries rigged up in his home at Port Huron and practised until he was quite skilful.

His service as a telegrapher began at Indianapolis, when he was eighteen years old. While here he made

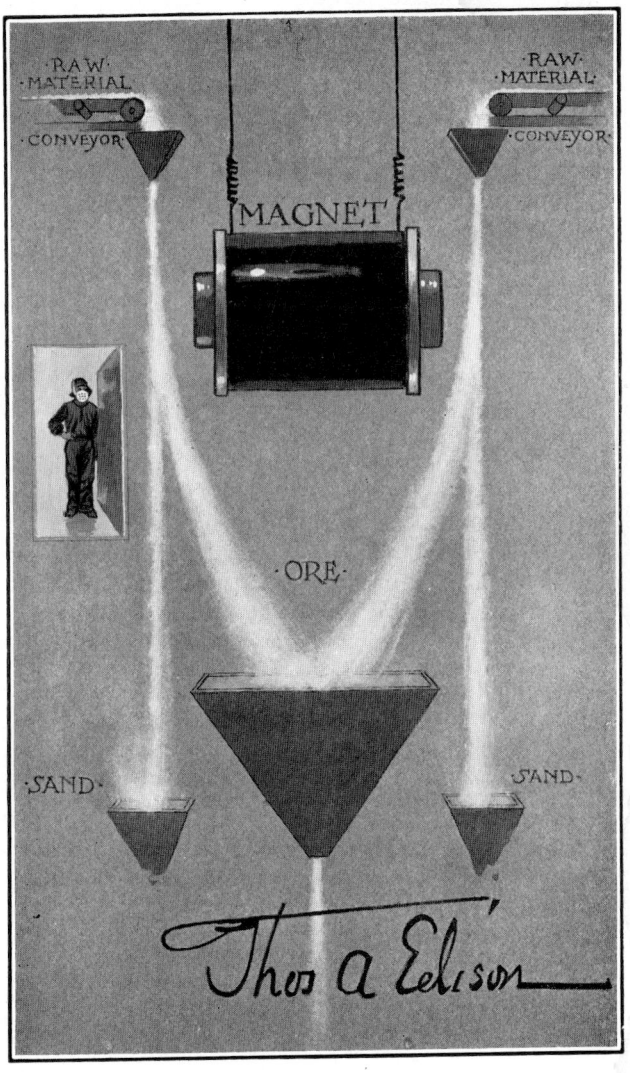

EDISON'S MAGNETIC ORE SEPARATOR
(From original sketch by the inventor)

HEROES OF PROGRESS 303

his first invention, this being an automatic register for receiving messages and transferring them to another wire. In this device lay the germ of the phonograph, the triumph of his later life. Constantly practising, Edison became very expert and swift as an operator, as usual, however, giving all his spare hours to his favorite study of chemistry. On one occasion, when he was night operator, and had to show that he was wide awake by sending the word "six" every half hour to the superintendent, he found time to devote to his books and experiments by contriving a device that sent the signal automatically. Unluckily for him, his clever scheme was found out, and he lost his situation.

From Indianapolis he drifted eastward, getting positions here and there, and finally reaching Boston, then looked upon as one of the most important telegraph centres of the country. He got a position there, and, as everywhere else, managed to do some chemical experimenting in his off hours. A legend is told of his experience in the Boston office which is worth repeating, even if its absolute truth cannot be vouched for. It is said that the spruce Boston operators were amused at the countrified aspect of the young Westerner who had been installed at a wire in the office and decided to have some fun at the tyro's expense. They therefore got a very rapid operator in New York to send a message at lightning speed to the newcomer, thinking to set him utterly at sea. To their surprise, Edison took the message with ease, and sent back an answer in still more rapid style, confusing the New Yorker and decidedly getting the laugh on the conspirators. This is a good story, whether it is fact or fiction.

Edison's genius for invention was now turned towards telegraphy, and while in Boston he made one of the greatest of inventions in that line, that of duplex telegraphy—the sending of two messages at once over a single wire. On this he spent many hours of his spare time, making many failures, and finding success very difficult to reach. From this invention he afterwards developed that of quadruplex telegraphy, by which four messages could be sent at once over the same wire, two in each direction, without interference with one another.

It was about 1868 that Edison began to be known as an inventor. He had given up his position as an operator, and had tried in vain to make his duplex telegraph work between Rochester and Boston. This failure was a sore trial to the inventor, who made his way in a down-hearted mood to New York, where, after trying vainly to interest the telegraph companies in his inventions, he established himself as an expert in telegraphy, ready to do any odd jobs that offered. One day the indicator of the Gold and Stock Company broke down, and the electricians of the company made long and vain efforts to adjust it. Finally Edison, hearing of their difficulty, offered his services and his offer was accepted as a forlorn hope. He was not long in discovering the source of the trouble, and soon had the line in working order again. This established his reputation as an expert, and business began to come to him from all sides. In 1871 he became superintendent of the company.

The trouble with the indicator suggested to his mind a new device, the printing telegraph for gold and stock quotations, and before long he had a shop at work in Newark, New Jersey, for the manufacture of his new instrument, the "stock ticker," designed for reporting in brokers' offices the prices of stocks on the exchange. It has since come everywhere into use. Money now began to come in rapidly to the inventor, his shop turning out the stock tickers and other devices, for which a ready market was found, and telegraph companies employing him in researches aimed at further inventions. The young experimenter of the Grand Trunk Railway train was making his way.

It was not until 1872 that full success was gained with the duplex telegraph. The quadruplex came later, also the electric pen. The latter is a hollow needle, driven by electricity and working like a sewing machine needle, perforating and inking the lines of a message on a number of sheets of paper.

In 1876 Edison made the great venture of his life. He proposed thereafter to devote his time solely to the work of invention, especially in the line of the electric light, and his reputation as an inventor had now become so great that he had no difficulty in interesting a number of wealthy capitalists in the project, they to supply the money and he the brains. A shop was built and equipped at Menlo Park, New Jersey, and there his experiments in this new field of labor began. They have since been kept up in this and other directions, his inventions being fairly multitudinous in number.

The arc system of electric lighting had some years before been invented and was coming into use. It was to the incandescent system that Edison applied himself, seeking to produce a satisfactory lamp for houses and stores. He began by using platinum wires in a glass bulb, but soon sought a better and cheaper material. Carbon was at length selected as having the highest power of resistance to the current. To prevent its destruction by oxygen, the bulbs had to be exhausted of air as completely as possible. Carbon fibres were tried from a great number of materials, carbonized bamboo being finally chosen. This gave lamps good for at least six hundred hours.

One great difficulty experienced in the use of the incandescent light was that, when the light was subdivided between many burners, the extinction of one light affected all the others. Edison finally overcame this difficulty, so that any light on his circuit might be raised, lowered, or extinguished without affecting the others.

Edison was an indefatigable investigator; when actively at work upon an intricate problem he fairly forgot the need of eating and sleeping. At one time, when his printing telegraph for some reason refused to perform, he worked for sixty hours without rest, eating nothing but some crackers and cheese as he worked. On another occasion all the electric lamps at Menlo Park suddenly ceased to burn. The problem annoyed him. He worked at it incessantly for five days, taking no rest himself and giving his assistants none. At the end of that time he had to go to bed, leaving the difficulty unsolved. He was worn out with chagrin and weariness. For fifteen hours he had worked without eating a morsel, and was surprised when it was suggested to him that food was in order. The trouble, in the end, proved to be that the vacuum in the globes was not sufficient, and long experiment was needed to gain a more complete exhaustion of the air. In this, as in almost everything he tried, Edison succeeded.

Aside from the electric light, the Edison inventions have been very numerous. He has taken out some 500 patents and invented machines of the most extra-

HEROES OF PROGRESS 307

ordinary character. He has perhaps a hundred patents in connection with telegraphy, including the duplex, quadruplex, and sextuplex system. Among the most remarkable of his inventions relating to sound are the microphone, by which the faintest of sounds can be detected; the megaphone, by which ordinary sounds can be heard at great distances; the carbon telephone; and especially the phonograph, one of the most marvellous of instruments, by which the sounds of the human voice can be registered and kept for reproduction at a future time. This has been remarkably developed since its invention. His kinetoscope is a development of the zeotrope, in which a continuous picture is produced by a swift succession of instantaneous photographs, taken forty-six or more per second. It has also had a splendid development, yielding what is known as the living picture. For a time he devoted himself to the problem of obtaining the iron from the iron-bearing sands of New Jersey by aid of the magnet. Large works were built to apply this process, but without encouraging success in the way of profits.

As an inventor Edison may truly be named a wizard. The world has never known his equal. He has made invention a business, and by the aid of a large capital, trained assistants, and incessant application, has succeeded in adding remarkably to the mechanical devices possessed by the world. He is untiring and unconquerable. He never lets go of a possibility of invention until he has exhausted it. His workshop is unique. He has gathered there everything that can be used in his experiments, and all the leading scientific journals of the world are indexed ready for instant use. He is equipped for any experiment that may suggest itself. His mind is never at rest. He says, in relation to his contract to manufacture a large number of his "stock tickers" at his Newark shop: "I was a poor manufacturer, because I could not let well enough alone. My first impulse, upon taking in my hand any machine, from an egg-beater to an electric motor, is to seek a way of improving it. Therefore, as soon as I have finished a machine I am anxious to take it apart again in order to make an experiment. That is a costly mania for a manufacturer."

He is one of the busiest men of the world, constantly at work, constantly devising. One of his latest productions is an improved electric storage cell for automobiles. Of his inventions he says: "These are only trials, with which we may accomplish still greater wonders. The very fact that this century [the nineteenth] has accomplished so much in the way of invention makes it more than probable that the next century will do far greater things."

A rather tall, compactly-built man is the famous inventor, with a somewhat boyish, clean-shaven face, to which incessant thought is adding lines of premature age. He cares little about dress, and usually manages to have hands and clothes stained with oil and chemicals. Somewhat deaf, he watches his visitor's lips closely to catch what he is saying. Kind and genial in disposition, he is patient in explaining his methods and results to inquiring visitors. On the whole, Thomas A. Edison is the most marvellous example of the American genius for invention.

FRANCES E. WILLARD, THE WOMEN'S TEMPERANCE LEADER

It was in the year 1873 that the women of America first became active in the war against drunkenness, which had been going on in this country, in the hands of men, for half a century before. A "woman's crusade" broke out in Ohio in that year and spread like a consuming fire through the middle West, ardent women advocates of temperance invading the saloons, praying and imploring and doing all in their power to break up the sale of strong drink and the vile habit of intoxication. Their labors led in 1874 to the organization of the Women's Christian Temperance Union, which since then has been the strongest force in the fight for this great reform. At its head for twenty years was the notable figure of the woman with whose life history we are now concerned, one of the ablest and noblest in the reform movements of the age.

Frances Elizabeth Willard came from the best New England stock, being a descendant in a direct line from Major-General Simon Willard, who came from England in 1636, was the founder of Concord, Massachusetts, and took a prominent part in early colonial affairs. Born at Churchville, New York, September 23, 1839, Miss Willard was taken by her parents to Oberlin, Ohio, in the following year, and in 1846 to Wisconsin. Here her father became a farmer and her mother was for many years engaged in teaching, and here her own education was obtained, it being completed in the Milwaukee Female College and the Northwestern Female College, from the latter of which she graduated in 1859.

As a girl she was full of vitality and energy, passing a very active outdoor life with her brother and sister, and being fond of riding, fishing, sketching, tree-climbing, and other outing occupations. Her mother encouraged these health-giving pursuits, by the aid of which the young girl laid up a stock of vigor which aided in carrying her through the strenuous duties of her later years. That she did not neglect intellectual pursuits we know from the fact that at the age of sixteen she won a prize from the Illinois Agricultural Society for an essay on "Country Homes," and that in college she was active with pen and voice.

At the time of her graduation Miss Willard was a resident of Evanston, Illinois, the chief suburb of Chicago, which remained her place of residence till her death. Her graduation was quickly followed by a period of teaching in the Northwestern Female College, where she served as Professor of Natural Science from 1861 to 1866, and during part of this time was the college dean. She taught also one year in the Genesee Wesleyan Seminary, of Lima, New York, and spent the years 1868 to 1870 in European travel. Her route covered the whole of Europe and parts of Africa and Asia, extending from Helsingfors on the north to Nubia on the south, and eastward as far as Damascus, while much of her time abroad was occupied in the study of language and of the history of the fine arts. Aside from rest and enjoyment, she gained new inspiration and mental development from the extended journey.

In 1871, shortly after her return to America, she was made president of the Woman's College of the Northwestern University, at Evanston. Her presidency of this institution is notable for the introduction under her auspices of a system of self-government by the pupils. This important educational experiment, of which she was the originator, proved so successful as an aid in discipline, that other colleges soon began to take it up, and it is now adopted in many of our institutions of learning. In addition to her duties as president, Miss Willard was also Professor of Æsthetics in the college during 1873-74. In the latter year she resigned, and shortly afterwards became identified with the temperance movement, to which the remainder of her life was devoted. She had already engaged to some extent in literary work, especially in her "Nineteen Beautiful Years," the story of the brief but inspiring and noble life of her younger sister.

Miss Willard's entrance into the field of labor which became the unresting occupation of her later life was a natural outcome of her sympathy with all movements of reform. She had signed the temperance pledge under her father's and mother's names while still a young child, but did not awaken to the need of entering actively upon temperance work until after the crusade of the women of Ohio in 1873, which she watched with warm approval.

The event which finally enlisted her energies in the cause was the ill-treatment of a band of women crusaders in the streets of Chicago by a rough party of men. Filled with indignation at this outrage, she declared the crusade to be "everybody's war," took part in it as far as her college duties permitted, and began speaking at temperance meetings, in so ardent and effective a manner that her services were soon much in demand.

Shortly after this Miss Willard resigned from the college in consequence of some lack of harmony in the faculty, and at once entered fervently upon temperance work. She made a journey East, conferred with the leaders in the cause, saw the mission temperance work in the slums of New York, became familiar with the extent of the evil and the character of the effort to eradicate it, and determined to give her life to this labor. While in Pittsburg she took part personally in crusade work, going to the saloons with a party of earnest women, kneeling with them on soiled bar-room floors, praying fervently, and pleading earnestly with liquor sellers to give up their soul-destroying business.

One day in 1874 two letters reached her. One was from a school principal in New York, asking her to take charge of a young ladies' department at a salary of $2400 a year; the other was from a friend at home begging her to become president of the Chicago branch of the Women's Christian Temperance Union, then just organized as an outcome of the crusade movement. It took her no time to choose between the salaried and the non-salaried offer. She at once accepted the latter position, flung herself ardently into the work, and in October, 1874, accepted the position of corresponding secretary of the Illinois section of the Union.

The formation of the Women's Christian Temperance Union was a new move in the temperance cause, a substitution of organized and systematic work, under womanly auspices, for the largely desultory work which had before prevailed, and it had a broad field before it. Miss Willard threw herself, body and soul, into this movement, became its leader and most energetic worker, and was elected president of the National Union in 1879, a post which she held during the remainder of her life.

A ready and pleasing orator, Miss Willard is said to have averaged one speech daily in favor of temperance and other reforms during the first ten years of her work, during which she visited every town of 10,000 and more inhabitants and most of those of 5,000 in the United States. In 1883 alone she is said to have addressed audiences in every State and Territory in the country, travelling thirty thousand miles through the land. Her work was begun without salary, other than such chance contributions as might come in, but as the Union grew more prosperous a regular salary was paid her for her arduous and incessant labors.

As the years went on, Miss Willard's evident ability and incessant activity led to her engaging in other reform movements and being given various positions of leadership. Strongly religious in sentiment, she was occupied in 1877 in aiding the evangelist Moody in his mission work in Boston, and subsequently took active part in other duties. In 1882 she was made a member of the Central Committee of the National Prohibition Party, and in 1883 organized a World's Women's Christian Temperance Union, with the purpose of carrying the crusade against strong drink into all parts of the world. Of this body also she was made the president.

Indefatigable in her labors, and constantly seeking for some new opportunity for effective effort, in 1884 she presented, under the auspices of the Union, a memorial to each of the four political conventions for the nomination of Presidential candidates. In the same year she took part in the founding of the Home Protection Party, organized for the protection of the home against the evils of intemperance, and became a member of its executive committee. The petition prepared by it was presented before the legislature of nearly every State.

A new field of labor now entered by her was that of the White Cross and the White Shield, for the promotion of social purity, upon which she spoke widely in the United States and Canada, engaging in it with her usual vital earnestness. She accepted the leadership of this movement in the Unions of which she was president, making this her special department till her death. An active member of the Methodist Church, she was sent as a delegate to its General Conference in 1887, and in 1889 was elected to its Commercial Council, but was refused admittance on some technical plea.

The World's Women's Christian Temperance Union, organized by her in 1883, spread until it had membership in thirty-five different countries, and a huge polyglot petition against the sale of intoxicating liquors and opium was distributed for signature, it eventually receiving the vast number of seven million signatures. Of these about 6,500,000 were in the United States, the remainder being from many countries covered by the World's Union.

The petition was presented to President Cleveland in 1895, and two years afterwards to the government of Canada. Its most effective and picturesque presentation was before a great World's Temperance Convention held in London in 1896, at which the monster petition encircled the entire hall and lay in huge rolls in front of the platform. Delegates from temperance societies of many different countries were present, many of them in their picturesque native costumes. Miss Willard and Lady Henry Somerset were the presiding officers of the meeting, which was a very large and highly enthusiastic one. But as for the vast petition, it need only be said that it proved of no effect, the sale of liquor and opium going on unchecked.

In 1893 Miss Willard was honored with the chairmanship of the World's Temperance Convention at the Columbian Exposition in Chicago. Recognition of her standing as a worker came to her in the honorary degree of A.M. from Syracuse University in 1871, and of LL.D. from the Ohio Wesleyan University in 1894. Her active work on the platform was kept up to the close of her life in all parts of the country, she making among her tours eight journeys through the Southern States, bringing together the women of the two sections of the Union in harmonious association under the white flag of the W. C. T. U., with its famous motto, "For God and Home and Native Land."

In these incessant labors the indefatigable president of the Union was always dignified, earnest, and inspiring, while as a temperance orator her powers were rare and fine. As a presiding officer her excellence was everywhere acknowledged, her grace and graciousness of manner, tact and judgment, quickness at repartee, and intellectual alertness, winning her universal respect and esteem at the meetings of the White Ribbon class.

Miss Willard did not confine herself to the lines of activity here mentioned, but engaged also earnestly in editorial and literary labors. Editorially, her work was done on the Chicago *Daily Post,* the Boston *Our Day,* and *The Union Signal,* the special publication of the W. C. T. U. She was also the director of the Women's

Temperance Publishing Association, of Chicago. Her books included "Nineteen Beautiful Years," already mentioned; "Glimpses of Fifty Years," "Women and Temperance," and a number of others. Of these, "Glimpses of Fifty Years" was of the character of an autobiography, and had a very large sale, more than fifty thousand copies being called for from all parts of the world.

Her persistent and unceasing labors in time told upon Miss Willard's strength, and for several of her later years she suffered from ill health. Despite this she kept diligently at work, and, though worn out with labor, presided at the convention of 1897. The exertion here required proved too much for her strength, and she died on the 18th of February, 1898.

We may close with an estimate of the character of this indefatigable worker for reform from Lady Henry Somerset, her intimate friend in the presidency of the World's Women's Christian Temperance Union:

"Capacity for work, untiring and unremitting, is one of the great characteristics which close friendship of these years has revealed; and save when sleeping I have never seen her idle. The secret of her success has perhaps lain in this, that she has set herself towards her aim and nothing would tempt her from the goal. 'She is ambitious,' is the worst condemnation of her enemies; but surely if there has been a noble and pure and true ambition it has been that of Frances Willard."

CLARA BARTON, THE RED CROSS EVANGEL OF MERCY

The famous Red Cross Society, founded in Europe in 1864 as a result of the Geneva Conference in 1863, did not make its way to America until 1881, its establishment in this country being due to the efforts of the noble-hearted Clara Barton, who was appointed its president. Most of us are familiar with the beneficent purpose of this society, to ameliorate the sufferings arising from war; but most may not know that twenty years before its founding in America Clara Barton was carrying out its ends and aims with an unselfish devotion which has rarely been equalled. If any woman in our land has earned a crown of glory by works of mercy and beneficence, none could be more deserving of it than this bearer of relief to the afflicted, the story of whose life we are about to tell.

The daughter of a soldier who fought under Anthony Wayne against the Indians of the West, Clara Barton was born in North Oxford, Massachusetts, December 25, 1821. She was educated in an academy at Clinton, New York, became a teacher, and quickly showed her progressive spirit and ability by founding at Bordentown, New Jersey, at her own risk, the first free school ever opened in that State. Beginning with six pupils, she had six hundred by the end of her first year, and had obtained the money to erect a new schoolhouse, at a cost of four thousand dollars.

Her life as a teacher ended in 1854, when failing

health obliged her to give up the absorbing duties of her school. Soon afterwards she obtained a position as clerk in the Patent Office at Washington, holding it till the outbreak of the Civil War, when the demands of the wounded and suffering appealed so strongly to her warm heart that she resigned her position and offered her services as a volunteer nurse. It was the first step in a long life given to this cause.

Seeking the hospital, the camp, the battle-field itself, she devoted herself unflinchingly to the distressing work she had undertaken, nobly facing the terrible scenes into which it brought her, and when the army began its Peninsular campaign in 1862 she went with it to the field, where she pursued her chosen work in a quiet, self-contained, and most efficient way, never flinching from the most arduous duties or the most harrowing scenes. Her earnest solicitation brought her supplies in abundance from the charitable, and all the resources of military trains and camp equipage were placed at her service, her noble and valuable work of aid to the suffering being everywhere acknowledged.

She was present on many of the battle-fields of Virginia, was eight months engaged in hospital duty on Morris Island during the siege of Charleston, was afterwards busied in the Wilderness campaign, and in 1864 was put in charge of the hospitals at the front of the Army of the James, her devotion to duty not ceasing until the war ended.

The close of the war brought her new work to do. At the request of President Lincoln she took up the arduous duty of searching for the 80,000 men marked on the army muster rolls as missing. In this service she went to the prison at Andersonville, aided the prisoners there upon their release, and continued the

DINING-ROOM AND OFFICE IN CLARA BARTON'S HOME
(The long box is her field kit)

work of identifying the dead until gravestones had been erected over the bodies of 12,920 men, and tablets marked "unknown" placed over four hundred more. This labor took four years of her life, during part of which she gave a series of lectures upon "Incidents of the War," in which she told to hundreds of thousands of interested listeners the facts of her thrilling experience.

It was while in Switzerland in 1869, whither she had gone for rest after her many years of hard work, that she first heard of the Red Cross Society. Every power in Europe had joined in the treaty which gave the members of this beneficent association immunity on the battle-field, and licensed them to care for the wounded of every creed and race, whether friends or foes. It was a work of mercy that appealed strongly to her sympathetic soul, and she promptly joined the society, entering quickly upon its duties, and devoting herself to them with the warmest zeal during the Franco-Prussian War.

After the capitulation of Strassburg, she accompanied the German troops in their entry into its streets, and there found the most urgent need for this mission of benevolence. There were many thousands of homeless and starving people within the walls, and her heart was rent with sorrow at the suffering visible on every hand. Systematic and energetic work was needed here, and Miss Barton earnestly undertook the task of seeking to relieve the distress that surrounded her. Food was supplied for the hungry, materials for thousands of garments were procured, and she set the hungry and half-clad women at work in making these into articles of wear, seeing that they were paid for their labor and thus enabled to obtain food.

Her work at Strassburg was quickly followed by similar work at Paris, where the outbreak of the Commune had caused wide-spread suffering and distress. Entering that terror-haunted city courageously on foot, she began her work with an earnestness that quickly won her recognition and protection among the warring elements, food and clothing being supplied her which she distributed with the judicious care born of long experience. The story is told that on one occasion a hungry mob, fiercely demanding food, had overcome the police in front of her dwelling. Opening the door, she spoke earnestly to the infuriated throng. Recognizing her as the bringer of relief to their families, their mood changed.

"*Mon Dieu*, it is an angel!" they exclaimed. Then they quietly dispersed, their wild fury tamed by the voice of this giver of food to them and theirs.

Miss Barton returned to America in 1873. She brought with her, as tokens of appreciation of her work, the Golden Cross of Baden, presented her by the Grand Duke, and the Iron Cross of Germany, presented by the Emperor, both of them in recognition of her invaluable services. In her native land, in which she was at that time the only member of the Red Cross, she earnestly applied to Congress to join in the international European treaty establishing this society, an effort in which she did not succeed until 1881.

As president of the American branch of the society, she proposed an amendment which vastly widened its scope. There was at that time no probability that the services of the Red Cross members would for years be called for by wars in America, and the duties of the society had been restricted to this purpose. Her pro-

HEROES OF PROGRESS

posal was that its scope should be widened so as to embrace all cases suffering from fire, flood, famine, pestilence, or disasters of any kind calling for relief.

Her amendment, which also embraced protection to Red Cross agents under duties of any nature, was agreed to by a conference of the society held at Berne in 1882, but was not adopted by any of the nations of Europe. Had the work of the society been confined to war, Miss Barton would have found little call for her services at home, but its new and broader scope brought her no end of duties, of the most diversified kind. The Michigan forest fires and the Mississippi Valley floods of 1882 and 1883 called for active relief work, which was conducted under her supervision. In 1884 there came the Louisiana cyclone. Later there was the Charleston earthquake, the drought in Texas, and that frightful disaster, the Johnstown flood. When the news of this terrible affliction reached her she hurried to the ground on the first train, and remained there for five months, having under her a force of fifty men and women, and vast sums of money being placed at her disposal, for use in giving relief to the suffering and destitute. Later the dreadful cyclone on the Sea Islands of South Carolina called for similar devoted services.

During part of this period Miss Barton held the position of superintendent of the Reformatory School for Women at Sherborn, Massachusetts, which was placed under her care in 1883. As evidence of the kind of work she did there, and the respect and admiration felt for her by the inmates, we may give the following incident told by a lady visitor to the institution. While she was being taken by the superintendent through the wards, a girl convict raised herself on her cot and gazed fixedly at Miss Barton.

"Well, what is it?" the latter kindly asked.

"Nothing. I heard you coming and just wanted to *look* at you."

It was a pathetic demonstration of the warmth of their feeling towards her.

In 1883 Miss Barton, at the request of a committee of Congress, prepared a volume entitled "History of the Red Cross Association." This was supplemented at a later date by a work similar in character, "History of the Red Cross in Peace and War."

In 1884 she attended the International Peace Congress at Geneva, as a deputy from the United States, and on two occasions subsequently was appointed by the United States Government to international conferences in Europe to discuss questions of relief in war.

Though the nations of Europe had not accepted the American widening of the purposes of the Red Cross Society, Miss Barton volunteered her services there on two critical occasions unwarlike in character. During the famine in Russia in 1891–92 the American Red Cross Society took active part under the auspices of its noble president in the work of relief. Food and clothing were obtained in quantities and widely distributed among the sufferers.

Again in January, 1896, moved by the frightful massacres in Armenia, she made an appeal for aid to the charitable of this country, and in February reached Constantinople, attended by five assistants. Here an appeal was made to the Sultan for permission to proceed to Armenia and relieve the distress there as far as could be done. A reluctant assent was given, with the demand that Miss Barton and her assistants should place the crescent above the cross on the badges worn by them. This being complied with, a gratifying change was visible, the government giving prompt and courteous assistance, while the messengers made their way without delay to the scene of trouble and rendered timely and important service to the destitute and injured sufferers.

Miss Barton's services during this mission of mercy were recognized by Guy de Lusignan, Prince of Jerusalem, Cyprus, and Armenia, through the decoration of the Order of Melusine, which he conferred upon her. In addition to this and the crosses of honor bestowed upon her at the close of the Franco-Prussian War, she received at intervals other valuable tokens of appreciation, including a handsome jewel from the Duchess of Baden, a medal and jewel from the Empress of Germany, a decoration of gems from the Queen of Servia, and a brooch and pendant of diamonds as a tribute of gratitude from the people of Johnstown.

In 1898 Miss Barton, at the request of President McKinley, proceeded to Cuba as a bearer of relief to the suffering and starving *reconcentrados* of that country, and in the war that succeeded she did valuable field work among the sick and wounded of the army in Cuba. In 1900 another demand for relief came from the sufferers at Galveston, where a vast ocean storm had inundated and ruined the city. Miss Barton, with her accustomed promptness, hastened to the scene of suffering, but the strain proved too much for her, now nearly in her eightieth year, and she broke down and was forced, for the first time in her long life of arduous work, to desist from active labors.

History does not contain many records of devotion to humanity and self-sacrifice in women surpassing that of Clara Barton, and she amply earned the high regard in which she was held. She was one of the few American women who won a European reputation, her name being known and revered from Paris and Strassburg to Russia and Armenia. In her own land she nobly earned her crown of fame.

ANDREW CARNEGIE, AND THE NEW GOSPEL OF WEALTH

THIS work is not designed as a record of the careers of men whose chief claim to distinction has been the accumulation of large sums of money. Astor and Girard have been spoken of as pioneers in this field, and the latter especially for the praiseworthy use made by him of his wealth. But in these later days of enterprise and the development of the natural resources of this country the opportunities for money making have greatly increased, and many have far surpassed these pioneers in the gathering of wealth. Some among these have died and left part or all of their money to found useful institutions, but of these examples of public service without self-sacrifice Astor and Girard must suffice. In our day there are some who are doing far better than this, giving their money while living, and it seems only just to tell the story of one of these. We select for our example Andrew Carnegie, the Pittsburg multimillionaire and free-handed giver of good gifts, a man who has converted benevolence into a business. We may here fitly quote an old writer who quaintly said: " To amass money and to make no use of it is as senseless as to hunt game and not roast it." If he had said " good use of it " he would have bettered his saying. Carnegie has put the idea into better shape in his new " Gospel of Wealth " motto: "A man who dies rich dies disgraced."

Andrew Carnegie is of Scotch birth, having been born in Dunfermline, Scotland, November 25, 1837.

In 1848 his father, unable longer to get work in Scotland, emigrated to America. He brought with him a sturdy republican in his young son, whose mind had been filled with democratic ideas by his uncle and father, both of them reform orators. The stories of Scotch history and English tyranny had been deeply impressed upon his mind, and filled him with hatred of tyrants and love of liberty. We may find the results of his early training in his notable book published forty years afterwards, "Triumphant Democracy."

Father, mother, and the two boys, Andy and Tom, duly reached their future home in Pittsburg, where Mr. Carnegie got work in a cotton factory, and where Andy, when twelve years old, began his business career as a bobbin-boy at the wages of a dollar and twenty cents a week. It was a modest beginning for one who was in time to become the owner of hundreds of millions of dollars. There have been several marvellous examples of money-making in our day, but that of the bobbin-boy of Pittsburg is one of the most extraordinary of them all.

We do not propose to give in full detail the story of Andrew Carnegie's progress to fortune. It is a tale that might be repeated in different words in the career of many living Americans, and may be dealt with somewhat briefly here. It is remarkable only in the vast wealth he accumulated, but the narration of enterprise and alertness in taking advantage of business opportunities has nothing in it new. There are many who have the abilities necessary to become very rich. There are few who have the opportunity to use these abilities. Carnegie was one of these few favorites of fortune.

Changes soon came in the boy's career. At thirteen

he was put at the hard work of firing for the boiler of a factory engine. At fourteen he was given a much easier position as telegraph-boy, with three dollars a week salary. His escape from the stoker's den to life in the open air was to the boy like an escape from purgatory to paradise. His leisure moments were given to practicing with the telegraph, in which he learned to take by sound instead of by tape, as was then much the custom.

The boy was apt and quick, and made such progress that at sixteen he was installed as an operator at a salary of three hundred dollars a year. It came in good time, for his father had died and he had to bear much of the weight of the family support. Thomas A. Scott, then superintendent of the Pittsburg Division of the Pennsylvania Railroad, gave him his next lift. Attracted by the alert intelligence of the young operator, he offered him a position as railroad telegrapher at ten dollars a month advance, and soon after gave him an opening to make an excellent investment in shares of the Adams Express Company. The offer was a good one, but the boy had no money. His mother, however, had a business head. She saw its advantages, and mortgaged her house to raise the four hundred dollars needed. She thus gave the boy his first step as a capitalist on a small scale.

When the Civil War broke out Carnegie was in his twenty-fourth year and had become private secretary and right hand man of Mr. Scott, who was appointed in 1861 Assistant Secretary of War, with charge of the important work of keeping the railroads steadily active. Promptness in the moving of trains, instant attention to stoppages and break-downs, etc., were highly necessary, and it needed a clear head and sound nerves to handle the military traffic and movements of troops. This was a heavy strain on Scott and Carnegie alike, and he was glad enough when his chief gave it up and returned to Pittsburg on the 1st of June, 1862.

There was one great opportunity in Carnegie's career of success that must be mentioned. Splendid opportunities came to him for profitable investments, and he was quick to take advantage of them, though never lacking in caution and judgment. His second investment arose from a gentleman on a railroad train showing him a model of a sleeping car he had invented. Carnegie was quick to see its value and to push it into notice, he taking an interest in the company, which in time gained a profitable business. Shortly afterwards he was advanced to the position which Mr. Scott had formerly held, that of superintendent of the Pittsburg Division of the Pennsylvania Railroad.

So far he had only been getting his foot firmly fixed on the highway of life, but now came the opening for an immense boom in his fortunes, far beyond his dreams. The coal oil business was then in its early days of activity, new fields were being rapidly opened, and Carnegie joined some friends in the purchase for forty thousand dollars of the Storey Farm, a piece of promising ground on Oil Creek. The well on it, then running one hundred barrels daily, proved in the end to be immensely valuable, gaining a value on the Stock Exchange of $5,000,000, and paying in one year the surprising dividend of $1,000,000—certainly a splendid return for a $40,000 investment.

Andrew Carnegie, now twenty-seven years old, was thus suddenly made a capitalist. He might have preceded Rockefeller as a great oil magnate but that

HEROES OF PROGRESS 329

his energies were turned in another direction. The wooden bridges then in use on railroads were for various reasons very unsatisfactory, and the Pennsylvania Railroad had just made a successful experiment with iron. This set its Pittsburg superintendent to thinking. There was going to be a business, very likely a large business, in iron bridges, and the first in the field would have the best chance. He decided to be one of the first, organized a company, and started the Keystone Bridge Works.

A big order soon came, to build an iron bridge over the Ohio River, with a three hundred foot span. Others followed rapidly, and the Keystone Company soon had to extend its works. Thus our shrewd Scotchman launched himself into what became a great business, and laid the foundation of what is to-day one of the finest iron and steel works in the world. Carnegie, inspired by the success of his first venture in the field of manufacture, now resigned his railroad position and devoted all his time and attention to the business he had given so timely a start.

The Keystone Company made very rapid progress. Orders came from all sides, and Carnegie, as its manager, kept it fully up to date in all particulars. The newest time and labor saving machinery was always put in, every promising invention was taken advantage of, and a far-seeing enterprise was visible in all its affairs.

But this establishment was far from exhausting all of Carnegie's energies. Another great opportunity came to him, and he was quick to grasp it. He made a visit to England in 1868, just at the time the Bessemer steel process had passed from the stage of experiment to that of success. He saw its vast prospective value at a glance. Steel had then in many directions, especially in rails, begun to replace iron. He himself had, while in the Pennsylvania Railroad service, made a very successful experiment in the hardening of iron rails by carbon. But the rails made from Bessemer steel were far superior to these, and he determined at once to take advantage of the new process. On his return to Pittsburg he set promptly to work in the erection of a great Bessemer steel plant. As he had been among the first in America to see that iron was about to replace wood in bridges, so he was one of the earliest to realize that steel was soon to take the place of iron. It was by his foresight in these two particulars that he laid the foundation of his enormous fortune.

We have here described the initial steps of Mr. Carnegie's progress to fortune, from the position of bobbin-boy to that of the chief proprietor of great industrial works. He might have stopped at this point. His fortune was large, his needs were small, he had abundance to live on in comfort or in luxury if he desired. But men who are on the highroad of prosperity do not stop. Ambition, more than actual desire for larger wealth, carries them on. They like to excel, to stand at the top, the admired of the world, and Andrew Carnegie was not free from this ambition. Great designs awakened in his mind and he hastened to put them into execution.

He felt that a great steel plant should take advantage of all available resources. It should own its own iron and coal fields and its own railways and steamships, so as to put itself fairly beyond competition. In pursuance of this scheme he built the great plant known as the Edgar Thompson Steel Works, on the Monongahela River; bought vast tracts of mineral land, much of it on the Great Lakes, hundreds of miles away; purchased a fleet of steamships to carry the ore from the mines across the lakes, and built a railroad four hundred and twenty-five miles long to carry coal and iron directly to his works.

The results of this enterprise are well known. The cheap steel rails turned out created an immense demand. The great works were swamped with orders. Their manager could not wait to build new ones, but purchased the plant of the neighboring Homestead Steel Company, whose immense foundries were close to his own works. He had reduced the cost of production to the lowest possible point. No concern in existence could compete with him in price. The home trade for steel was in his hands, and he stretched out to grasp the trade of the world. A genius in practical affairs, he kept this enormous business under his own control, and the millions of his wealth grew until they became overwhelmingly large.

We must stop here. We cannot follow the steps of progress of the titanic plant which rapidly grew up. It must suffice to say that by 1900 it included ten different concerns, three of them of enormous size, with a total of 45,000 employees. We must step forward to the early years of the twentieth century, when a Steel Trust with enormous capital was formed, its purpose being to control all the important works in the country. First of all stood the vast Carnegie plant. The " steel master " was ready to sell. He had always resolved to retire before old age came upon him. He could and did make his own terms, being given for his interest the enormous sum of $250,000,000 in bonds on the properties of the United States Steel Corporation, bearing interest at the rate of five per cent.

Mr. Carnegie had spent more than sixty years of his life in getting. Now began his era of giving. His views in regard to the use of money he has himself tersely expressed: " The day is not far distant when the man who dies, leaving behind him millions of available wealth which was free for him to administer during life, will pass away unwept, unhonored, and unsung, no matter to what use he leaves the dross which he cannot take with him. Of such as these the public verdict will be: *'The man who dies thus rich dies disgraced.'*"

How to give for the best good of mankind was the problem before him. He strongly opposed indiscriminate charity, as likely to do far more harm than good, saying, " It were better for mankind that the millions of the rich were thrown into the sea than so spent as to encourage the slothful, the drunken, the unworthy." It was his fixed idea that men should be helped to help themselves, and this has been his view in all his giving.

In this he followed what many look upon as a mistaken method, believing that to establish libraries and thus get men into the habit of reading, at once keeping them from more harmful enjoyments and cultivating their minds, was the best way in which he could distribute his money. Perhaps a difficulty of getting books in his younger days may have inspired him to this. Certainly most of his gifts have been in this direction, and he has made himself a power in the work of advancing the education and adding to the knowledge of the world.

Let us briefly state the results of his gifts during the past five years. The libraries founded by him in the United States number nearly eight hundred, and those abroad more than five hundred, their total cost being about $40,000,000. The splendid Carnegie Institute founded by him at Pittsburg consumed $7,000,000, the Polytechnic Institute $2,000,000, and the pension fund for steel works workingmen $4,000,000. Scotland, his native land, has been remembered with $15,000,000 for the benefit of its university students, and Dunfermline, his birth-place, with $2,500,000. More recently he has branched out into new fields of beneficence, establishing a fund of $5,000,000 for the benefit of those who perform deeds of heroism, $10,000,000 to pension off superannuated college professors, and $10,000,000 to establish a National University at Washington, its purpose being to encourage discovery by aiding those engaged in original researches. These are his greatest gifts. There are many smaller ones. The total is estimated at considerably over $100,000,000.

This is what Andrew Carnegie had done up to 1906 to avoid the disgrace of dying rich. It will be seen that he kept firmly to his theory of not helping directly those able to help themselves, and did nothing to help those unable to help themselves, except in the way of pensions. But he was hale and hearty yet, his ideas seemed spreading, his wealth remained enormous; no one could say what views he might take as to its ultimate disposal. Whatever else may be said of Andrew Carnegie, he must be given the honor of being a pioneer in establishing the theory that it is the duty of every rich man to use his wealth while living for the benefit of mankind. At the present day there are many following his example, doubtless largely inspired by his action, and the time may come when no very rich man will permit himself to die disgraced in this manner.

Mr. Carnegie has not confined himself to money

making and money giving. Since he left business he has enjoyed himself in a sane and moderate way. He has purchased a castle and an estate in Scotland, where much of his time is spent, and where he keeps wide awake to all the events of the world. He has always been an able thinker and a ready writer, having an incisive and picturesque way of expressing himself and taking broad views of political and other affairs.

He has long been addicted to literary pursuits, and has written a number of interesting books. One of these, " Round the World," contained a lively description of a journey westward around the seas and continents. " Our Coaching Trip," issued in 1882, was a rambling and agreeable story of a drive through England and Scotland. " Triumphant Democracy," already spoken of, shows him to have become a true American in grain, however he may prefer to dwell in his native land. Finally we may name the " Gospel of Wealth," in which he lays bare his sentiments about many of the economic problems of the day.

Here we have Mr. Carnegie. He is still with us and may long remain. And he still holds in hand much the greater part of that vast store of wealth with which he has set out to do all the good he can, in consonance with his own ideas of doing good. The world has benefited much from his beneficence; it is likely to benefit much more. He will win a crown of honor if he succeeds in establishing as a worthy rule his theory that " he who dies rich dies disgraced."

BOOKER T. WASHINGTON, PIONEER OF NEGRO PROGRESS

NEAR the end of the days of slavery, on a plantation in Franklin County, Virginia, was born a negro boy who was destined to lift himself, by moral and mental strength, into the ranks of the great men of the world. He is the sole representative which we can give here of a race that numbers more than nine millions of people in the United States. Freed from slavery only forty years ago, not yet freed from ignorance, the negro race has had little opportunity to develop the powers it may possess. Frederick Douglass, an able and brilliant orator of the times before the war, was the only man of negro blood who raised himself to a national reputation before the coming of Booker T. Washington, of whose striking career it is our purpose now to speak.

Born in a tumble-down log-cabin on an old Virginia plantation, the boy named came into a world in which he was expected to play so small a part that no record was kept even of the year of his birth. All he knew of it was that it was some time in the years 1858 or 1859. His father, a white man, he never knew. He knew no name except Booker, by which he was called during his few years of slave life on the plantation. A mere toddler as he was, only six or seven years old when the war ended and freedom came, he was kept busy at odd jobs, cleaning the yard, carrying water to the men, taking corn to the mill, and, as he says, at times falling from the horse with his bag of corn and sitting in tears by the wayside until some one came along to lift him up again.

Schooling was not thought of for any one with a black skin, though the little slave boy already felt a thirst for knowledge. He tells us how he would carry the books of his young mistress when she went to school and gaze wistfully through the door into the school-room, closed against all of his color, but which seemed to him like a paradise to which he was denied entrance.

The slaves, he tells us, knew well the purpose of the war. They had a system of wireless telegraphy of their own, by which they often heard of events in the field before their masters. The fact that "Massa Linkum" had set them free was quickly spread among them, and when the war ended and they could move about without hindrance, many of them hastened to test their new liberty by leaving the plantations on which their lives had been spent.

Booker's reputed father, who had been a slave on a neighboring plantation, made his way to West Virginia, where he got work in the mines and soon sent for his wife and children. Here little Booker was put to work in a salt furnace. His childish desire to learn grew intense as time passed on. The art of reading seemed something magical to the child, who had an alert brain under his sable skin; and, getting possession in some way of a book, he pored over it intently, with no one to help, for all around were as ignorant as himself. All he succeeded in doing was to learn the alphabet from it; the joining of the letters into words was beyond his childish powers.

Some time later a young negro opened a school in the vicinity, but, to his keen disappointment, his father would not let him go, insisting that he should keep at work. Determined to open the closed door of knowledge, he managed to get some lessons at night from the teacher, and appealed so earnestly that his father finally consented to his going to day school for a few months, if he would work in the furnace until nine o'clock in the morning and for two hours in the afternoon after school had closed.

Little Booker was willing to do anything to gain an education. His thirst for knowledge had grown with his years, and there was no danger but that he would be a diligent student. But his first day at school brought him in face of a distressing difficulty. When the teacher called the roll he learned that every boy there had at least two names. He felt a deep sense of shame at the fact that he had only one. He had never been called anything but Booker, and knew of no other name. But a native shrewdness made him equal to the situation. When the teacher asked for his name he calmly replied that it was Booker Washington, appropriating the name of the Father of the Country without a qualm of conscience. Later on his mother told him that his real name was Booker Taliaferro, but he clung to the name he had adopted, and has ever since been known as Booker T. Washington.

From the salt furnace the boy was transferred to a coal mine, a change, in his opinion, much for the worse; but a few months later he got a place as servant in the house of Mrs. Ruffner, the wife of the mine owner. Mrs. Ruffner had the name of being a hard mistress, with whom no servant would stay more than a few months, but Booker soon found that the trouble was more with the servants than with the mistress. What she demanded was that they should keep things clean and do their work promptly and systematically. When her new boy learned what she wanted he did his best to please her, and instead of a harsh taskmaster found her considerate and just. He stayed with her a year and a half, and might have stayed much longer, for he had made Mrs. Ruffner a kind friend, but for a new desire that stirred his soul.

One day, while in the coal mine, he had heard two miners talking about a great school for colored people somewhere in Virginia. He heard also that worthy students could work out part of their board and be taught a useful trade. The news filled him with an intense eagerness to go to this wonderful school, and in the fall of 1872, when he was thirteen or fourteen years old, he determined to get there if it was possible.

His mother strongly opposed the idea, and gave her consent only after long pleading. But the colored people of the vicinity favored it, education seeming to them like an inestimable treasure. Some of them helped the boy with a little money, and at length, with a very slender purse, he set out on his long journey to Hampton, five hundred miles away.

He had expected to ride there, but his first day's journey in the stage coach showed him that his funds would not carry him a fifth of the way, and he changed riding for walking, except when he could beg a ride. He reached the city of Richmond at length. His pockets were empty, and Hampton still far away. No lodging was to be had for a wandering colored urchin, and that night he slept under a raised part of the board sidewalk. The next day he earned a little money

HEROES OF PROGRESS

by helping unload a vessel at the wharves, and this he kept at for several days, still sleeping under the boards. Years afterwards, when he visited Richmond as a distinguished man, he sought out this spot in the streets and looked with pathetic interest upon his first sleeping place in Virginia's capital city. When he reached Hampton at length, he had just fifty cents with which to get an education in the famous institute.

A sorry picture was the vagrant student when he presented himself tremblingly before the head teacher of the institute. Ill-clad, begrimed, hungry-looking, he waited with sinking heart while others were admitted, but no attention paid to him. At length, after a weary probation, the teacher looked him over disapprovingly, and put a broom into his hands, telling him to sweep one of the recitation-rooms. Now young Booker's severe training under Mrs. Ruffner served him well. He swept and dusted that room so thoroughly that when the teacher, a Yankee housewife, came in she could not find a speck of dust hiding anywhere. "I guess you will do to enter this institution," she said.

The boy had swept his way into her good graces. She offered him a position as janitor, which enabled him to pay his board, and was ever afterwards his good friend. General Armstrong, that faithful friend of the blacks who was at the head of the institution, was so pleased with the earnestness and intelligence of the boy, one of the youngest under his care, that he induced a friend to pay the $70 a year for the little lad's tuition, and thus he was fairly launched upon the highroad of education.

That Booker worked hard we may be assured. His diligence, fidelity, and studiousness won him friends on all sides. He got work outside during the vacations, and after two years paid a visit home, only to see his mother die. She had been a good mother to him, and he mourned her loss.

His term at Hampton ended in 1875, but his connection with the institution did not cease, for after a time he was made a teacher in the night-school and also put in charge of the Indian inmates. The opportunity of his life, for which he had been unwittingly preparing, came in 1881, while he was still night-school teacher at Hampton. An application had come to General Armstrong for some one to take charge of a colored normal school at Tuskegee, Alabama. The kindly superintendent, who knew well the capability of his night-school teacher, offered him the position, and Booker, with some natural hesitation, agreed to try.

Tuskegee was a town of about two thousand population, nearly half of them colored. It was situated in the Black Belt of Alabama, negroes being plentiful and education sparse. The legislature had voted an annual appropriation of $2000 to pay the running expenses of the school, but when the new teacher reached Tuskegee he was disappointed to find that no building and no equipment had been provided. There were plenty of scholars, but that was all.

Booker went to work with a will, determined to make the most of his chance. The best place he could get for a school-house was an old shanty near the colored Methodist church, and here he opened with thirty students, ranging from fifteen to forty years of age, most of them having already served, in some fashion, as school-teachers. The roof was so leaky that when it rained one of the students had to hold an umbrella over him as he taught.

HEROES OF PROGRESS 341

After three weeks Miss Olivia A. Davidson came to the school as a co-teacher—a bright girl, with new ideas, who afterwards became Mr. Washington's wife. Booker Washington was a born man of business from the start. After he had been in Tuskegee for three months an abandoned plantation near by was offered for sale for the low sum of $500. He determined to obtain it if possible, and succeeded in borrowing from the treasurer of the Hampton Institute $250 for a first payment. The remaining sum was raised by various measures in time to make the final payment and secure the property.

The mansion house of the plantation had been burned down. The buildings remaining consisted of a cabin which had been used as the dining-room, a kitchen, a stable, and an old henhouse. The latter two were used for school purposes, and the others as residences. The first animal obtained was an old, blind horse. It was the pioneer in a troop of animals which now embraces over two hundred horses, oxen, and cows, about seven hundred hogs, and many sheep and goats, while the original tumble-down buildings have been replaced by a large number of well built structures, nearly all erected by the students themselves.

The new principal was a man of ambitious views and genius for affairs. His first daring undertaking was to build a $6000 school-house without a dollar of capital. But he had already won a reputation for ability and integrity and help came in. The necessary lumber was supplied by a dealer in the vicinity who insisted on sending it and waiting for pay. Contributions came from many sources, and the building was completed and paid for. By this time the strenuous and self-sacrificing efforts of the young teacher and the remarkable results he was achieving with the smallest means were becoming known and appreciated throughout the country, and aid began to come in from many sources. He made in subsequent years frequent lecturing tours in the North, describing with simple eloquence the character and needs of his work, and obtaining in this way the annual amount necessary for its prosecution.

His purpose was to develop at Tuskegee an educational and industrial school, teaching the essential elements of education while making each student familiar with some trade, and in this he has had so signal a success that he is looked upon as having solved the problem of the future of the negro in America. It has throughout been his purpose to make his students capable, self-supporting, and self-respecting, a design which has been carried out to a highly gratifying extent, while the present school at Tuskegee has given birth to various offsprings in which the same methods are pursued.

All the ordinary trades are taught in the institution, especially the various branches of farming. Twenty-five separate industries are carried on by the students, the object being to train the colored youth in self-supporting occupations, while the girls are taught the branches most useful to them. Washington holds that the race problem will be solved when the negro becomes a valuable workman and financially independent, and he has done noble work in the effort to bring this about.

The leaky cabin with which he began is now superseded by forty or more handsome and well adapted buildings, large and small, all but four of which have been erected by student labor, even to the making of the bricks and the sawing of the planks. The thirty students with whom he began have increased to over eleven hundred, and his solitary labors have been replaced by the work of some eighty instructors, while the old shanty of 1881 has grown in the short space of twenty years to an extensive group of edifices, and his fragment of meeting-house ground to a broad estate of 2460 acres, the whole valued at over $300,000, and with an endowment fund of $215,000. This looks like a magical result from the work of the ragged and penniless boy who made his way on foot to Hampton Institute in 1872, and we cannot but look upon Booker Washington as an extraordinary man.

This was the state of affairs in 1900. Since then the development has continued, and the endowment fund has been greatly increased by the generous gift from Andrew Carnegie of $600,000, to be used as Mr. Washington wishes, except that he and his wife shall be provided for out of its proceeds. Carnegie says of Mr. Washington: "To me he seems one of the greatest of living men, because his work is unique, the modern Moses who leads his race and lifts it through education to even better and higher things than a land overflowing with milk and honey. History is to tell of two Washingtons, one white, the other black, both fathers of their people."

Carnegie is not alone in this opinion. There are many who look upon Booker T. Washington as one of the greatest of living men. He has won the respect and admiration of the South as well as of the North. He went far to win the South by his highly effective address at the opening of the Atlanta Exposition of 1895. The *Boston Transcript* said of this speech: " It seems to have dwarfed all the other proceedings and the Exposition itself. The sensation it has caused in the press has never been equalled." Its purpose was to show how the whites and blacks could live together in harmony in the South.

Since then Tuskegee has become a place of pilgrimage for our Presidents on their journeys through the land. President McKinley visited it, with the general approbation of the people, and in 1905 President Roosevelt did the same. In history there are few examples of so remarkable a career as that of this Moses of the negro race.

THEODORE ROOSEVELT AS AMERICA'S ALL-ROUND MAN AND CHAMPION

THE opening of the twentieth century marked the beginning of a great era in American history, one in which the most mighty and famous of the world's republics began to spread its wings afar and make its voice heard from the Arctic to the Antarctic seas and to the bordering lands of the Atlantic and Pacific oceans. The time was at hand for new men to arise, new doctrines to be proclaimed, new rights and duties to be set forth. The world, which had long been divided between the East and the West, continents with separate ideas and institutions, was to meet and join, and enter upon the preliminaries of a vast struggle for power and dominion on one side, for human rights and justice on the other—the most stupendous contest of nations the world had ever known.

Many men of might and ability took part in this revolutionary movement, men with advanced aims and claims, men of wide thought and mighty purpose; and among them all rose one great warrior for the right, who on the very threshold of the century was raised to the high position of President of the United States and who while the century was still in its infancy was hailed the world over as one of the supreme figures in history, a man of unsurpassed ability in all fields of government and statesmanship and all-round daring and endeavor.

Such a man was Theodore Roosevelt, a born fighter, but not on the field of battle. His war history was a very brief one, it being that of his picturesque charge up San Juan Hill in Cuba during the Spanish-American war. But his vigorous contest against graft and dishonor, his long and sturdy battle for reform, his demand of equal rights for all men, a square deal for high and low, rich and poor, gave him a standing in world politics that made his name a household word throughout the nations, and in his journey through Europe after his hunting trip to Africa brought him warm invitations from the kings and emperors of that ancient continent. His journey there was a continued ovation, marked by the cheers of multitudes in foreign nations and the crowding of thousands to gaze upon this simple American citizen, a man without rank or power, for his term of presidential rule was then at an end. But the people hailed him as their friend and champion, the man who stood for the masses against the classes. Whatever the warrant for his prominence, he stood in the limelight of the world's applause, a man of supreme significance in human affairs.

Theodore Roosevelt, to the story of whose active and varied career we must give a somewhat extended notice, was born in the city of New York on the 27th day of October, 1858, of old Knickerbocker stock, a descendant from Klass Martinson Van Roosevelt, who made his way from Holland to New Amsterdam in 1640. He inherited from his father his love of outdoor life and his warm interest in the doings and claims of the " common people," but had a fight from the beginning, a battle for health and strength. A pale, delicate lad, weak in body and short of sight, he looked like one born for an indoor life. But below this lay an unusual store of that native energy from which strong men are made. No indoor career for him. He determined to outlive his normal weakness, to equal his

THEODORE ROOSEVELT IN HIS LIBRARY AT OYSTER BAY

companions in health and strength, to take full part in outdoor sports and exercises of all sorts. He tramped over hill and dale, learned to swim, row and ride, traversed the forests and studied their secrets, and grew up to be a hardy lad, all his natal weakness overcome.

When he was but six years of age his love of outside nature began to declare itself and as well his later enjoyment of a good, hard fight. He developed a love for adventure, was fond of stories of animal life and gained as useful an education in the wilds and woods as in home and school. He himself tells us: "My father, all my people, held that no one has a right to merely cumber the earth: that the most contemptible of created beings is the man who does nothing. I determined to be strong and well and I made my health what it is. By the time I entered Harvard College I was able to take my part in whatever sports I liked. I wrestled and sparred and ran a great deal while in college, and though I never came in first I got more good out of the exercise than those who did, because I immensely enjoyed it and never injured myself."

As a boy he was a busy reader, especially of stories of adventure. Cooper's Leather-Stocking Tales he devoured greedily, declaring later, "Why, man, there is nothing like them. I could pass an examination in the whole of them to-day."

He entered Harvard at the age of eighteen and did his best while there to "hit the line hard." His tastes in study lay towards gaining a knowledge of living things, men and animals. Later he devoted himself to history and political principles. It was common with him to pick up a book and become so absorbed in it that a cannon's roar would hardly have awakened him to his surroundings.

Before he left college his love of books led to his writing a book of his own—and certainly no boyish one. Having read a history of the naval battles in the war of 1812, he found it so one-sided, so unduly pro-American, that he made a special study of the subject and followed this by writing " The Naval History of 1812." This was no schoolboy exercise, but was so carefully and capitally done that it is still regarded as an authority upon this topic. In 1880 he graduated, not at the top of his class, but at a very reputable distance from the bottom.

Such, briefly, is the story of Roosevelt's early life—his career of preparation. It was very quickly followed by one of operation. After a short journey abroad, in which he took a tramp afoot through Germany and climbed the Jungfrau and the Matterhorn, he returned home again, ready to take his full part in the battle of life. He began by a brief term of law study in the office of his uncle, Robert B. Roosevelt, but at the same time took part in the political affairs of his district, and with such remarkable ability that he was elected a state representative before the end of the year.

Thus placed, in 1881, at the age of twenty-three, he took his seat in the New York Assembly in the following year, the youngest member of the House. Boy as he seemed, he was not long there before he became a centre of political storm and stress of his own stirring. He found the Assembly rotten with corruption, deep and intrenched, which had remained undisturbed for years, it being sustained by a large majority of the membership. The minority needed a leader. It quickly found one in young Roosevelt, who plunged into the campaign with such force and energy that he quickly made himself the undisputed advocate of their views.

The New York city government at that time was stagnant with fraud, and a new and reformed charter was sadly needed. It was in favor of this that the young champion began his battle, fighting for it unflinchingly during his three terms in the Assembly and saving the people hundreds of thousands of dollars, which he wrenched from the hands of the grafters. His chief victory had to do with a choice bit of graft in connection with the elevated railway ring, sustained by the attorney general of the State and by Judge Westbrook, of the Supreme Court.

On April 6, 1882, Roosevelt began his legislative career by rising from his seat in the House and demanding that Judge Westbrook should be impeached. The young statesman was squelched by his numerous opponents. But he pounded away day after day, and with such effect that a knowledge of the scandal spread through the state, his opponents were forced to yield to public opinion, and Roosevelt won by a vote of 104 to 6. In the end, however, the delinquent officials escaped by a whitewashing report.

Another demand then in vogue was civil service reform, alike in state and nation. The first intelligently drawn bill for this purpose offered in the New York Assembly was presented by Roosevelt. It was carried in 1883 and signed by Governor Cleveland at nearly the same time that the civil service bill passed by Congress was signed by President Arthur.

Roosevelt was by this time looked upon by all parties as a man of power and ability. He had thrown his hat into the ring in the cause of reform, and the ringsters were far from eager to take it up. His energy had so impressed his party that George William Curtis, a fellow delegate, said of him: "You will know more of him later; a good deal more, or I am much in error. He is just out of school almost, and yet he is a force to be reckoned with in New York. Later the nation will be criticizing or praising him. He will not truckle nor cringe. His political life will probably be a turbulent one, but he will be a figure, not a figurehead, in future development."

Such was the verdict passed by an able critic on Roosevelt in 1884, four years after his graduation from college. With this year his legislative career ended. He had from boyhood been eager to see the great West, and now broke loose from settled civilization to take a long holiday in this favorite realm of the pioneer, the land of the cowboy and the hunting field. Seeking the frontier of Dakota, he established a cattle ranch of his own, where he spent two years, living in a rough log house of his own building, dressing in cowboy attire, caring for his own herds and finding high enjoyment in the wild life of the hunting field. It was the first of his three notable periods of adventure in the world's greatest hunting fields. Here also he devoted some time to authorship and writing "Hunting Trips of a Ranchman," "Ranch Life and Hunting Trail" and two works of biography, lives of Thomas Hart Burton and Gouverneur Morris.

Roosevelt had other adventures than those of the hunting field. Various interesting stories are told of his life during those two years in the wilds. Of these his encounter with one of the "bad men" of the West is oftenest told. This tough, well primed with whisky, invited all in a saloon which the young rancher had entered to drink with him. Roosevelt declined, saying that he did not care to drink. But when the tough drew a pistol and flourished it in the face of the tenderfoot, the young rancher rose as if to obey. In a moment more the "bad man" was laid on his back by the force of a potent left-hander from the spectacled, "foureyed" stranger, while the pistol was kicked from his hand across the room. When the bully regained his wits he felt as if an elephant had trod on him, and he gave up all interest in that hard-hitting tenderfoot.

The Wild West holiday ended suddenly in 1886, when news reached the rancher that the independent citizens of New York had nominated him as their candidate for mayor of that city. That night he packed his trunk and the next day bade good-by to his life on the plains and set out for the East, to embark again on the sea of politics. His fight was brief but vigorous, there being two other candidates in the field. One of these, Abram S. Hewitt, was elected. But Roosevelt had made new capital for himself. As evidence of the effect of his brief career on the public mind we may quote a remark of Andrew D. White, president of Cornell College, who said to his class in the early eighties:

"Young gentlemen, some of you will enter public life. I call your attention to Theodore Roosevelt. He is on the right road to success. It is dangerous to predict a future for a young man, but let me tell you that if any man of his age was pointed straight for the Presidency, that man is Theodore Roosevelt."

The young Assemblyman was now fairly launched on his great political career. He had sown the seed; the time was fast coming when he would reap the harvest. In the years that followed promotion came rapidly and he played a prominent part in public life. Having carried a civil service reform bill through the

New York Assembly in 1884, he was appointed on the Civil Service Commission by President Harrison in 1889 and was made chairman of that body. He went into the work with all his native energy, remained on the commission for six years and during that period kept things on the jump. When he entered the commission there were 14,000 officials under civil service rules. When he left there were 40,000. Of his work in it Mr. John H. Proctor, one of his fellow-members, said:

"Every day I went to the office as to an entertainment. I knew that something was sure to turn up to make it worth my while, with him there. When he went away I had heart in it no longer."

When he left, to engage in a new line of work, President Cleveland warmly congratulated him on the able service he had rendered.

The new duty that came to him was that of president of the Board of Police Commissioners of New York city. This was a task that strongly appealed to him. There was strenuous work to be done. So corrupt had the police board become that it needed an earthquake to shake it up. Its new president, young and boiling with energy, was this earthquake. A reform administration, that of Mayor Strong, was then in power, and soldiers of reform were needed to carry out its plans. The new commissioner was the man for the place. He went into it with his wonted energy, and stirred up the evils that prevailed with a vigor never before seen in that special field of duty. The whole country looked on, for the young and ardent reformer had by this time won a national reputation. Corruption was deeply planted in the soil of the police department and it was not easy to uproot. There was a system of blackmail by policemen and officials, including the non-enforcement of the Sunday liquor law and other evils, to be handled. Dishonesty at elections was one of these evils, and it needed vigorous labor on the part of the commissioner to overcome it. All this and more Roosevelt had to deal with during his two years of duty in the police presidency, and he did so with a vigor that brought the prevailing corruption largely to an end. Disorder and bad administration prevailed before he entered the board. When he left it these had been overcome and New York had a well-trained and ably organized force of blue-coated public protectors, whose honor, ability and devotion to duty were beyond question. The police force thus organized was the ablest and cleanest the metropolis had ever known, loot and blackmail had ceased to exist, and for the first time in years decency and honesty prevailed in the New York police department.

Such was the state of affairs in 1897. In that year men of ability in other fields were in demand, and Roosevelt was one of the first called into the national service. The barbarities of Spanish rule in Cuba brought up questions with which the United States had to deal, and another President, McKinley, found it desirable to call the young New York reformer into the national service, as aide and assistant in the threatened conflict. It was important to make the American navy ready for any contingency that might arise, and strong and competent men were needed to take hold. McKinley, in consequence, appointed Roosevelt Assistant Secretary of the Navy, looking upon him as the man best fitted for the post.

The American naval service had been allowed to fall into decay after the civil war. A new navy was in the making, but it needed men of capacity and energy to take care of its development. Roosevelt was amply qualified for this task, and though bearing the minor rank of assistant, he soon made his force felt through every branch of the department.

The chief and most important work done by him was that of collecting arms and ammunition and insisting on the gunners being well trained in marksmanship. He felt that war was coming and that it was his duty to see that the naval force was fully prepared for it. The ships must be put in order and the foreign coaling stations well supplied with fuel. It was largely due to his activity in this direction that Dewey was able to make his prompt movement from Hongkong to Manila when the war broke out. Of this we have testimony in the statement of Senator Davis, then head of the Committee on Foreign Relations.

"If it had not been for Roosevelt," said the Senator, "Dewey would not have been able to strike the blow that he dealt at Manila. Roosevelt's forethought, energy and promptness made this posible."

In respect to the efficiency of the men at the guns may be related an anecdote that outlines in picturesque shape the work done by the ardent Assistant Secretary. Shortly after his appointment to the post he asked Congress for an appropriation of $800,000 for ammunition. The appropriation was made, but, to the surprise of the members, the Secretary was in a few months again before them demanding more money for powder. This time he asked for $500,000.

"What has become of the other appropriation?" he was asked.

"Every cent of it was spent for powder and shot,

HEROES OF PROGRESS 355

and every ounce of powder and shot has been fired away," he replied.

"And what do you propose to do with the $500,000 you now want?"

"I will use every dollar of that, too, within the next thirty days in practice shooting."

It was costly practice, but it paid. It was mainly due to it that the gunners were able to fire true and straight the next year at Manila and Santiago.

"It is useless," Roosevelt said, "to spend millions of dollars in the building of perfect fighting machines unless we make the personnel which is to handle these machines equally perfect."

This work, these ideas, were soon to prove their utility. Early in the next year the battleship Maine was blown up in Havana harbor and sent to the bottom with nearly her entire crew. While attempts were made to settle the hot controversy that followed by negotiation, many felt that war was the only probable outcome, and the energetic and capable Assistant Secretary lost no time in preparing for all contingencies. It was he who selected Commodore Dewey to command the squadron in Chinese waters, saying to those who objected to the commodore as only a well-dressed dude:

"It does not matter what kind of clothes and collars he wears," declared Roosevelt; "the man will fight. He is the man for the place. He has a lion heart."

He not only sent Dewey to Hongkong, but he kept his fleet there also. When the Olympia was ordered home Roosevelt objected so strongly that the order was repealed.

"Keep the Olympia," he cabled to Dewey, "and keep full of coal."

He saw clearly what was in the air and was determined that the small American navy, so far as his power over it extended, should not be caught napping.

Roosevelt's foresight was fully justified. The war came, and without hesitation the fighting Secretary plunged into it, resigning his post without hesitation and preparing to take part in the contest as a soldier. Chains could not have held him back. He had in his veins too much of the berserker blood for that. All his life he had been fighting, alike in the assembly, on the ranch, in the police and other official duties, and in the naval department. Now had come the opportunity to fight on the battlefield and he hailed it with the zeal of a born warrior.

"There's nothing more for me to do here," he said to his colleagues. "I've got to get into the fight myself. I have done all I could to bring on the war, because it is a just war. Now that it has come, I have no business to ask others to do the fighting and stay at home myself."

But he went into it in a way that won him the attention and admiration of the whole nation. It was a happy idea of his to enlist the regiment named the "Rough Riders," consisting of cowboys, hunters, Indians from the West, athletes, football players, oarsmen from the East, even the society men of athletic training. It was such a body of horsemen as the world had rarely seen, and the name of "Roosevelt's Rough Riders" swept like a cheer from end to end of the land. They were, unfortunately, unable to show their prowess as horsemen, being out of their native element on foot, but the name clung to them. "Roosevelt's Weary Walkers" was the humorous title they chose for themselves, after three long and dreary months in the Cuban jungles.

This name was one that had more truth than poetry in it.

Roosevelt had for several years been a member of the National Guard of New York, in which he had risen to the rank of captain. He had ample warrant to make himself colonel of his new regiment, but he preferred to serve as lieutenant colonel, choosing his friend, Colonel Leonard Wood, an officer of the regular army, to take command. At a later date Wood was promoted to the rank of general and Roosevelt succeeded him as colonel. During all his after life the title of "Colonel" clung to him.

The story told of Roosevelt and his men, after reaching the battlefield in Cuba, near Santiago, was one of picturesque activity. Up San Juan Hill they stormed in the face of the intrenched Spaniards, who poured down upon them a hot fire of shells and bullets. Roosevelt in the lead, the Rough Riders and the Tenth Cavalry all on foot, charged with wild yells through the hail of gunfire. On they went, faster and faster. Suddenly Roosevelt's horse, stopped by a bullet, fell in a heap, but in an instant the rider was free from the saddle, landing on his feet and charging onward afoot, sword in hand. The top of the hill was reached. The Spaniards in their trenches were so dazed by the daring and audacity of the Americans that they had no heart to wait for them. Wavering for an instant, they turned and ran, their works being quickly overrun. More than half of the Rough Riders had been wounded, but their daring leader was untouched. He had passed triumphantly through his baptism of fire.

That brilliant charge practically ended the fight, Santiago soon after surrendering. There was but one more event in which Roosevelt figured in Cuba, this a month or more later. The victors were suffering from an attack of malaria, but they were uselessly kept in Cuba. Roosevelt—then a colonel—boiled over with indignation, finally writing a " round robin," which his men signed, and in which he protested against the keeping of his regiment in that pestilential climate. This protest, with a vigorous letter, was sent to General Shafter, and though it met adverse criticism, had the desired effect. The men were recalled, and with this event the war experience of the Colonel and his rough-riding regiment came to an end.

Almost every war has its popular hero, and the Cuban war was no exception. The dramatic picturesqueness of the cowboy regiment, with its telling title, and the newspaper story of its spectacled leader charging up San Juan Hill, yelling and firing, hit the fancy of the American people from Maine to California, and Roosevelt became its hero in the West as Dewey did in the East. A place for the Colonel, thus standing on the pedestal of public appreciation, was ready. New York state needed a new governor, and Theodore Roosevelt was the man of the hour. The Citizens' Union was the first to nominate him, but he declined the compliment, saying that he was a Republican and proposed to stand by his colors. The nomination of the Republican party followed and he carried the election by a majority of 18,000 over Van Wyck, the Democratic nominee.

Governor Roosevelt held the office thus given him for two years. As to his administration we may quote from Dr. Albert Shaw, the editor of the "Review of Reviews." The clear-headed editor said:

"He found the state administration thoroughly political; he left it business-like and efficient. He

HEROES OF PROGRESS 359

kept thrice over every promise that he made to the people in his canvass. Mr. Roosevelt so elevated and improved the whole tone of the state administration, and so effectually educated his party and public opinion generally, that future governors will find easy what was before almost impossible."

We must deal very briefly with his record as governor thus characterized. A larger and wider field of action awaited him. He was on his way to the Presidency, which years before had been predicted for him, though no indication of this high elevation was yet visible in his career. As governor little was achieved in his first year in the way of practical reform. He was feeling his way and the utmost he was yet able to do was to see that no bad laws were enacted. During the second year his hold on the situation grew stronger and much new and beneficial legislation was carried through. But there was ample work before him still, important reforms which he was eager to have enacted, and which he deemed essential to the well-being of the state. Therefore, when in 1900 there was suddenly held before his eyes the glittering lure of the Vice-Presidency of the United States he was not at all pleased with the prospect. His work at Albany was not yet finished, and he was not the man to desire to be shelved in the seat of chairman of the Senate, a sleepy dignity for so active a man. He had it in mind to be again a candidate for governor of New York, a post promising live work to be done, and to be laid on the shelf in this manner was a compliment that failed to appeal to his taste.

The date of 1900 was that of the second nomination of McKinley, this nomination being seconded by Roosevelt at the convention in a strong speech. Hardly had he finished his address before the convention hailed him as its choice for Vice-President— to his consternation rather than his approval. Senator Depew, of New York, who was not anxious to have Roosevelt remain in the governor's chair, took the opportunity to drawl out: "In the East we call him Teddy." At this the applause was roof-rending. "Teddy Roosevelt! Teddy Roosevelt!" was shouted to the skies. Calls for a vote arose from all parts of the convention. It was quickly taken and under the circumstances could end but in one way. McKinley and Roosevelt were chosen as the Republican candidates for 1900.

The nomination was sorely against his will. He did not want the office and he well knew the purpose of Depew and others who were pressing him into it. He strongly objected to accepting the nomination, and was finally persuaded to yield to the demand only under strong pressure. Not a man in the hall dreamed of the real issue that awaited, and that before the first year of the term would end the tide of events would sweep Roosevelt into the Presidential chair. When the day of election came the vote for the candidates showed a plurality of 850,000 votes and an electoral majority of 137. Only twenty years had elapsed since his graduation at Harvard College and less than twenty years since the beginning of his political career.

It was, as we have said, on the threshold of the twentieth century that Theodore Roosevelt attained the highest office in the gift of the American people. Taking office with McKinley in March 4, 1901, the opening year of the century, the year had about a third of its length to run when the hand of an assassin brought the term of McKinley to an end and launched Roosevelt upon a career of which his opponents had not dreamed when they planned to remove him from an active into a passive position. On Friday, August 13, when word was sent adrift that the victim of the assassin's bullet was fast sinking, Roosevelt was away on a tramp and hunt in the New England mountains, no one knowing just where he could be found. Hours passed before he was discovered, and it was near evening when the news of the fast approaching death of the President was brought to his ears.

The nearest railroad station was thirty-five miles away, with a rough forest road between, and it was the morning of the 14th before the station could be reached. It was not until 1.40 P.M. that the fast-driven train reached Buffalo, where the tragedy had been enacted. He reached there to find that the President had passed away and that the late Vice-President was now President of the United States. He was the youngest man in the history of the country to win this exalted office, being still less than forty-three years of age. But he had lived what seemed a long life since his schoolboy days and few people before him had held so many important offices in so brief a time.

During his first term of office as President the new head of the American government sought to follow in the footsteps of his predecessor and avoid any radical legislation of anti-McKinley type. Yet a man of his energy could not well help taking firm hold of such compelling conditions as confronted him. His first radical act was to invite Booker Washington, the famous negro educator, to take dinner with him. Though this was not the first colored man to sit at table with a President, the act aroused a storm of denunciation in parts of the South. Again, when a coal-strike broke out in Pennsylvania, Roosevelt broke all precedents by stepping into the breach and by his influence bringing the labor war to an end. Most significant of all was his act when the Republic of Colombia refused to sustain the action for the building of the Panama Canal and the State of Panama declared its independence in consequence. Roosevelt hastened to recognize this act. His impatience of delay in this instance ran away with his judgment, and his haste gave rise to a situation whose ill results remained vital for many years later. Other acts of a radical character might be mentioned, but the above will suffice to show that the new President was a very live man. He might cause mischief by overhaste, but the man who charged up San Juan Hill was not likely to sin on the side of overdelay.

In his second term as President, Roosevelt felt no longer under obligation to carry out the policies of his predecessor. He was now the direct, instead of the indirect, choice of the people and was free to carry out the promises of his platform. This he did without hesitation, the platform being broad enough to enable him to work for all the reforms in which he felt an interest. And aside from the interest of the party and the country there were world-wide matters that appealed to him. A desperate war was going on between Russia and Japan, one which the nations of Europe made no effort to bring to an end. In 1905, the year of his inauguration, Roosevelt

Copyrighted, 1911, by Munn & Co., Inc.   Courtesy "Scientific American"
BIRD'S-EYE VIEW OF PANAMA CANAL LOCKS

HEROES OF PROGRESS

took this matter in hand, stretching across the two oceans the olive branch of peace. Thus, while Europe dallied and delayed, America acted. Both the belligerents wanted peace, but neither ventured to act, and it was left to President Roosevelt to bring this about in the Portsmouth Peace Treaty of September 5, 1905.

The world, as well as his country, had been watching and admiring the career of the American President, and this bold venture into world politics brought him distinctly into the limelight of world events. It seemed a simple thing to do, but no other nation had volunteered to do it, and the act gave Roosevelt and the United States an international prominence they had not hitherto attained. Roosevelt's direct reward for it was the Nobel prize in the following year for the best work in the interests of peace.

As for his own country, one of his most important acts was the organization of the National Conservation Commission for the preservation of the natural resources of the country, which were vanishing at an alarming rate. Wasteful modes of lumbering and devastating fires were destroying the forests; the coal supply was disappearing through bad handling; the fisheries were being exhausted through ignorance and greed; the fertile soil was being washed away into the streams; all was going wrong, and all sadly needed righting. It was due in great part to the initiative of President Roosevelt that this wastefulness has been overcome and the vast natural wealth of the country conserved.

This was one of the Roosevelt policies. There were others of equal note. Among these may be named his favorite dogma of good citizenship and a square deal for all men. To this may be added the control of corporations and the reign of law over that of force and fraud; the arbitration of labor disputes; the larger good in place of the system of temporary expediency; national defense and the need of a strong army and navy; and the development of international arbitration and world-peace, to be gained by some measure like the league of nations, now so widely advocated and developed.

Theodore Roosevelt was, as we have entitled him, in every respect an all-round man. Any duty offered him he was ready to undertake and whatever he did was well done. Few men have been called upon to handle such a diversity of public duties and none have dealt with them more efficiently. As a politician, a handler of men and public affairs, he was unsurpassed. As rancher, hunter, soldier he was as active and capable. As for his spare time, he had none. Every minute was occupied. He was a devourer of books and a maker of books. Any one who would like to test his power in the author field must read his " Winning of the West." This is the ablest of the many books that came from his pen. As a writer of presidential messages and an orator, he was practical to a marked degree. His method of dealing in this field had in it nothing of the imaginative and ideal. He was thoroughly direct and literal. In his speeches every point was well made, flung straight out and aimed to hit its mark like a bullet. His messages were long—verbose some thought them. But he had a wide field to cover and it was his effort to cover it fully and ably. While he

HEROES OF PROGRESS

spoke apparently to Congress he had a far wider audience in view than that of the Capitol.

At noontide of March 4, 1909, the official life of Theodore Roosevelt came to an end. It had extended for a quarter of a century and all that he had done had been done ably and capably. He was ready for a holiday; but the holiday was, like the man, full of that "Strenuous Life" of which he was an ardent advocate. There was no war with foreign countries to plunge into, but there was the war with wild beasts. He had many years before fought with the beasts of the "Wild West," but he had long felt an eager desire to grapple with the most ferocious and perilous of all animals, those of the wilds of Africa, the lion and leopard, the rhinoceros and elephant, and the host of other creatures with which the African continent abounds.

He lost no time. On the morning of March 23, less than three weeks after leaving the presidential chair, he set out from Oyster Bay, his Long Island home, on the long journey to Mombasa, the East African landing place of his projected hunting trip, in company with the party of skilled hunters who had been chosen to accompany him to this huntsman's "promised land." Among them was his son Kermit, not skilled in hunting but with all the ardor of youth. The expedition had been equipped by the Smithsonian Institution of Washington, which was to be repaid by the series of African animals which the party hoped to collect. As for Roosevelt and his son, he paid his own and Kermit's way.

Mombasa was reached on April 21, the voyage lasting somewhat less than a month. In addition to the leader of the expedition and his son, the party was made up of Colonel Edgar A. Mearns, a retired officer of much skill and experience as a naturalist; Edmund Heller, also a skilled huntsman and collector, and J. Alden Loving, of whom the same may be said. It is not our purpose to tell the long story of this hunt. It must suffice here to say that it was highly successful, and the results of it are now to be seen at the United States National Museum at Washington, instituting an admirable series of African mammals. The most we can here say is to speak of some of the perils of the party and its leaders.

The locality of the hunting ground sought by the Roosevelt party was in the Uganda district of British East Africa, north and northeast of the great Lake Victoria Nganza, a region lying five hundred miles by rail from the Pacific coast, and a true hunter's paradise, as it abounded with game of all sorts and sizes and of every grade of temper, from the ferocious lion to the gentle giraffe and antelope, the latter in a great variety of species.

It was not lacking in scenes of peril, and more than one member of the party found themselves in danger from the lions, leopards and other beasts that fell victims to their bullets. The endurance of the Colonel was notable. He was ready at any time for a thirty-mile ride on horseback or a long tramp on foot, and after a hard day's work afield and a hearty meal at its end, might have been seen, pen in hand, writing away until after midnight. Yet when day dawned again he was often astir before sunrise, ready to take the field. His comrades were amply justified in speaking of him as " a glutton for work."

More than once the eager hunter rashly invited death, and would have met it but for the vigilance of

HEROES OF PROGRESS 367

his trained comrades, his eagerness drawing him into imminent danger. On one occasion he found himself facing a herd of elephants some twenty in number. He raised his rifle against one of the largest of these and was on the point of firing when Selous, a skilled hunter of African game who had joined the party, gave him hasty warning:

"Don't shoot! On your life, don't shoot! A bullet will bring a charge of the herd and we may be trampled to death. Follow me."

A safer spot being reached, Selous bade the risky sportsman to climb a tree and followed him hastily into its branches. In a few minutes the great beasts came crushing through the tall reeds bordering their path. Selous now told his excited companion how to aim, and Roosevelt, Winchester in hand, brought down the great beast with a half dozen balls from his trusty weapon, the giant tusker falling dead close to the tree which held its hidden foes.

Other perilous situations had to do with the rhinoceros and the black-maned lion, only a hasty and fatal shot saving the incautious hunter when charged by one of the latter. His greatest peril came from a herd of buffaloes, a fierce African species of this animal, a herd of some eighty or more of these beasts charging into the plain and facing the party of hunters. The peril was imminent. Had the brutes pushed on with their accustomed fury not a man would have escaped alive. A single shot would have been sure to provoke an attack. As it proved, it was rather curiosity than fury that moved the animals, and after a brief interval of suspense they turned and rushed away across the plain. The danger had been great and none of the party wanted a second similar adventure.

This memorable visit to the domain of the world's most varied centre of beast life was followed by an experience of a quite different kind. Nearly a year was spent by the Colonel in the hunting field, in which he made many narrow escapes, yet came through without a scratch. His journey homeward was by way of the Nile, reaching the outposts of civilization at Khartum and Cairo and landing in Naples on April 2, 1910. Europe was waiting for him with a welcome which few travellers had ever experienced. No man in the world at that time was so much talked of or bore so great a reputation as Theodore Roosevelt, and the ruling kings and emperors of the European continent were eager to greet the man from over the ocean who then stood foremost in the world's regard.

The first potentate to greet and honor him was King Victor Emmanuel of Italy, in the capitol of the old Roman Empire. The second was Francis Joseph, ruler of Austria and Hungary. Both of these did their utmost to pay him every honor, as a man fully their equal in dignity. Next in his route came the Republic of France, with its President, M. Fallières, as his host. Thence he made his way to Holland, the home of his ancestors, passing through Belgium and visiting Brussels on his route. Wherever he appeared he was greeted with the heartiest applause and dealt with as a full equal in dignity with the potentates he visited. Denmark, Norway and Sweden, the Scandinavian Kingdoms, welcomed him with warm enthusiasm, and Germany came next in his route, with Emperor William, the then all-powerful Kaiser, as his host. Little did the latter and his people at that time dream of the change that was to come upon them during the decade which had then been entered upon.

England was the final European country in his route. Here a different reception awaited him. King Edward VII, its monarch, had just died, and the whole country was in deep mourning. Roosevelt had a brief interview with King George, the new monarch, but the dead king still awaited burial and all greetings and festivities were for the time at an end. But while his reception was a quiet one, he was visited by various of the royalties of Europe whom the late king's obsequies had called to London and by many of England's dignitaries. Of his experience there the event that most pleased him was a tramp with Sir Edward Grey through New Forest, a picturesque and romantic woodland near Southampton. Grey was a keen angler and a skilled ornithologist, and at nightfall, when they reached their hotel, rain-soaked and mud-spattered, Roosevelt said to a friend:

"My day in New Forest with Sir Edward Grey was the crowning experience of the whole three months."

During this journey through Europe the American visitor took the opportunity to make a series of orations, some of them extended lectures, in which he gave remarkable evidence of his breadth of view and his familiarity with history and international affairs. Of these we can give only the titles of the most significant.

His lecture before the University of Paris was on the appropriate subject of "Citizenship in a Republic." That delivered in Norway was on "A World League of Peace," it being the occasion of the presentation of the Nobel Peace Prize. He advocated a condition of national affairs resembling the now-advocated League of Nations for the maintenance of peace. Others were: "The World Movement," before the University of Berlin, and "Biological Analogies in History," the Romanes lecture at Oxford University, the whole showing a broad acquaintance with historical and political subjects.

This ovation in Europe formed the culminating phase in Theodore Roosevelt's career. His subsequent life showed a gradual decline in influence and popularity, though to the end he had a vast multitude of admirers at home and abroad. With this final period of his life we must more briefly deal. After his return home he made a journey through the Middle West in which he lectured on a radical system of national politics which he denominated the "New Nationalism." Returning to his native state he made an unsuccessful effort to carry it for the Republican party, and then withdrew for a time from public affairs, devoting himself to editorial duties on the *Outlook* periodical.

In 1912 he took a leading part in the Presidential campaign of the Republican party, but met with strong opposition in the convention and ended by withdrawing from the party and forming a new one, which took the name of the Progressive party. While campaigning for this party he was shot by a lunatic at Milwaukee and narrowly escaped death. So great was his energy, however, that he did not let the bullet stop his speech. He was defeated in the election and again withdrew from public life.

The following year found him again abroad, this time in South America. This continent presented no great hunting field, like that of Africa, but the broad basin of the Amazon River and its tributaries constituted a field of discovery in considerable part unknown and awaiting investigation. After a visit to the great southern capitals, Rio de Janeiro and Buenos Ayres, in both of which he was given a flattering reception, he plunged into the great tropical realm of southern Brazil with a party of adventurers of his own type, and made his way through that pestiferous climate northward towards the mighty Amazon, enduring a multitude of hardships, but none sufficient to subdue his ardent spirit and love of strenuous adventure.

What he had chiefly in view was to find and explore an unknown river which had been touched upon by some travellers but never traced or described. This he succeeded in doing, after undergoing a series of arduous and dangerous experiences, tracing the stream from its head waters northward to its junction with the Amazon. In honor of his exploit it was named after him by the Brazilian authorities, being entitled the Rio Téodoro. He was to pay rather dearly, however, for the honor, as he left Brazil infected by a tropical fever from which it is doubtful if he ever fully recovered.

The later experience of Colonel Roosevelt was marked by severe criticism of President Wilson's "watchful waiting" policy in Mexico, and by a strong anti-German attitude after the European war broke out, especially after the sinking of the *Lusitania*, which he held to demand an attitude on the part of the United States far more dominant and hostile than the long-drawn-out diplomatic policy of Wilson and his advisers. War, in his view, was called for a full year before it came.

In the presidential campaign of 1915 efforts were made to bring about harmonious relations between the Republican and Progressive parties, with Roosevelt as their candidate. The Republican leaders, however, opposed this movement and chose Charles E. Hughes, a Supreme Court Justice, as their candidate. Roosevelt now declined the nomination of his party followers and supported Hughes with much of his old fire and energy, but not with his accustomed success.

With the re-election of Wilson the public career of Theodore Roosevelt came to an end. After war had been declared against Germany he showed an eagerness to take an active part in it, but President Wilson checked his aspirations. The best that the champion of San Juan Hill was enabled to do was to send his four sons to represent him on the battlefield—one of them to his death, as it proved.

During his active and ardent career Roosevelt had burned his candle at both ends, and at the close of his sixtieth year his power of endurance was practically at an end. Death came to him suddenly and unexpectedly on January 6, 1919, removing from the field of human affairs one of the most energetic, capable and remarkable men that the world had ever known, an American " to the manner born."